Studia Fennica
Folkloristica 18

The Finnish Literature Society (SKS) was founded in 1831 and has, from the very beginning, engaged in publishing operations. It nowadays publishes literature in the fields of ethnology and folkloristics, linguistics, literary research and cultural history.

The first volume of the Studia Fennica series appeared in 1933. Since 1992, the series has been divided into three thematic subseries: Ethnologica, Folkloristica and Linguistica. Two additional subseries were formed in 2002, Historica and Litteraria. The subseries Anthropologica was formed in 2007.

In addition to its publishing activities, the Finnish Literature Society maintains research activities and infrastructures, an archive containing folklore and literary collections, a research library and promotes Finnish literature abroad.

Studia fennica editorial board
Markku Haakana, professor, University of Helsinki, Finland
Timo Kaartinen, professor, University of Helsinki, Finland
Pauli Kettunen, professor, University of Helsinki, Finland
Leena Kirstinä, professor, University of Jyväskylä, Finland
Hanna Snellman, professor, University of Jyväskylä, Finland
Lotte Tarkka, professor, University of Helsinki, Finland
Johanna Ilmakunnas, secretary of the board, Finnish Literature Society, Finland

Editorial Office
SKS
P.O. Box 259
FI-00171 Helsinki
www.finlit.fi

Venla Sykäri

Words as Events

Cretan Mandinádes in Performance and Composition

Finnish Literature Society • Helsinki

Studia Fennica Folkloristica 18

The publication has undergone a peer review.

The open access publication of this volume has received part funding via Helsinki University Library.

© 2011 Venla Sykäri and SKS
License CC-BY-NC-ND 4.0 International

A digital edition of a printed book first published in 2011 by the Finnish Literature Society.
Cover Design: Timo Numminen
EPUB: eLibris Media Oy

ISBN 978-952-222-261-9 (Print)
ISBN 978-952-222-778-2 (PDF)
ISBN 978-952-222-777-5 (EPUB)

ISSN 0085-6835 (Studia Fennica)
ISSN 1235-1946 (Studia Fennica Folkloristica)

DOI: http://dx.doi.org/10.21435/sff.18

This work is licensed under a Creative Commons CC-BY-NC-ND 4.0 International License.
To view a copy of the license, please visit http://creativecommons.org/licenses/by-nc-nd/4.0/

A free open access version of the book is available at http://dx.doi.org/10.21435/sff.18 or by scanning this QR code with your mobile device.

Contents

	PREFACE AND ACKNOWLEDGEMENTS	7
	Note on transliteration	17
I	INTRODUCTION	19
	Mantinádes in Crete: a poetic tradition across the time	19
	In the crossroads of composition and communicating	25
	Rhymed poetry	26
	Short, communicative forms	27
	Research on mantinádes and related traditions	28
	Local literature and discourses on mantinádes	35
	Research as engagement	37
	Research questions	37
	Fieldwork	39
	Methodology and methods of research and analysis	43
	Ethical considerations	48
	Data	49
	The field	50
	Local terminology	51
	Outline of the chapters	52
II	THEORETICAL FRAME OF INTERPRETATION	54
	The register	57
	Focus on performance	61
	Performance arena as a frame of experience	61
	Contextualization	61
	Strategies of meaning	62
	Dialogism	64
	Creativity and competence	65
	Conceptualizing improvisation	69
	Perceptions of improvisation among folklore scholarship	70
	Improvisation in music	73
	Improvisation and metrical registers	75
	Poems as text and process: the double-identity	79
III	CRETE AND TRADITIONAL PERFORMANCE CONTEXTS.	81
	Crete as historical, social and cultural setting	81
	Cretan music, dance and song	86
	Rizítika songs of the western Crete	92
	Shared performance arena, the *gléndi*	93
	The traditional *gléndi*	93
	The *gléndi* and the dances in eastern Crete	96
	The *gléndi* in the rizítika area of western Crete	97
	Poetic confrontations	98
	Transformations of the *gléndi*	100
	Casual singing events	104
	Kantáda	115

IV	THE POETIC LANGUAGE	117
	Origins of the metrical structure and the emergence of the mantináda	117
	Poetic form and means	121
	Thematic contents	127
	Couplets as building blocks	132
	Mantinádes "continued" (sinehómenes)	132
	Narrative songs	135
V	THE MULTIDIMENSIONAL PERFORMANCE	138
	Recited performances	139
	Poems embedded in speech	141
	Stories of past performances	146
	Presentation of poetic inventiveness	149
	Performance as gendered and shared experience	150
	Participation, improvisation and meaning	152
	Thematic continuation	153
	Statements/ideas enclosed in the imagery	154
	Contextual relevance	155
	Internal fitting	156
	Written and media contexts	157
	Written arenas	158
	When television substituted the paréa	159
	Mobile phone messages	160
	Individual and shared: problems implied by the double-identity in modern arenas	161
VI	COMPOSITION	162
	Internalizing the tradition	162
	Local definitions of composition	166
	Rhyming and structuring the verse order	168
	Inventing meaning through rhyme	171
	The ideal of coherence: building an image	172
	Motivations for composing	176
	Verbal interaction	177
	Composition for emotional self-expression	180
	Capturing a theme	182
	The creativity of making the point: reframing	185
	Commanding a poetic world as a productive language	191
VII	A THEORY OF DIALOGIC ORAL POETRY	195
	Dialogic oral poetry	195
	Individuals and tradition	196
	Four aspects of creativity	198
	The self-dependent poem and the economy of tradition	200
	The plural aesthetics of performance and composition	202
	From oral to modern performance arenas	205
	Performative, contextual and textual dialogue	206
BIBLIOGRAPHY AND PRIMARY SOURCES		210
INDEX		220

Preface and acknowledgements

The Cretan rhyming couplets, the *mantinádes*, are short, compact poems which contain an independent message created either for the needs of a particular occasion, or to encapsulate a larger proverbial, philosophical or lyrical idea. This research approaches the mantinádes as a special poetic language, a *register*, and studies how these extemporized or memorized units are performed and composed, and also explores the larger principles that underlie the communication, self-expression and creativity in the genre.

The need for studies on short, conversational traditions to balance the understanding of oral poetry has been acknowledged in several sources. New approaches to longer narrative, epic and mythic traditions and to improvised contest poetry have provided in-depth insights into the dynamics and aesthetics of composition in performance, as well as to the processes of encoding and decoding of the textual units within performative discourses. Short poetry genres that favor spontaneity in communication and constant production of new texts, however, appeal to quite different human needs.

In Greece and the surrounding Mediterranean areas, several especially anthropological articles and books based on fieldwork carried out in the 1970s and 1980s, already provide good insights into the uses of the compact units of oral poetry. When I encountered the mantinádes in Crete at the end of the 1990s, I felt there was a need for an up-to-date study that would address the change that had been created by the adaptation of the poetic activities in the modern society during the past twenty to thirty years. Yet an even greater gap in the literature was the need for a comprehensive study presenting this type of poetic register and its use in traditional performances and composition. In addition, it was clear that the significance attributed to the new, seemingly context-less performances in the written and mass media arenas was intimately drawn from the ideals immanent in the traditional poetic expression; furthermore, many Cretans were fluent in both arenas. This meant that any conclusions could only be inferred from a full image of the tradition.

The need for a comprehensive study was further enhanced by my experience that mantinádes were at the same time an overwhelmingly versatile and uniformly conceptualized song and speech genre in Crete. Indeed, the couplet model has been widespread in the southern Greek islands since the fifteenth century and it is still popular and living, especially in Crete. Although significant differences have existed until the 1980s in the performative practices between the different parts of Crete concerning how, where and with which instruments mantinádes were sung (if instruments were used), the rhyming couplet model is something that is felt to be emblematic of the entire island of Crete. Besides their being exchanged in culturally institutionalized singing events, these poems are widely composed for personal pleasure, and they occur embedded in casual speech to an extent which points to a language-like conception of the poetic model.

The initial motivation for this research was thus to provide a descriptive book which I would have wanted to have found when I first became aware of the tradition. This took place when I spent five months at the University of Crete in Rethimno as a foreign exchange student of Modern Greek in 1997. In hindsight, I am happy that I did not find a book published on this topic. What ensued from my becoming familiar with a living field at such an early phase of my studies was that I was able to follow a path of folklore studies which combined periods of fieldwork and related studies throughout my master's thesis and doctoral dissertation work. I had the opportunity to stay in Crete for several longer periods, and later visited the island once a year, with the overall fieldwork covering a total time span of twelve years. As a result, I acquired very different layers of data through fieldwork and the data interacted with my academic learning. Even the most basic information on the situations and the ways in which mantinádes were performed all had to be constructed through fieldwork conversations, and these conversations soon led to an extended academic discussion on the ideas and values of poetic self-expression.

When I first began this study in 1997, the ethnopoetics and performance-centered approaches to verbal art were becoming established in Finnish Folklore studies that provide the scholarly background for framing the research questions in this study. The earlier studies on mantinádes carried out by Samuel Baud-Bovy (1936), Anna Caraveli (1982, 1985) and Michael Herzfeld (1981, 1985a, 1985b) helped me to understand the plurality of the poetic experience, to ground and focus my perception in the field, and to go for more than was easily available. To ground my own inquiry as an *ethnographic register analysis* of the mantinádes, as I conceptualize this research now, I was primarily assisted by the close analysis of these researchers' fieldwork. I was also able to combine Albert Lord's model (1960) of seeing the register from the singers' point of view with the later approaches of John Miles Foley, who had brought the study of the metrically defined oral poetry methodologically to a new starting point (esp. 1991, 1995). I could further enlarge this methodological and theoretical basis by drawing on Charles Briggs' comprehensive study on the conversational Mexicano genres (1988).

In Crete, however, my attention was particularly captured by the locals' eager introduction of the poems as poems in their own right. When I inquired about mantinádes, especially old people often recited to me poems. These separate poems were performed with great pride, often accompanied by an intense, affirmative eye-contact or even by the phrase: *See, it has a lot of meaning*! The people clearly valued the way these miniature poems captured an idea as such; they were also well worth performing. The discourse to which they bound the poem was, however, not evident from the situational, circumstantial context, to an outsider like me, and several times I continued to wonder *why* the particular poem that was performed was so meaningful. This motivated me to search for an explanation for the cultural and artistic values and processes beyond those types of performances that were explained to me as being culturally institutionalized. I therefore turned to search for the factors that were the basis for their perceptions, the creating of their meanings, in addition to the actual performative realizations. I was encouraged to envision such a task as a creative intellectual challenge, especially by one of Michael Herzfeld's phrases: "Context, by which the meaning of a text is locally recognized, may be verbal as well as circumstantial or social: words, too, are 'events'" (1981:139). The title of this study, *Words as Events*, includes an acknowledgement of this intellectual challenge.

When I was conducting the early stages of my fieldwork in 2001–2003, I also had the opportunity to participate in analyzing the Finnish *kalevala-meter* lyric poetry in the folklore archives. I worked with the researcher Senni Timonen for short periods of altogether eight months.[1] The perception of an essentially language-like characteristic of the poetic tradition in Crete was very similar to this experience. The analysis itself, the depth of Senni Timonen's experience, and our detailed conversations during our joint work, all made me intimately familiar with another flexible poetic register, as well as with the creativity of the poetic self-expression as a vehicle for diverse processes of problem solving and consolation. Timonen's long research career culminated in a dissertation on the *kalevala-meter* lyric poems in 2004. In addition, a year later, the dissertation by Lotte Tarkka on the singing of the *kalevala-meter* poetry as a cultural system in the historical Vuokkiniemi parish posed new interpretations which were also near to my own research questions. Although my fieldwork periods in Crete and concerns with the short forms of oral poetry separated me from the mainstream of contemporary folklore research in Finland, the work of these researchers, as well as that of Lauri Harvilahti, and of my peer, the doctoral student Kati Kallio, kept me constantly in connection with the broader ideas of oral poetry.[2]

Interpreting the threads of evidence that emerged from my fieldwork first took several paths beyond the core areas of the folklore discipline, or even linguistic anthropology, which is closely related to the sphere of this

---

1 After a period of archive practice that is required in the folklore studies, I continued in the Finnish Literary Society for a total of eight months (2001–2004) in a project of indexing the thematic units of the *kalevala-meter* lyric poetry. This work consisted of going systematically through the related poetic motives and their appearance in the individual poems. The work was carried out sub-group by sub-group from preliminary handwritten cards by checking the references and by writing a comment on each motive.

2 Of the Finnish scholars, Lauri Honko is also widely known for his research on epic poetry (esp. 1998) and Pertti Anttonen (1994; 2009) and Tom Dubois (1995) have contributed to the research on Finnish oral poetry from an ethnopoetic perspective.

study. I had few practical models to study the spontaneity emerging as a characteristic of the tradition and the Cretan impressions seemed to fall only partially within the perspectives given by other studies. I participated in seminars organized among the social sciences and education, semiotics and philosophy, and ethnomusicology and dance, and these gave me specific insights from those areas of study. Some of these concerns proved to be useful for verbalizing the characteristics of the Cretan tradition; others showed that several disciplines currently share the very same issues concerning human thinking and self-expression that I encountered in my research. One of the terms which made me look outside of the core of the folklore research was improvisation. My use of that term was initially questioned by both my mentors in a seminar in October 2003, and after reconstructing what it can signify regarding the tradition of mantinádes, in the final writing period from April 2009 to March 2010, it also introduced me better to the literary and text-centered folklore research history. The biases of this paradigm, something I first envisioned as a subject of a brief historical exploration, still turned out to be at odds with conceptualizing the creative personal agency particularly in composition – and this agency therefore grew into a major theme of the present study.

Through an ethnographic register approach, this study aims to clarify the ways in which the productive poetic tradition of the mantinádes allows creativity and an experience of meaningfulness for the poets and performers. I felt very early on that the "restrictions" of the structure played a decisive role in generating impulses of creativity, and along with the inconvenience I felt over the lack of information about the poetic registers and their role in several anthropological studies capturing sociocultural themes, I noticed that the basic problem of the research available was that it did not grant access to the world of resources available to the performers and composers of poetry. By a register approach, I therefore mean that I will focus on the poetic language, the register, as well as on how, where, when and by whom, to whom and between whom, this register can be used. This type of focus on the dialectical relationship between the system and its individual usages is, of course, not new, but already present in the Prague School's early approaches towards sociolinguistics from the twenties and thirties (see Fine 1984: 31–32), and in particular in the discussion carried out by Jakobson and Bogatyrev (1980 [1929]) on reshaping the meaning of Saussure's terms *langue* and *parole*.

Ethnographic means that this aim is endeavored through the experience of individuals engaged in the tradition. The orientations to this experience are constructed here by combining the researcher's observation and participation in the performances to focusing on these matters in repeated conversations. The present study therefore examines how the contemporary people in Crete understand and conceptualize their own tradition. In other words, this analysis will explore how they still practice or recollect the collective singing and acoustic musical ways of celebration and entertainment that form their very recent past, how they perform and compose these poems today, as well as how they value the access to this shared potentiality and evaluate its individual renditions.

As Steven Caton observes, the ethnographic appropriation of an oral poem concerns two distinct but interdependent processes: understanding and interpretation. Whereas native speakers may be confronted by the challenge of interpretation while they may automatically understand the expression, a foreign ethnographer is also confronted by the problem of understanding. This understanding concerns a complex set of linguistic features as well as background information on the concrete and cultural references. (Caton 1990: 16–18; see also Caraveli 1982)

Understanding is also a primary method in most human research. But unlike many other types of ethnographic work, in this type, the participation in the conversations and knowledge production, is the essential prerequisite for understanding to a degree which also stands firmly and visibly in the final product. Several ethnographic studies, and essentially those on short forms (Briggs 1988; Caton 1990; Herzfeld 1981), were of great help in making me conscious that rather than a disadvantage, my engagement in the research dialogue would be the necessary tool for grasping the ways in which people express themselves in this kind of speech genre. Understanding the several, often very elliptic levels of the apt poetic expression demanded that I learn a profound system of the ideals of communication in Crete and essentially their verbal ways of challenging the interlocutor to engage in the discourse. In brief, the dialogic structures of the tradition were also imposed on the structure of the fieldwork. After accepting to learn not just new information, but a new way of communicating, being a foreigner was nonetheless very rewarding. The advantage is that people are motivated to explain and explore in conversation things which normally are self-evident.

As a foreign student of the mantinádes, however, I have had the benefit of receiving help from a native Greek within easy reach. After the initial period of studies and preliminary fieldwork in Rethimno in the spring 1997, my attempts to understand the Cretan and Greek music led me to become acquainted in May 1999 – when I had already organized my return to Rethimno for studies and fieldwork for the academic year 1999/2000 – with the percussionist Yannis Hadziharalambous, an Athens-born expert in the Balkan and eastern rhythmical traditions, who later become my husband. By that time, he had lived in Crete for most of the preceding eight years, and his sharp ear and his insider experience of the deeply idiomatic Greek and Cretan expressions have complemented my pursuits in indispensable ways.

Being a couple facilitated enormously our move to a village environment. During March and April 2001, we stayed for the first time in a small village which came to be my temporary residence during all the longer and shorter periods of fieldwork until the end of 2007. The village is situated in the Milopotamos valley, and I will refer to this community in the following pages simply as the 'Village'. In March 2003, I completed my master's thesis on the mantinádes (Sykäri 2003) and in the beginning of the 2004, I received a doctoral research grant for three years from the Finnish Cultural Foundation, which allowed me to plan a long-term study and to return to Crete for eight months that same year. Although I was unable to carry out my research exclusively in the Village, we rented the same house again because in this village, I felt truly welcomed, and the house with a garden which I could tend as my own, as well as the great mountain views, provided a well-needed nest. Although a deep sympathy towards my being Finnish has contributed to my easy acceptance in many fieldwork situations, these outermost corners of Europe are socially and culturally very different, which becomes more evident during a longer stay. For most of this time, my partner accompanied me in my fieldwork, providing help in the transcription of the recordings and in the everyday means of conversing and understanding the peculiarities of the idiomatic and dialectally complicated linguistic expressions.

Before my stay in the Village, my informants had been mainly men, who still were much more easily contacted in Crete. I was therefore happy to continue the close relationships with the two ordinary village women, Despina Papadaki and Agapi Moshovaki, who had became important informants during my first stay in 2001. Both women were in their early seventies at that time. Together, these friends introduced me most practically to their everyday verbal dexterity and to their creative associating through memories. Still at that time, Despina spontaneously composed ex tempore, although her memory and health already started to fail her. She also recurrently explained to me her moral principles by reciting her poems. Agapi had the skill to complement any situation by inserting a poem from her inexhaustible poetic reserves. Having lived all her life in this Village, she also used to contribute to our discussions with stories of past performances. I am happy that these women, to whom my gratitude has grown so great over the years, wanted me to use their names, although, unlike most of the other persons featuring with their name in this book, they are known as performers only within their close circles.

Later, the decision to stay in the Village brought still one more advantage: I became familiar with Kostoula Papadoyanni, a middle-aged woman talented in composition, whose growing ambition I was able to follow and I conversed with her over a five-year period. She also has the extraordinary skill to verbalize the processes of composition, providing a unique source for an extended discussion on these matters. By placing special emphasis on the insights that I had developed due to my familiarity with these three women, I wish to point to the fact that although men may be principal actors in musical public performances, both sexes equally speak the shared poetic idiom.

One of those composers with whom I had the pleasure to talk several times over the years is Mitsos Stavrakakis from Iraklio. His grasp of analysis in our conversations helped me to understand the background and mental frame of reference which the contemporary adult male poets have in their traditional singing events. As a consequence, his insightful descriptions of the traditional ways of singing and communicating occupy a special place in this work. I also enjoyed the expressive sarcasm of Aristidis Heretis from Anoya during our several meetings starting from 1999. Yet another contributor, beginning in 2004, was the instrument builder Antonis Stefanakis from Zaros and my conversations with him widened the scope of the village life and expressional means. In addition, Katerina Kornarou, born in the region of Merambello, later married in Milopotamos, provided me with hours of recollections of her childhood and youth in eastern Crete, and performed her mantináda and song-compositions during our conversations. Another valuable source of information, who began contributing in 2004, was Yorgos Sifakis from Rethimno, and he has also given me many hours of his time for our detailed conversations. His recent contribution in providing me with audio material that was recorded in the singing events complements the present study in indispensable ways.

The role of the aforementioned *mantinadolóyi*, mantináda-composers, and the specialists of the tradition, with whom I could talk repeatedly, has been fundamental in my understanding of the mantinádes. In the various regions of Crete, I also conversed with Aleksandra Pateraki (Dzermiado), Kostas Kontoyannis (Rethimno), Kostas Mangoufakis (Ano Vianos), Lefteris Kalomiris (Anoya) and Nikolis Nikiforos (Rethimno), and many others. Several performers in Crete, who welcomed my passing by with creative challenges, remain anonymous, because in most of these casual meetings, I did not ask their names or their permission to disclose their identification in this study. Many of these anonymous performers, however, indeed helped me recognize the power of the casual recitals of poems as *performances*. Naturally, I had in-depth conversations with several people in the Village from 1999 up to 2009.

In addition to these poets and performers, many people have contributed to my work by informing, helping, advising and conversing with me during these twelve years. For example, Ross Daly and Yannis Tsouhlarakis helped me find some relevant bibliography and interviewees. In November 2005, the violinist Vangelis Vardakis with the laoúto-player Manolis Liapakis from Ierapetra, offered me an in-depth introduction to the cultural sphere of eastern Crete and to its different music, dance and singing traditions. The traditions of western Crete were originally disclosed by several people in Frankokastello and Sfakia during my early trips in 1997–1999, and in the spring and summer of 2006 by Stelios Tsiburakis from Hania, and his mother Irini and father Maximos, a recognized performer of the rizítika songs and mantinádes of his time.

Besides all these people who helped me understand the tradition and register of the mantinádes, other people assisted in getting started and organizing the fieldwork and living arrangements in Crete. During the spring 1997, my friend Judy Preston, a student at the University of Birmingham at that time, accompanied me on many of the early experiences. A rethimniot friend, Manolis Papadakis, took me like a family member to various events, village weddings and parées. Later, especially three people helped me far beyond the normal boundaries of friendship and played decisive roles in my fieldwork: Roula Koumentakakou, Mihalis Troulis and Vasilis Kalivianakis. Without the trust of Mihalis, and the practical help, the friendship and genuine interest of Roula and Vasili at various problems and times, I would have returned home many times. In addition to their concrete help, these three people and their families were irreplaceable for maintaining my spiritual resources.

In the academic world as well, several people have contributed to the practical side of my research: Risto Pekka Pennanen, a friend throughout this project, got me in contact with Chris Williams, who through e-mail directions kindly instructed me on the basic knowledge of Cretan music during the winter 1998–1999. Chris then connected me to Alexis Politis, a professor and now manager of the Department of Philology at the University of Crete. All three have read and contributed to this manuscript at various stages.

The staff at the Department of Folklore Studies at the University of Helsinki has always been extremely positive towards my research. Professors Anna-Leena Siikala and Satu Apo encouraged me in several seminars in which I first presented my ideas. Docent Pertti Anttonen has read my drafts and has offered very helpful, constructive criticism. Docent Lauri Harvilahti has been my supervisor from the first seminar for my master's thesis, guiding me to the essential literature right from the beginning. Having carried out long periods of fieldwork in several countries himself, he warmly welcomed my idea for extended fieldwork and always supported my own, independent processes of analysis and digested forms of reporting of them in academic studies. During the last years of finalizing my arguments, I received close assistance from my second supervisor, Professor Lotte Tarkka, who has read every single clause I have written several times. In addition to this, with her I could very easily ask various questions and problems that I was formulating in casual conversation. This was particularly significant to me, since it allowed me to continue the production of knowledge through the dialogue that I had internalized during my fieldwork. If I ever felt lonely in relation to the academic discourse during the long fieldwork periods, her keen interest and skills as a conversant have significantly warded off this feeling. For the same reason of allowing detailed discussion both on the subject matter and on the research process, the friendships I have shared with the researcher Senni Timonen and the doctoral students Kati Kallio and Joonas Ahola has been highly valuable to me. So many evolving ideas took form while exchanging thoughts, reading and commenting on other's papers, and particularly with Joonas, through our discussions on theories and concepts. I also benefited greatly from the conversations with the anthropologist Timo Kaartinen during a year-long seminar on linguistic anthropology, as well as with Professor John Miles Foley during his visits and seminars in Helsinki in 2006 and in Viena Karelia in 2007.

A special privilege of the academic process is provided by the pre-examination of the doctoral dissertation by two specialists before its final submission for public defense. Thus the moment I really needed a dialogue from the outside, I was able to entrust my manuscript to the criticism of Pekka Hakamies, professor of folklore studies from the University of Turku, and Michael Herzfeld, professor of anthropology from Harvard University. Their reports verified that some of my central arguments were already accessible, and they both gave me valuable ideas for strengthening my vague arguments, as well as for shaping and correcting the final text. Unfortunately, I did not have time to adapt some of the additional bibliography referred to by them. Michael Herzfeld has also kindly accepted to be my opponent in the final task of my doctoral defense. It is hard to express my appreciation for the opportunity of having an opponent whose vast experience in the field and

A view from the garden, Milopotamos, spring 2006. My daily solitary tending of my landlord's small garden balanced the extroversion of the fieldwork and also created extended emotional ties to the Village. In the beginning, the villagers were astonished at my sense of duty for a garden not my own – something which in the long run certainly contributed to their approving attitude towards me.

whose insightful writings about the specific social and cultural environment of my subject matter have initiated and served as points of reference for so many ideas taken under examination in this study.

I extend my profound gratitude to all these direct contributors to my study; to the funding institutions, the Finnish Literary Society and the Finnish Cultural Foundation, whose generous fellowships first enabled me to undertake this long-term study and then to carry it on to the end; and to the Finnish Literary Society, who decided to publish my study in the series of *Studia Fennica Folkloristica*. My warmest thanks are due to Jussi Korhonen, who initially planted the seed for my interest in Modern Greek culture during the Modern Greek language classes at the University of Helsinki. I also wish to thank all the doctoral students and staff of folklore studies, who have contributed to a pleasant working atmosphere at the University of Helsinki, the staff of the Finnish Literary Society's library, as well as Johanna Ilmakunnas for her editorial skills and patient guidance through the process of preparing the manuscript for printing. I am grateful to Manolis Tzirakis for generously sharing with me some photographs from his private archives, which were collected during his biographic study of some famous Cretan dancers and musicians. Although most of these photographs are not dated, they add valuable depth to the historical description. Finally, Kate Moore helped me with the English text. I am profoundly grateful for her professional, yet cheerful contribution. All errors that remain are naturally my responsibility alone. Translations of the Cretan poetic texts are my own, and the responsibility for all decisions concerning the linguistic forms is my own.

The support and joy of my friends and family made this all worthwhile. Special heartfelt thanks go to my husband, Yannis Hadziharalambous. We met during the initial stages of this project, and during 1999–2005, he participated in my fieldwork on several occasions. He has been the first one to inspect the correctness of the metrical lines, as well as the chief conversant and support in each phase of the study. In addition to this study, our extended stay in the Village and daily living in a countryside house with a garden had another consequence: after these years, living exclusively in town was unthinkable – besides sharing the life that produced this study, Yannis now kindly shares the loan for our own garden and country house in Finland.

Note on transliteration

The transliteration of Modern Greek presents well-known problems. For the purposes of this study, I have adopted a phonetic system based on the pronunciation of Standard Modern Greek, however, I also maintain certain conventions and simplifications that help to recognize the original Greek text. The poetic texts are written as they were sung in the recorded material or recited in conversations, which means a good deal of lexical, morphological and phonetic inconsistency. The dialectal Cretan pronunciation is however not specifically noted, except in a few cases, which made the dialect very explicit. The individual word accentuation, which in Modern Greek is marked in the written language, is preserved in transcription (apart from proper names), and it helps in following the meter of the poetic texts (introduced in Chapter 4). When two or three vowels are pronounced together, thus occupying one syllable in the metrical line, a hyphen is entered between the words: *ke-an* ("and if").

A key to the transcription:

Α α	= a	Ν ν	= n	αι	= e
Β β	= v	Ξ ξ	= ks	ει	= i
Γ γ*	= y or g	Ο ο	= o	οι	= i
Δ δ*	= d	Π π	= p	ου*	= ou
Ε ε	= e	Ρ ρ	= r	αυ*	= af or av
Ζ ζ	= z	Σ ς	= s	ευ*	= ef or ev
Η η	= i	Τ τ	= t	μπ*	= b or nb
Θ θ*	= th	Υ υ	= i	ντ*	= d or nd
Ι ι	= i	Φ φ	= f	γγ, γκ	= ng
Κ κ	= k	Χ χ*	= h	γι *	= y
Λ λ	= l	Ψ ψ	= ps	τζ	= dz
Μ μ	= m	Ω ω	= o		

*Pronunciation:

γ, (→y), like the *y* in the "yes", preceding either [e] or [i]
    (→g), in all other cases; does not correspond to any sound in English
δ, like the *th* in the English word "there"
θ, like the *th* in the English word "that"
χ, like the *ch* in the Scottish word "loch"
ου, between "put" and "boot"
αυ, ευ, = af, ef, before the consonants π, τ, κ, φ, θ, χ, σ, ξ, ψ and at the end of the word; av, ev, before a vowel or any other consonant
μπ, ντ, = b, d, in the beginning of the word, (n)b, (n)d in middle of the word

γ + unstressed [i] when followed by a vowel, like the *y* in the "yes"

Note: the vowel [i] may become non-syllabic if unstressed and followed by another vowel (pronounced as the *y* in "yes" or *h* in "huge"). For example, the word *kardiá* [karðjá] has two syllables (c.f. the improvised form *kardía* that has three syllables).

A full introduction to the pronunciation of Standard Modern Greek is available in: *Greek: An Essential Grammar of the Modern Language* by Holton, Mackridge and Philippaki-Warburton (2004: 1–10).

I Introduction

Mantinádes in Crete: a poetic tradition across the time

On a walking day trip in southern Crete at the end of May 1998, I had stayed in a *kafenío*[1] to rest. It was midday and already very hot, and the path I had chosen randomly had twisted upwards. In the *kafenío*, three-four elder men, apparently frequent guests of that place, were having a leisurely conversation with the owner, who looked very tired. After sitting a long while, enjoying the shade in a relaxed atmosphere, participating at times in the conversation, I began to feel hungry. Upon my inquiry, the owner agreed to prepare a simple lunch of what the house had to offer: salad and eggs. The other men left one-by-one to have lunch at their homes and the owner started cooking for me as well as for himself. He explained that his wife normally had a cooked meal available every day, but now she had traveled to visit their adult children in Athens. He also told me that he was very tired because he had stayed up until the early hours singing with a *paréa* (a get-together of friends) in the nearby village. After a short while, the owner and I enjoyed our meal over a conversation about the local products. I praised his home-made wine, which gave him the opportunity to treat me by bringing out a tasty older wine, a *marouvás*, too. The pride over his home-grown and produced products evidently raised his spirits and suddenly in middle of our casual conversation, he got the idea that I must stay and join the *paréa* that evening. I thanked him for his offer, but told him that it was not possible; I had to return to Rethimno by bus in the afternoon. He kept on persuading and I kept rejecting his offer, until he burst into the following mantinádes:

> *Is' ómorfi, íse sklirí / íse ke pismatára*
> *Ke pos pligónis mia kardiá / de dínis mia dekára*
>
> You are beautiful, you are hard / you are stubborn, too
> And that you hurt one heart / you don't give a penny

---

[1] A traditional coffee-bar where men pass their time.

I was very taken by his summoning of the poetic tradition for help, and I told him as my excuse that he must understand that I was not able to stay; having a long, exclusive relationship with my partner, I could not hurt him by staying and partying with a man who was a stranger. Now this comment made him resort to exploiting all his poetical soul to depict my thought:

> *Horísame prosoriná / mi hásis tin elpída*
> *Ma tin kardiá mou kivernás / sa naftikí piksída*

> We separated temporarily / don't lose your hope
> Since you govern my heart / like the compass the seaman

> *Horísame, de sou zitó / elpída na mou dósis*
> *Móno ta tósa mistiká / poté na min prodósis*

> We separated, I don't ask you / to give me any hope
> Just that all those secrets / you never betray others

> *De tha mas ksehorísoune / i stratiyi ts' Evrópis*
> *Yatí agapithíkame / ís ton anthó tis niótis*

> We cannot be separated / by Europe's generals
> Because we fell in love / in the bloom of youth

> *'Ithela ná 'me sínnefo / na me fisá t' ayéri*
> *Na me fisíksi mia vradiá / kontá sou na me féri*

> I wish I were a cloud / to be blown by the wind
> To be blown one night / and brought by your side

The poems he recited illustrate the romantic idea of a long relationship and focus on the theme of temporary separation. The second poem, although also reflecting a long relationship, somehow departs from this schema; it is inserted by the immediate thematic pull of the ideas and words "separation" and "hope", which is characteristic of a singing event – or even as a symbolic hint to the possibility of a deviation from fidelity. I told him that even though his mantinádes were great, I soon had to leave. I then asked him if I could write down these verses (which I did). When he realized that I "knew" what mantinádes are, he became very enflamed: he would recite me thousands of them if I stay! But finally I got up to leave, and he was disappointed and commented:

> *Pollá ta déndra pou anthoún / ma líga pou karpízoun*
> *Pol' ín' ekíni p' agapoún / ma líyi pou kerdízoun*

> Many are the trees that bloom / but few the ones that bear fruit
> Many are the ones who love / but few the ones who gain

In Crete, these rhyming couplets, the *mantinádes*, are still widely used to clothe one's argument in a sharper, more expressive form. On this occasion, my interlocutor responded to the challenge of my sudden presence in middle of an ordinary midday, of our conversations and the change these made to his everyday routines, by changing the code of speech, as well. He colored our dialogue with a set of traditional poems: first as a provoking statement, then as creating a confidential, understanding but also romantic atmosphere, and in the end, with an interpretation of that frustrating situation. Even if my staying was just an impulse that occurred to him at the moment, the poetic discourse took up that challenge very seriously. From my part, I was able to downplay the seriousness and to stress the flirting playfulness. He tried to persuade me, but in this case, the negotiation of a shared frame of reference did not alter the course of real life as to the suggested proposal of joining the *paréa*. This exchange did, however, make me decide to carry on after a preliminary study on mantinádes and to embark upon a full-length folkloristic study.

The rhyming couplet form became established in Crete in the fifteenth century when the island was governed by Venetia and along with the new Western literary models, the end rhyme was introduced. The end rhyme bound two of the already established Byzantine *dekapentasíllavo* (= of fifteen-syllables) metrical lines to a new flexible poetic unit. Except in Crete, this versatile couplet model has been prominent in all the Southern Dodecanese islands, in Cyprus and until the enforced population exchange of 1922–3, in the Greek communities of Asia Minor. On all these islands, couplets have been the vehicle for flirting and love matters, especially for the young people, in festive occasions and dance, as well as for the extemporized commentary of social relations and undertakings of the fellow villagers.

In Crete, the poetic idiom has left its mark to all the significant communicative, festive and recreational events. Up to the 1970s, poems were sung in the village and life cycle festivities along with the local music, which until then, was performed acoustically. Frequent musical get-togethers, *parées*, formed another major frame of performance for men. In everyday communicative situations, extemporized utterances were formed by those who could, while a selection of crystallized poems served the others in their emotional, normative and philosophical expression.

Significant differences emerge in what was valued and these divide Crete geographically roughly into three main areas. In eastern Crete, as in the nearby islands of Karpathos and Kasos, oral communication seems to have emphasized immediate textual improvisation. A special center of plurality in musical violin styles and well-known for verses that were improvised is Sitia, and these verses were openly sexually oriented,[2] mocking and teasing. Central Crete shares the improvisatory music tradition with eastern Crete, especially the musical genre *kondiliés*, although the main musical instrument was the *lira*, instead of the violin, and this region is characterized more by the philosophical and poetic weight of what is said. In western Crete, except the along the coast and especially the small town of Kastelli (Kissamos),

---

2 This applies only to male *parées*, the presence of a woman would turn the focus elsewhere (051102).

A paréa gathered around a festive table with Yerasimos Stamatoyanakis on the lira, and Yannis Markoyannakis on the laoúto. Early 1980s. Photo private collection of Manolis Tzirakis.

where musicians were hired for major festivities including dance, the main form of entertainment was the singing of slow, crystallized, unaccompanied choral songs called the *rizítika*. Mantinádes were combined with these in performance, and reciprocal contests also took place.

Another distinction is apparent between the high mountain areas and the lowlands: the different sources of livelihood and correspondingly social structures also divide these areas in relation to their focus on communication. In the past, the performances could thus have quite different parameters in the different communities regarding the contents and style, as well as to how serious a conflict could be created by the one wrong mantináda.

The differences in the local codes of performance likewise determined the women's freedom to participate in public events: In Crete, the western Hania and Sfakia, and generally the mountainous pastoral areas, are well-known for extreme patriarchy, as well as for the submission of female participation in public discourses. In stark contrast, in eastern Crete, in the agricultural and fishing lowland cultures, active female participation in public performance was a rule as long as the traditional performance practices were held (chiefly until the 1970s). With the contemporary transfer of the public poetic dialogues to the mass media arenas, women now have attained an equal public position as performers and poets.

The composition of mantinádes in Crete has gained even new prevalence today, albeit in a changed society and among changed ways of communication. This change in the ways of communication, as well as the crucial role of the idiom in Cretan oral communities until just thirty years ago, is described (referring to central Crete) below by Mitsos Stavrakakis, 1999 (991202):

Today, a lot of people are engaged in mantinádes. But they are not engaged with the same feeling as before. Because all has changed: the way people behave, the way they love, the way they fall in love; the way they communicate has changed completely. That is, when I was in the village (…), the only way you could communicate with the other, with the other sex of course, because mainly the motives to make mantinádes were the erotic motives, first of all! That is, when young, the way you could communicate was, either you played mandolin and sung old mantinádes that you liked, mantinádes for your eyes, the one…or you made your own ones; when the existing mantinádes did not satisfy you, you made a personal own one. And this way you little by little understood if you had in yourself this poetic talent, which here they say, the most of us have. (…) Now what comes to the quality of the verses, this differed from person to person. That is, somebody caught senses that others would not catch, or made a mantináda and decorated it with such beautiful words that you admired it, so. The basic thing I want to underline is that this way of self-expression was the only one possible to you, there were no other convenient ways to express yourself than making, thus, mantinádes, and in succession, singing them in a *paréa*.

In Greece, the beginning of the 1980s marks a major change in the modernization and privatization of life. Intense urbanization had begun already in the 1950s, but at the beginning of the 1980s, cars became a common possession, allowing people to move during their free time, and the oral, acoustic entertainment in recreational events was increasingly exchanged for the entertainment provided by television and professionals. Starting in the seventies, the entertainment in the life cycle and village feasts changed completely. The acoustic arenas were then left to professional musicians now equipped with amplifiers and therefore removed from the middle of the square to a bandstand, and gradually the feasts were organized more and more in special commercial feast houses, the *kéndra*. On these occasions, audience participation takes place mainly through dance. In verbal communication, mantinádes rarely figure today as a spontaneous face-to-face self-expression – this is no longer crucial for the veiled or roundabout ways of communication of the highly regulated social relations in the village communities.

Although the processes of modernization have reduced the participative, collective events of singing mantinádes, and the poetic culture does not automatically touch everyone, mantinádes are nevertheless today far from being conceived as something of the past. On the contrary, the composition of poems continues, although the ways and environments in which many of them are performed have changed. The contemporary adult generations still have a vivid experience of the village practices, and significant past events are eagerly recollected by citing the mantinádes performed in these events. Appearing in public, the mantinádes continue to be the emblematic mould for song in the lively local Cretan musical tradition. New generations learn the productive form now especially from live and recorded musical performances and from written sources. Mantinádes are also a central subject in the shared arenas provided by the mass media, especially on the television and radio shows, which are broadcast daily during the winter-season, and where people can send in their own compositions. Apart from the prominence of the poems in these public arenas, personally composed and heard poems are widely presented among friends and family members. These are exchanged by mobile phones as text messages, and they regularly arise as subjects in conversation and emotional self-expression. Contemporary poems therefore occur in a full continuum of styles that span from spontaneous and traditional styles to all the more written-oriented and figuratively complicated. Correspondingly, differences of opinion exist between people who are critical towards the modern style poems and their lack of a clear message and musicality[3] on the one hand, and on the other, those who see that the more poems there are, the more good poems and poets will arise in the course of time.

Crossing borders in a changing society and changing communication is possible due to the mantinádes being essentially a tradition of productive poetry and that the poetic expression lives markedly through an individual experience of meaningfulness. The fact that a local tradition is cherished is further enhanced by the Cretans' pervasive claims for cultural idiosyncrasy and their extensive focus on performative self-definition and compact, witty verbal expression. Mantinádes are flexible and offer an option for creativity in several ways. Although we can acknowledge the significance of the poems in the past oral societies as a means of interpersonal communication, the key to a full image of the register is provided only by reviewing its value as a means of inventive, artful self-expression as well.

The subject of the mantinádes can be any matter relevant to human life and they also appear in many styles. They can be ephemeral products, which celebrate the associations born on the spur of the moment, or appreciated poetry, which enclose an independent poetic image and stay in the local oral repertoire. The number of people talented in ex tempore composition is restricted, and those in oral composition in general might be much the same as in any average peasant or contemporary society. However, since the tradition is widely shared in the community and easily accessible, more people can try and develop their skills. Moreover, once created, the poetic units are compact and easy to remember and they can be picked up and used by a much larger group of people than just the specialists. Poems can be sung, recited or be thought utterances. The creative challenges that draw people to mantinádes are the verbal, artistic play with words and structures in the building of an image, the cognitive skills in making a point, and the experience of taking part in a dialogue. All this is a cycle in which the special way of speaking and formulating one's thoughts is perceived as making everyday moments something *more*.

---

3   Musicians often remark that these new poems cannot be sung (e.g. 051102). By this, they either refer to the elliptic balance between the vowels and the consonants or, especially, to the too complicated syntactic organization of the sentence constituents. In the latter case it is difficult to make sense of the meaning, since in a singing event, one cannot hear the whole couplet at once (see Chapter 3).

In the crossroads of composition and communicating

As a verbal tradition, mantinádes thus occur in the crossroads of improvised, rhymed poetry and short, communicative folklore genres. The latter, consisting of proverbs, proverbial sayings, anecdotes, aphorisms and the like, often referred to as the minor genres of folklore, are best known as rather fixed texts: existing units which are embedded into speech to form an authoritative utterance. Although, for example, proverbs in their traditional diversity have mainly disappeared from contemporary societies, the idiomatic formation of the lexical units as a natural tendency of language is always close to common experience. Since these forms are normally more concise than mantinádes (the common quatrain format) and they do not have a similar authority as poetry as the mantinádes have in Crete, I have limited the research of these genres as being beyond the scope of this study, although the questions of their lexical variance and contexts of use significantly overlap with those of the present inquiry (c.f. Kuusi 1963; Lauhakangas 2004).

Besides the identity of mantinádes as short, memorized entities, which can be embedded into spoken or sung discourses, mantinádes are essentially a register of individually composed oral poetry. This idea of the oral composition of poems is no longer familiar to the public at large in Western societies. Moreover, in Western societies, folklore is typically conceived as consisting of material with familiar, recurrent plots and thematic units, and/or historical and mythical knowledge. By comparison, the metrical forms which are directed towards spontaneous, improvised expression are less well-known. These forms, although once very popular in most communities, and although as "traditional" as the forms of greater scholarly prestige, are largely absent in folklore research because their fluid, ephemeral aesthetics were less appreciated by the researchers of the earlier literary folklore research paradigms. These composed traditions are emblematically based on a special productive poetic and stylistic idiom, which makes new production possible and the units recognizable, even when the linguistic forms used are close to everyday language.

The term *register* has become established to denote the special way or style of speech – in the research for oral poetry, this refers to the special, characteristic metrical and poetic vehicles of performance (Halliday 1978, Hymes 1989, Foley 1995; see Chapter 2). Oral poetry registers are based on natural linguistic forms and on the flexibility these offer to the composition in each case. In the present study, my own larger frame of reference concerns especially the registers which have as their basis a linguistic idiom syntactically flexible because the verbs are conjugated in person and the substantives in cases. As I noticed earlier, although this study focuses exclusively on the Cretan rhymed couplets and the Greek *dekapentasíllavo* meter, I have also worked with the Finnish poetry in *kalevala-meter*, as well. Both these metrical models have offered their structural and semantic potentials for a very long time (*kalevala-meter* is purported to be over two thousand years old and *dekapentasíllavo* is well over a thousand years) in the community. They are both by nature multi-purpose: they have been used to render poems and songs with thematically more or less fixed contents ("folk songs"), to compose topical verses on current local themes, as well as to make short, communicative entities. Familiarity with *kalevala-meter* poetry gives me a parallel vantage point for a metrically elastic and semantically associative register.[4]

In this study, I will thus apply the concept of register to verbal traditions based on metrical models. When discussing metrical registers of oral poetry, their productivity is also necessarily a part of the focus. Therefore, although certain registers and genres are more *explicitly* productive than others, it is difficult to transfer the colloquial understanding of such productivity unambiguously to the naming of the separate categories in research. The registers specifically used for the extemporization of poems are often referred to as *improvised oral poetry* (Armistead and Zuleika 2005; Garcia et al. 2001). As I will adopt a wider perspective on the notion improvisation in this study, I will use the notions *productive register* and *register-based tradition* as tools to focus on the topic of conscious composition. I will discuss these subjects in detail in the next chapter.

Rhymed poetry

Rhymed poetry is a familiar phenomenon in many countries. In addition to nursery rhymes, dance songs, popular songs and rhymed art poetry, in many cultures (and all those culturally connected to Crete), the explicitly productive registers are rhymed. According to my experience, these rhymed registers can be categorized into four main groups:

(1) contest poetry[5]: improvised oral poetry composed on the spot, containing a set or free number of rhyming verses or couplets and often sung competitively by (chiefly male) performers in organized casual or ritual events;
(2) longer narrative poems and songs, often historical, romantic, or humoristic: especially topical verse[6], composed by known individuals and often (but not exclusively) transmitted as texts; ballads;
(3) short, compact couplets and quatrains;
(4) an intermediate group in length and style: thematically connected sets of a few couplets (in Crete called just "songs" or *mantinádes sinehómenes*, "mantinádes continued"; in Crete, also separate genres like laments and lullabies)

---

4 For the variation among genres of *kalevala-meter* poetry, see esp. Tarkka 2005; forthcoming in English; for the structural and semantic variation in composition, see Harvilahti 1992; 2004; also Timonen 2005. For *kalevala-meter* and poetry in *kalevala-meter* in general, see Siikala and Vakimo 1994.
5 For an exhaustive description, see Miner 1993; also quoted in Zemke 2005: 84–85.
6 For the poetry often referred to as local or contemporary, I will use the expression topical verse, coined as a translation of the Finnish term *aikalaisrunous* or *rahvaanrunous* by Lotte Tarkka and Leila Virtanen (Tarkka, forthcoming).

The subject of this book is the third group, represented by mantinádes as independent units of one couplet. However, in performance and composition, they can also be "continued" to a set of few couplets (case 4). I will discuss this phenomenon as well as how other types of rhymed oral poetry are both similar and different. Although significant differences in length, style and way of performance and production distinguish these forms of oral poetry, they are all explicitly and directly based on the use of a productive, rhymed register. These *register-based* poetic traditions have as their primary aim to reflect the contextually arising themes of everyday life in the composition of textually new entities.

Although competent individuals play a significant role in bringing durable innovations to register-based traditions, the composition and performative uses of these registers are open to everyone in the local communities. Since the expression and style are explicitly based on specific linguistic idioms and bound to them and the shared experience of their use as poetry, these traditions are mainly very local and often they indeed highlight the local or group identity by referring to insider knowledge very elliptically. This is one reason why these traditions, even those that are versatile today, have remained predominantly unnoticed by scholars and by the public at large outside the specific linguistic groups who are performing them.

An important aid for textual improvisation and the key to recognizing the change in the mode of speech is the end rhyme. Although these types of poems are familiar in most cultures chiefly as sung within the frames of special singing events, end rhyme gives a clearly recognizable form to even a casual utterance. Furthermore, end rhyme helps to distinguish the accentuated expression when the form is short (a couplet/quatrain), the register resembles natural language and the poem is recited in unexpected performances on the spur of the moment. Besides the rhyme, what is typical for each genre is a fixed metrical or rhythmical pattern in which the spoken or sung verses are adapted. Rhyme patterns are different according to the traditions and to what is natural for the language. Thus, for example, in the mixed Greek and Turkish societies of the Asia minor coast, until the population exchange of 1922–3, the Greek rhyming couplet of two fifteen-syllable lines (often called *amanés,* plural *amanédes*)[7], which is often conceptualized as four half-lines with the typical quatrain pattern a,b,c,b, had an equivalent in the Turkish language (*mani*, plural *maniler*) in quatrains of 7 syllables, rhymed mainly as a,a,b,a (Bartók 1976: 203)

Short, communicative forms

If academic research has not fully recognized how the longer, mythical and historical forms are embedded into the interactive, communicative

---

[7] *Amanés* refers primarily to the vocal improvisation in a certain style, but commonly also to the corresponding poetic text which, although metrically equivalent with the mantináda, has a plaintive style and concentrates on certain typical themes (see Pennanen 2004 for details of this subject).

verbal acts, the shorter, communicative forms of oral poetry may have suffered from this lack of contextualization even more. During the earlier text-centered paradigm in folklore studies, scholars collected short poems, such as the mantinádes or the Latvian *dainas*, as well as proverbs and other minor folklore productions, but although their variation and versatility could be documented, the social context of their use was rarely focused on.[8] Although the performance-centered paradigm in the 1980s had already emphasized the various aspects of the interaction of the text and context in performances, as well as the performer/audience relationships, research was directed mainly at the narrative and ritual traditions. Two anthropologists, Michael Herzfeld (1981a; 1985b) and Charles Briggs (1988), have thus pointed out that the actual local focus on eliciting a *situated meaning* by using short, communicative genres was still absent in research. Both researchers, while concentrating on short, communicative genres in their research, have criticized heavily the way that the text-centered paradigms had neglected to research the dialectical relations of the textual and contextual features in performance (Herzfeld 1981a: 116; 1985b; Briggs 1988: 370–373). Moreover, Herzfeld and Briggs demonstrated that textual and contextual elements are always interdependent: the "experience is ultimately seamless" (Herzfeld 1985b: 216), and performers "interpret both traditions and social settings, actively transforming both in the course of their performances" (Briggs 1988: 7). Both researchers also emphasize that the performers focus on this interactive communicative competence (Briggs 1988: 3–4, 6–7; Herzfeld 1981a: 116; 1985b).

Research on mantinádes and related traditions

Much of the information and the analysis in this study has taken shape in the conversations I have had with Cretan informants during my fieldwork. As I mentioned earlier, mantinádes have been a part of the oral traditions in all the southern Dodecanese Islands, and they are one of the versatile traditions which foreign researchers have remarked on earlier. My fieldwork was therefore also informed by several earlier, particularly analytic insights into this tradition.

An important corpus of Greek folk songs and music was collected and analyzed by the Swiss ethnomusicologist and philologist Samuel Baud-Bovy in the 1930s. Baud-Bovy found the mantinádes to be the only fertile genre at this time of his doctoral fieldwork, and they formed the most important body of living folk songs. In his dissertation (1936), Baud-Bovy's conclusions concerning the longer songs are influenced by a search for origins and for ways of diffusion, a methodology belonging to the historical-geographical school of research. However, the metrical form

---

8 For the collection of *dainas*, see e.g. Vikis-Freibergs 1989: ix–xiii; for the variance of proverbs, see Kuusi 1963; for the research on the social contexts of proverbs, Lauhakangas 2004: esp. 11–12; 42.

and the versatile format and improvisation that are typical of mantinádes are described by Baud-Bovy in details that are still valid. Indeed, that part (1936: 313–394) of his dissertation features one of the most comprehensive sources on the structures and methods of rhymed oral poetry.

Michael Herzfeld's research on mantinádes (1981, 1985b, also 1985a: 141–149), as well as Anna Caraveli's publications (1982, 1985), attest to the focus on meaning as the primary characteristic of this register. These articles were important contributions to the dynamics and indigenous meaning of the poetic communication. Anna Caraveli Chaves' doctoral thesis (1978) researches the questions related to the live performance of love songs and laments and her work is based on a corpus of earlier recorded material (for laments, see also Alexiou 1974). Caraveli's later articles (1980; 1982; 1985) focus more practically and analytically on the living Greek song tradition, and especially on mantinádes. They offer a window to the ritual performance situation of the mantinádes in a wedding in the neighboring island of Karpathos (1985), to women's social poetic practices in Crete (1980), and to general methodological concerns relating to the high referentiality of the Greek folk song performances (1982). Many of her observations have been very helpful regarding the performance situation, singer and audience co-operation, and the relation of textual and extra-textual elements.

The anthropologist Michael Herzfeld is known as a critical analyst of the Greek nationalistic tradition of folklore research (1982a) and of anthropologic research in Greece (1987), as well as of many forms of Greek cultural practices, both on the local and national level.[9] From the perspective of my study, what is particularly significant is Herzfeld's focus on mantinádes and their meaning as a part of the local communicative means. One of these concerns is included in his study on a Cretan mountain village in the Milopotamos area (1985a), in which Herzfeld presents the socially crucial role that manly performativity plays in these pastoral communities. In two methodologically influential articles (1981a, 1985b), Herzfeld concentrates on the indigenous views of meaning in the performance of mantinádes. References to these studies will be recurrent in the present analysis.

The improvisation of mantinádes as a critical communicative discourse in singing events is the subject of the dissertation (1991) of Pavlos Kavouras, a Greek anthropologist educated in the United States. This musical-anthropological research concentrates on the singing of mantinádes as "poetics of exile," a discourse concerning the difficult social tension arising between the islanders and the visiting and returning emigrants in Karpathos. The distinct nature of the tradition of improvised mantinádes and music in the (until the last decades of the twentieth century) isolated, high mountain town of Olimbos in Karpathos is also well known to several musicians and poets in Crete. However, the social reality in this neighboring island of Crete, divided by heavy emigration, is very different from that in Crete.[10]

---

9 In addition to those mentioned here, among his many publications, see e.g. the following: 1974; 1981b; 1983; 1986; 1990; 1991a; 1991b; 1992; 2004.
10 As described by Kavouras, the expatriated villagers in Karpathos, returning yearly to enjoy summer vacations, wish to find the island as it was when they left. In Greece the

Kavouras' dissertation and fieldwork, which was conducted at the end of the 1980s, reflects one of the last periods and Greek collectives where improvised communication was still a central phenomenon in collective feasts.

Like Anna Caraveli in her article on a wedding *gléndi* (1985), Kavouras presents the singing of the mantinádes and the *gléndi* in Karpathos as being highly ritualistic in nature. In Crete, a similar fame is attributed to the male *parées* in some of the villages, for example, in the village of Korfes in the Department of Iraklio (Papirakis 2005). Chris Williams, who has researched the Cretan tradition both in Crete and among the succeeding generations of the expelled Turko-Cretans in Turkey, proposes that due to this ritualistic character, the habit of men gathering to singing events can have its origin in the practices of the Islamic Bektashi Sufi order. Bektashism has been influential in Albania, where similar singing events have been popular at Prespa Lake (Sugarman 1988: esp. 34, note 4), and there is also evidence of its presence in Crete. (Williams 2003) As remarked by Sugarman (1988: 34, note 4), it is likely that the event structure of the singing among the Prespa Lake Albanians is:

> modeled upon those of the Bektashi Sufi order. In the Near East both secular and religious gatherings of this type are generally associated with men, whereas Presparë use this structure, with some modification, for both men's and women's occasions. Ultimately, however, Prespa men's gatherings retain a much closer affinity to their Near Eastern counterparts than do women's gatherings.

In addition to the southern Greek islands, anthropologists conducted fieldwork in several areas around the Mediterranean during the 1960s–1980s. Most studies were concerned with social and family relations, addressing especially the questions of honor and shame.[11] At that time, a time span shortly preceding or parallel to the recent social change in many of these countries, it was still also possible to encounter the poetic traditions integrated into the social discourses of the communities in this area.

Throughout the entire Balkan area, the rhyming couplet and quatrain formats have played a major role in social discourses. Jane C. Sugarman, as referred above, analyzes the Prespa Albanian singing events organized among men as a ritual get-together (1988) and those connected to weddings (1997); among these, men can begin singing a song type referred to as the *bejte* (transcribed as *bete* in 1988) "a type of short, extemporized couplet, generally with a teasing theme, that may be added by singers to the end of

---

emigrants hold their right to vote, and in the reality of the small island, the large percentage rate of voting emigrants thus have the power to hinder the modernization desired by the islanders. In Crete, instead, the visiting and returning emigrants have had a significant role in bringing new influences, for example, to the local music (see Chapter 4).

11 For ethnographies concerning Greece, see Du Bouley 1974; Dubisch (ed.) 1986; Loizos and Papataxiarchis (eds.) 1991; for honor and shame, Campbell 1964; Pitt-Rivers 1971; Peristiany 1966; Gilmore 1987; Peristiany and Gilmore 1992.

a song; pairs of singers might also exchange such couplets in a short contest" (1997: 347).

In her book on wedding and funeral rites in Romania, Gail Kligman (1988) analyzes the use of traditional or improvised rhymed couplets as communication during rituals, but she remarks that they are also used in informal social interactions and in correspondence. These couplets consist of either of seven syllable lines or more commonly, of eight syllable lines, and they can be enlarged to triplets. This type of poetry is practiced by women and men alike, although, since women are the ritual specialists, their poetry is emphasized in this work on ritual poetry. (Kligman 1988: 13–16) According to the examples presented throughout her book, these couplets or triplets tend to form clusters of two, three or four.

The variation in form of the Balkan couplets and quatrains is concluded by Béla Bartók (1976: 196–197) as follows:

> The Turkish rural folk texts have rigorous stanza structure with fixed rhymes, similar to the Hungarian, Czech, Slovakian, and Ukrainian folk texts; and at variance with the Bulgarian and Serbo-Croatian ones in which no text-stanza structures or rhymes occur, and the Romanian which have rhymes but no stanza structure.

Turkish text stanzas always consist of four text lines, most often of eight syllables, and the rhyme pattern is characteristically a,a,b,a or a,a,a,b. Furthermore, the Mediterranean and Hispanic areas have widely cherished the quatrain form exactly similar to the Cretan mantinádes, e.g. the *Spirtu Pront* in Malta (Herndon and McLeod 1980), and the *copla* and other forms referred to by a variety of names in Spain (e.g. Armistead 2005; Fernandez 2005; Christian 2005; Trapero 2005; see also Mintz 1997).

Anthropologists conducting fieldwork further in the Arabic countries also reported on the importance of the conversational poetic traditions. The work of Steven C. Caton (1990) on the improvised Yemen verse duels and on the versification tradition as social and political acts suggests a close affinity with the socially charged styles of the Cretan (and generally southern Aegean island) mountain people's traditions. However, Caton as well as Sowayan (1985) witness an exclusion of affective, romantic and erotic verses in the men's oral poetry practices, while in Crete, these form a popular and appraised core of the expressive culture, especially among men. Moreover, Lila Abu-Lughod (1986) shows that emotional verses are composed and sung among the Bedouins, among the weak of the society, by women and young men. A collection of verses by Clinton Bailey (2002 [1991]) also presents a good variety of themes in the verses composed and transmitted among the Bedouin in Sinai and the Negev. Bailey shows that love verses and erotic histories are also among the popular poems in these communities. Other contributions in this field include research on the Arabic traditions of singing quatrains at weddings as ritual and entertainment. These are extensively analyzed in articles by Jargy, Haydar, Sbait, Sawa, and Sowayan in the special volume of Arabic oral poetry in the journal of *Oral Tradition* 4 (1989).

The quatrain is a strong form that occurs from the Mediterranean all through Eastern Europe up to Finland[12]. The Russian *tshastushkas* are still versatile, especially as bawdy mocking songs.[13] In 2001, the journalist Jussi Konttinen described a situation in the village Berozhok (published in the Finnish daily newspaper *Helsingin Sanomat*), where a mother and her son playing accordion competed by taking turns in singing *tshastushkas*. Konttinen remarks that the most popular songs are those most obscene, and although in this situation the son regards the obscenities not to be suitable for the strangers' ears (to the journalist and the female folklore students present), this is the direction in which the singing quickly steers. This article by Konttinen coincided with the political questions raised by Anna Politkovskaja and was motivated by the commentary on the freedom of speech in Russia. Konttinen concludes that (translation by the present author) "in a *tshastushka*, the freedom of speech is restricted only by the rhyme form. Anyone can create and sing them; in them, one can say anything aloud. Both women and men sing *tshastushkas*." He continues that in this particular case, the mother confesses that some drinking would help her formulate her songs better; normally the *tshastushkas* are sung during festivities and drinking sessions (Helsingin Sanomat August 26, 2001; see also Sokolov 1950).

In Finland, where the *kalevala-meter* had been the privileged meter of all oral song, the end-rhyme and stanzaic forms were introduced in the beginning of the seventeenth century.[14] These new song models, spreading to Finland chiefly from Sweden along with the European models, were first parallel to the *kalevala-meter* poetry but later rendered the latter outmoded. The "new folk song", mainly in the rhymed quatrain form, *rekilaulu*, was popular as oral poetry until the beginning of the twentieth century. Anneli Asplund (2006: 152–153) notes that the popularity of the *rekilaulu* is connected to the development of youth culture. Correspondingly, the main thematic contents of these rhymed quatrains concerned love and the relations between boys and girls. Furthermore, Leea Virtanen (1973: 156) observes that the two core areas of the rhymed *rekilaulu*, southern Ostrobothnia and Karelian Isthmus, are also those where village fights flourished. In other words, the lively youth culture and the socializing lifestyle of the densely populated villages made singing events and versatile rhymed quatrains popular. Virtanen observes that in the Karelian Isthmus, unmarried girls

---

12 Also the German language areas *Schnaderhüpflit* (Harvilahti 1985).
13 The lack of material translated into other languages unfortunately still renders the Russian research widely unattainable. Apart from the introduction given by Sokolov in 1950, I have not managed to find any research on *tshastushkas* in either English or Finnish. In order to enclose a reference to the contemporary practice, I will therefore refer to a recent article on the theme.
14 The earliest documents (dating back to the first decades of the seventeenth century) on the changing folk song culture and the use of end rhyme in Finland come from the court sentences received by the singers and composers of mocking songs (Asplund 2006: 109–114). This phenomenon is well known in many countries, e.g. the Icelandic saga-literature; the punishments for mocking rhymes were coded in the Icelandic law before the thirteenth century (Ahola forthcoming).

sung in their own groups, and boys in theirs. Rhymed songs were widely composed and used as mocking songs and, as described by Kati Kallio (né Heinonen), the male villagers in Ingria could gather for improvised singing sessions, in which the humorous, obscene contents were fueled by their consumption of alcohol (Heinonen 2008). The boys' preference to sing under the influence of alcohol is also reported by Virtanen (1973: 151–152). In Russian Karelia, the quatrain form was named short *pajo*, and remains to this day only as a fixed-phrase poetry. In addition, the unrhymed Latvian quatrains, the *dainas*, were extremely metaphoric, lyric and crystallized poems (see Harvilahti 1985; Vikis-Freibergs 1989).

To summarize, the rhyming couplets, or the quatrains that are equivalent in length with the Cretan mantinádes, have served or still serve in several linguistic areas as fixed or improvised songs in life cycle rituals, dance, entertainment, lyrical self-expression, duels, satire and improvised commentary. These forms are therefore particularly noteworthy in that they are closely connected to people's expressive needs in the spheres of life which concern their immediate, personal experience of being a member of their community. In many cases, normally among men, the consummation of alcohol has helped them open up, and the quatrains/couplets have served as means of contesting the narrow limits of the self-expression in the closely-knit and highly regulated village communities.

While most collectively shared traditions of oral poetry, including the productive couplets and quatrains, have nearly or completely died out during the modernization and urbanization processes which even the last East European and Mediterranean countries have undergone during the last decades of the twentieth century, several forms of improvised contest poetry flourish locally. These are practiced today in the Arabic tradition, in the Spanish and Portuguese speaking groups, in Southern Italy, and internationally in the form of freestyle rap (esp. Yacub 2007; Armistead and Zuleika 2005; Garcia et al. 2001; Zedda 2009; also Palonen 2008). As these sources show, improvised contest registers are chiefly used by experienced performers in organized singing events or at ritual events, especially marriages. Research on improvised rhymed poetry mainly concentrates on describing and analyzing the performance and composition in the framework of these events. Far less is known of how such productive, rhymed registers were or are carried over into everyday life (if, as I suggest, many of them are).

Although the above-mentioned studies offer valuable insights into the communication in poetic form, they still offer very little information about the conversational and casual uses of the poems. Therefore, the comprehensive research of the linguistic anthropologist Charles Briggs on the short, conversational forms in a Mexicano community (1988) makes an essential point of reference for several discussions in the present study. This research has especially influenced the perception of how traditional textual units are contextualized into speech events in practice. This detailed analysis of conversational forms and the dialogic elements inherent in them has given me a readiness to observe the dialogism of communication even in a very different society and register.

Characteristic of the research on the improvised and communicative genres is that the perception and research has often been coincidental; scholars have encountered these traditions during a longer residence in a community, often due to some other original research task. Lila Abu-Lughod (1986: 25) makes this very evident by stating:

> Listening and observing everyday life and social interactions both in public and in the intimacy of the domestic world, I had noticed that people often sang or punctuated their conversations with short poems. Everyone showed great interest in these poems and often seemed moved when they heard them. At first I ignored them, since I had no interest in poetry. I had come to study the patterning and meaning of interpersonal relations, in particular between men and women, so I merely jotted in my fieldnotes that people seemed to love reciting some sad-sounding short poems. After a few incidents, however, I began to wonder what these poems meant and why they were so valued by the Bedouins. I began to pay attention to them."

Even the folklorist Roger Abrahams comments on the finding of the urban male performance genres among the African-Americans: "This ingroup material did not come to my notice until I had lived in the neighborhood for many months" (1970: 6). (See also Abu-Lughod 1986: 24–31; Caton 1990: 4–5; Kligman 1988: 17–24) Inversely, I am sure that many short conversational forms and improvised uses of other registers have historically remained largely unnoticed due to the short visits, pre-determined targets or the collectors' inadequate language skills.

Academic researchers from outside the community are not the only ones to notice these verbal traditions; the interest among the inside-group can be noteworthy. This is the case in Crete as well as in the contemporary Hispanic and Portuguese speaking areas and Arabic societies. On the one hand, this interest seems to be as "text-centered" as it was among the folklore researchers until the second half of the twentieth century. In Crete, a focus on the poems as *poetry* is visibly important and writing down the poems and making collections of texts is a current task, as it has been all throughout the twentieth century. On the other hand, the inside group feeling seems to be strong among these register-based traditions. For instance, people in Crete generally suppose that similar verbal forms are not practiced by other peoples – one invariably encounters this attitude both in conversations and in the local written texts. The significance of such traditions as capital for local identity is thus underlined. It is therefore no surprise that live oral poetry is currently popular in communities such as Crete, Palestine and the Basque country, all famous for their maintenance of local identity, or among sub-cultures, such as rap-music.

Local literature and discourses on mantinádes

Foreign and Greek scholars have been widely interested in Greek folk poetry during the early years of establishing the Modern Greek State and during the earlier twentieth century. As in several other countries, this interest served ideological purposes and while focusing on the ethnic and mental unity of the people, strove to find the original forms of the folk song rather than to describe its versatility and variation. A reader will be able to become familiar with the history of collecting and publishing of Greek folk poetry through the comprehensive work of Alexis Politis (1984), as well as through the insights of Michael Herzfeld (esp. 1982). Sifakis (1988: 135–146) also offers a survey of the research on the poetic means of Greek folk poetry.

Until the 1990s, the Cretan way of writing about any form of tradition, just as the mainstream of the discourses on "tradition" when verbalized in festive and seminar speeches even today, typically contains an outspoken frame of regionalism, patriarchy and religious pathos. Most contributions were directed at advancing these types of values and at constructing a cultural past rather than analyzing or providing information on the actual contemporary traditions. From the beginning of the 1990s, methodologically more solid studies that were based on ethnographic and archive work started to appear, and these are available today on the subjects concerning local history, traditional occupations and other ethnographic themes. Publishers such as the University of Crete, Vikélia Vivliothíki (Municipality of Iraklio), and the Historical-Ethnographic Association of Rethimno can be acknowledged for these matters. These studies are, however, still interested quite exclusively in historical perspectives and consequently, contemporary themes are rare.

One of the most dramatic aspects for the Cretan cultural life concerns the ideological battle concerning the originality and place of the violin as a "Cretan" musical instrument. The well-known collector and publisher of Greek folk music, Simon Karas who, as argued by Konstantinos Papadakis (1989), had never personally been in Crete, came to the conclusion that the violin was a newly introduced instrument, which was taking power over the "original" instrument of folk music, the *lira*. As the director of the folk music programs on the radio, Karas managed to ban the use of the violin on the radio in 1955. His opinion was largely adopted by researchers and in the long run, by the locals in the other districts of Crete. The battle over the originality of the lira was very pointed at the turn of the twenty-first century, and only very lately it seems that most people have became informed of the role of the violin in eastern and western Crete. I am not familiar with the development of this juxtaposition in the Greek academic circles, but I was surprised to find that this ideological injustice was not historically contextualized in the otherwise so skillfully edited recent edition on Samuel Baud-Bovy's field work in Crete (Baud-Bovy 2006) – it becomes clear that his impressions, as well as his assistants, before and during the fieldwork conducted in 1953–54, are drawn directly from Karas.[15] Among foreign

---

15 For critics on the research policy of Karas, see also Brandl 1991.

scholars, the most often cited presentation of Cretan musical and song traditions is that of the musicologist Yorgos Amaryanakis (1988), which until lately was also the most accessible publication. Amaryanakis was originally from Ierapetra, and his introduction thus also pays attention to the role of the violin. During the last few years, several new introductions to Cretan musical instruments and dance forms have occurred. (e.g. Dalianoudi 2004; Nikolakakis 2007; 2008: Papadakis M. 2002; Petrakis 2009; Tsouhlarakis 2000; 2004; For Cretan music and dance, see Chapter 3)

As for the Cretan oral poetry, the literature available contains short introductions (Amaryanakis 1988, Beaton 1980), local publications of seminar papers (Moutzouris 2002), collections of poems (Lioudaki 1936; Droudakis 1982; Pavlakis 1994), studies and instructions on the correct Cretan dialect and expression in the composition of mantinádes (Kafkalas 1992; 1995; 1996; 1998) and a good wealth of publications of individual, composed poetry. The first major collection is that of Maria Lioudaki from 1936[16]. Lioudaki's collection is especially interesting in that it documents the poems in their original, dialectal form. Whereas collections of poems have been available throughout the twentieth century, they have appeared without information on the performers or on the performance situations and therefore mainly serve the local interests. During the last decades, however, a few studies have addressed the tradition of a village or region from the perspective of the individuals and these works offer a more pronounced idea of the times still accessible through oral history. The recognition of a composer's identity and the performative contexts of the poems and music are brought to the fore, for example, in a book presenting *mantinadolóyi* from the Korfes village by Papirakis (2004) and in a study on the local musicians from the end of 1800 and early 1900 by Diktakis (1999).

The collections of poems, however, make an interesting case. They can be criticized with reason as products of scholarly interest that overlook the essentially context-sensitive determination of the meaning of the poems in the village practices (Herzfeld 1985b). This orientation is nevertheless not the full picture from the perspective of a significant user group of these collections: by the Cretan composers and performers, with whom I have discussed this matter, the collections are not regarded as being examples of performances but that of a reserve. Thus the collections also reflect the evaluation that is evident in this indigenous contextualization of the poems: texts are both individually situated arguments and a shared property and potentiality. I will later refer to this emblematic aspect of the mantinádes as the *double-identity*. The ability to improvise and make references during a performance is based on a wide reserve and knowledge of existing texts, and collections serve as one of the reasonable sources for developing the ability to perform. Although poems have been learned from oral sources, whenever possible, people have also absorbed poems eagerly from written

---

16 An earlier local edition was published already in 1933. The edition I have is not dated; I refer here to the date of the first edition; a second edition was published in 1971 (for Lioudaki's bibliography, see Papadaki 1992: 197–203, and for her unpublished manuscripts and collections, Papadaki 1992: 201–220).

sources. Today these constitute, in addition to the poems heard in musical performances (live and recorded) and television and radio programs, the main source for embracing the tradition.[17] I will discuss this perspective in more detail in the next chapter, and return to the concern in Chapter 4.

The work of Mihalis Kafkalas has had an enormous impact on the writing and publishing of mantinádes. Kafkalas was himself a *mantinadológos*, with an interest in cultivating the poetic and linguistic expression of the mantináda in a correct and rich traditional Cretan idiom. Beginning in 1988, he held a monthly "competition of mantináda" in a Cretan newspaper, *Kritiká Epíkaira*, criticizing and evaluating the mantinádes sent to the competition. His influence is apparent in the enthusiasm of several contemporary composers to look for expressive local Cretan words and expressions. Kafkalas has published an article (1996) and a book (1998) based on these evaluations and focuses on the general outlines of the rules of composition with detailed examples. Moreover, Kafkalas has written a contemporary description of the Cretan dialect, with reference to mantinádes and to the poetic language (1992), and provides a comprehensive presentation of Cretan adverbs (1995). The exceptional diversity in the use of adverb forms is a distinctive characteristic of the Cretan idiom and a telling example of the morphological variation available for the poetic register.

In central Crete, two periodicals, *Kondiliés* and *Ksathéri*, appeared in the beginning of the twenty-first century and serve today as major forums for local interests in terms of contemporary musicians and poets, biographies of past musicians, as well as for the various kinds of presentations of the traditional and contemporary forms of the musical and verbal tradition.

Research as engagement

Research questions

At the beginning of the 1930s, Milman Parry attempted to find a living analogue to explain the classic problem of the Homeric question and the *oral* composition of these exceptionally long and elegant narratives in verse, which he came to suspect to be oral, especially after becoming familiar with the ethnographic studies of his contemporaries (Foley 1988:10–18). In the continuation, his student Albert Lord set up to explain in detail, first in his dissertation in 1949, and then in the *Singer of Tales* (1960), how this oral technique works, and how it was different from the written.[18] Lord explained this in a thorough way to convince his readers, as he knew that to his audience, the oral composition in a performance was completely unknown. This unfamiliarity with the process of oral composition remains much the same today, and the presentation of the productive register and processes of composition are therefore central issues in the present study.

---

17 See also Yacub 2007.
18 For a full bibliography, see Foley 1988: 36–40.

The research available on the oral composition of poetry concerns especially the composition of the narrative, epic poems and the rhymed contest poetry. The work of Milman Parry and Albert Lord stimulated extensive discussions on formulae, formulaic expressions and systems, themes, and other units of oral composition (see Foley 1985). The Basque poets and researchers (Garcia et. al. 2001; *Oral Tradition* volume 22, the Basque Special Issue, 2007) and Nadia Yaqub in her work on Palestine verse duelling (2007), have recently increased the detailed, firsthand knowledge of rhyming and the aesthetics of extempore composition. Since a full utterance among these traditions is a lengthy epic narrative or is constructed of several couplets or fluid verse improvisation, none of them places similar demand on coherence, which is the ideal characteristic of a mantináda[19]. In this study, I will therefore focus on defining the elements that are significant in the successful composition of an independent, semantically impressive couplet.

The basis for composition is register. As for mantinádes, the end rhyme plays an emblematic role, as it does in so many similar traditions worldwide. In addition to the question of rhyme and rhyming, and the examination of the ideal identity of the couplet as a clearly bound, self-dependent unit, one target is to address how the tradition and the register have changed when the composition is currently practiced and the poems are performed in a literary form and environment.

As the previous pages mentioned, short, explicitly communicative registers have existed widely in human societies, although during the earlier text-centered research paradigms, researchers and collectors did not notice this or they did not regard such registers as valuable or appealing[20]. During these research paradigms, the co-existence of traditions in a society was rarely the interest of the collectors, who rather encountered the wealth of the forms extremely selectively. Even where such communicative poetries intruded in the situation, pens were rather put aside and tape recorders were turned off until the performer took up the more archaic forms and often epic, narrative and mythic songs that were the target of the researcher. This was made explicit by the researcher Janika Oras in relation to the Estonian folklore collection practices in the twentieth century.[21] The predominant task for me has been to formulate a theory of the spontaneity, creativity and improvisation I witnessed in the field but I have realized has been largely lacking in the accounts of folklore scholarship.

Finally, what forged my personal attachment to the tradition was the growing awareness of the poems essentially as tools for dialogue: the

---

19 The composition of a thematic group of couplets, often called a "song", is also common in Crete; see Chapter 5.
20 Basing on the researchers' field notes and diaries, Kati Kallio, (Heinonen 2008) presents a telling survey of the selective aesthetics of the Finnish fieldworkers who collected song texts and melodies in the 1800–1950 in Ingria.
21 Presentation in the seminar: Kirjoitetun ja lauletun runon tutkimuksen metodologia ennen ja nyt, organized by the Finnish Literature Society, Helsinki September 6–7, 2007; see also Oras 2008, esp. 95–96.

realization that the mantinádes characteristically embodied a dialogic emphasis both in terms of the construction of the poem, the text, and the contextualization of a given text in a performative situation. For a long time, however, I could not capture the multi-facetness of the implicit performative and of the other dialogues going on in Crete: people living among an active poetic culture do not need theory or explanations. The pervasive thread running through this study is to find these dialogues. Behind setting out to define the plurality of the ways in which the individual members of the Cretan communities can engage in meaningful dialogues through this tradition, my goal is to capture something essential in the relationship between individuals and a verbal tradition. What does an oral tradition, and particularly a productive register of rhyming couplets, give to an individual perceiver, performer or composer? By trying to analyze the full complexity of my experience with mantinádes, I hope to help others who encounter these kinds of poetic models, either in print or in practice, to grasp more than the "simple rhymes."

Fieldwork

This study is based on long-term ethnographic fieldwork which began in 1997 and has continued ever since; my last visit to Crete and the discussions I engaged in occurred in September 2010. This lengthy period, however, forms three rather separate phases. The phases are different with regard to the nature and amount of my familiarity with the tradition, the consequences of forming the knowledge, as well as the organization of fieldwork and the closeness of the contacts, on which the production of the research data is grounded. Each of these factors has contributed to this research in significant ways.

The first phase covers the years 1997–2001. The first impulse to inquire upon the local folklore actualized during the spring season of 1997. I had arrived in Crete as an exchange-student primarily to improve my language skills and to advance my Modern Greek studies, but as folklore was my main subject at the University of Helsinki, I looked for local forms of oral poetry, and my intention was to complete a seminar paper on this topic for Modern Greek studies while in Crete. My first introduction to the mantinádes was Michael Herzfeld's book, *The Poetics of Manhood* (1985a), which examines the distinct nature of the people in a certain mountain village in central Crete. Although this study reflects a community with rather extreme opinions and habits even in the Cretan context, its focus on performativity and improvisation as central characteristics of the local ideal of being in a society is transferable to the entire island of Crete to a significant degree. This book prepared me to find – if I was yet to find twenty years after Herzfeld's fieldwork – a tradition of short, poetic units applied to socially significant, circumstantially defined acts of reciprocal communication.

The early inquiries however made me face very different kinds of speech acts. In the descriptions given to me by any Rethimniot, the main frame for the poetry performance was explicitly entitled to singing in *paréa*, informal get-togethers of groups of friends or relatives, and on festive occasions, such as at weddings and village feasts, although it was clear that these had already been transformed some decades ago. In one village wedding, I witnessed that even though the music and songs performed during the dance were now left exclusively to professional musicians, during the late hours, at the end of this occasion, a group of men gathered and took the microphone to sing their own verses, very much like I was told would happen in a traditional *gléndi*. My perception was, however, that the singing of those cheerfully drunken men turned more inwards in their self-expression than in communication between themselves or the audience. Many people eagerly narrated situations of past performances, where mantinádes where used to make a point, and these recollections implicitly showed how much the well-timed, situated performances and extempore composition were appreciated. Especially older people often quickly responded to my curiosity by simply reciting a single poem. One old man, a shopkeeper, used to recite me the same poem over and over again, pointing to the meaning that it has. Although I later came to understand that these seemingly harmless images often reflected people's profound conceptions of life, with the criteria I had in my mind at the time, I was hardly able to appreciate these as *real* performances.

After this initial period of studies, I returned to Rethimno for several short holiday trips and finally from August 1999 until June 2000 for a year of fieldwork and Modern Greek studies. The pretext to ask about mantinádes had turned out to be a good way of engaging in conversation with even occasional acquaintances. By now, my interest was also oriented towards writing my master's thesis on mantinádes and during the autumn of 1999, I conducted several organized, tape-recorded interviews in Rethimno, Iraklio and in the region of Milopotamos. The adaptation of Greek as the everyday language with my partner helped me to quickly gain more fluency in communication in the standard Greek language, and his presence in the conversations with people with heavy dialectal expression helped me make sense of many more demanding encounters. Together with another friend who worked as a teacher in a village primary school in the lower Milopotamos area, I visited this Village, in which we had the opportunity to find a house and stay during March and April of 2001. In the Village, the old women Despina and Agapi, to whom we were directed in the first place by a young woman who did not feel herself suitable to inform me about the theme, provided me with the essential practical introduction both as to the appearance of mantinádes in conversation and to the norms of communication. In addition to this, in our first meeting, I took over the task to write down on my portable computer, the hand-written sheets containing Despina's notes of her poems. These poems were phonemically hand-written and because it was difficult even for my Greek husband to transcribe them, we met several times to go through and discuss the poems. Among other things, these discussions turned out to be complete elementary lessons on the versatility of the form.

There was very little literary material and research on mantinádes to work from. On the basis of what I found, as well as my preliminary

Embracing the ethnographer. From this early period of our collaboration, the elderly women Agapi (left) and Despina (right) invited me to share their concerns in both our mantináda-oriented conversations and in our everyday discussions. Photo by Yannis Hadziharalambous, April 2001.

fieldwork, I completed my master's thesis in March 2003. Since the "field" had became a part of my life much before I had any idea of a large-scale academic study, and since understanding the way people communicate with mantinádes developed hand-in-hand with my language skills, this early period of learning closely followed the communicative structures of the tradition itself.

The second period encompasses the years 2004–2006. With the help of a three-year research grant, I was now able to make a long-term plan for doctoral research and to settle down in Crete for the period of May to December in 2004. We settled in the Village again, I bought a used car, and during this time, as well as during the next two years, this Village was the base from which we conducted field trips to other areas at times. In 2005, I returned to Crete four times for stays lasting from two to six weeks, and in 2006, for two stays of three and four weeks. During the year 2004, we lived in the Village together with my husband, who participated in many conversations especially during our trips outside the Village. Later I returned to the Village mostly by myself and also toured the island alone. By now, "we" formed a household in the Village, but also my "independent" Finnish character was accepted.[22] In addition to participating in the Village's shared

---

22 In the beginning, if I was alone for only one night, the people were concerned about how I could sleep alone in the house – especially since there was a direct view from the house towards the graveyard. Until lately, few of the village women drove a car alone, nor did they take long walks to other villages or in the olive groves, which I took daily.

Lasithi plateau. A major circuit in eastern Crete in November 2005 was constructed around a few pre-arranged targets, but complemented by several ex tempore inquiries. The latter often started in the local kafenío, and sometimes, like here, ended there as well. Here my partner, Yannis, interviews the last local player of the folk instrument askomandoúra, bagpipes, about the procedure of preparing the goat skin to make the bag. The other men urge him to fetch the instrument but he maintains that it was broken. Photo by the author.

activities and associating more tightly with a small circle of families, my gardening, composting, cooking and wine-making activities linked me to the everyday conversations of the village. This period is characterized by an amassing of experience in a wide variety of contexts: casual conversations, interviews, festive occasions, seminars on Cretan music, my husband's musical activities as a teacher and performer, trips to other regions, and the reading of the daily newspapers, etc.

The third period of 2007–2010 is characterized by short stays and long separations, since I could return to Crete and the Village only for short stays each September or October. Meanwhile, the relationship and conversational interaction with some of my key interlocutors become even more pronounced. During the year 2007, and after a pause of fifteen months again from April 2009 onwards, I concentrated on formulating the academic discussion in my dissertation. During these short visits each year, I was able to complement the images I was building with the help of revisiting my interlocutors' earlier, tape-recorded words at home; I could also test and discuss the ideas surfacing from this data and my intellectual process of interpretation and contextualization of the data, as I had done during the earlier years as well.

Methodology and methods of research and analysis

The primary data is thus chiefly produced during ethnographic encounters through the methods of participant observation, casual conversations and occasional organized interviews: intersubjective action and encounters. This type of intersubjective knowledge production among human sciences is today mainly conceptualized on the basis of a hermeneutic epistemology. Within cultural studies, this concerns especially the moderate hermeneutics outlined by Gadamer. According to Gadamer's hermeneutic principles, we have to recognize "*the priority of the question* in all knowledge and discourse that really reveals something of an object" (2004 [1975]: 357). This means that to question is to reveal the indeterminacy of that questioned. The dialectic of questions and answers is the basis for interpretation, which consequently proceeds in an open-ended hermeneutic circle. Moreover, the interlocutors' fore-understanding (or prejudice) is always present in the communicative interaction. In a hermeneutic process, that fore-understanding is however not an obstacle, but, when the existence of such fore-understanding is recognized and accepted, the necessary basis to which the engagement in such process can adhere (Gadamer 2004 [1975]: 356–371).[23]

The methodological move from positivist to hermeneutic epistemology brought into focus the ethnographer's own participation and reflection. The concept of dialogical methodology has become one of the chief ways to define that the data is produced in the interaction between the ethnographer and his or her interlocutors in the field (Vasenkari 1996; Vasenkari & Pekkala 2000). During the last decades of the twentieth century and pointedly among American anthropologists, the adaptation of the metaphor of dialogue (Marcus and Fischer 1986) also brought about serious debates over the quality of the dialogism of both the ethnographic interaction and the following de- and recontextualizations of the data. (Crapanzano 1992; Mannheim and Tedlock 1995; Tapaninen 1996; Vasenkari 1996; Vasenkari and Pekkala 2000)

My own methodological models for carrying out fieldwork and situating myself in the study as a necessary tool for grasping the underlying patterns and values of verbal communication comes directly from preceding researchers of short, conversational genres. The anthropologists Michael Herzfeld and Charles Briggs have been in the forefront, not only in pointing to the text-context interdependency of the verbal art they studied (Herzfeld 1981a; 1985b; Briggs 1988), but also in requiring methodological rigour and discussion over the terminological inaccuracy, false intimacy and the power over the outcome of the research (esp. Herzfeld 1987; Briggs 1986; 1988).

In an ethnographic study of a verbal tradition, the dialogic form of discourse and knowledge production makes the researcher and his or her understanding a primary vehicle for the knowledge produced. Charles Briggs (1988) notes three points in which this becomes palpable, and much as

---

23 See also for a detailed adaption of Gadamer's hermeneutics to the research of textualized material in Mikkola 2009: 45–53.

explained by Gadamer, serves the goal of understanding: (1) the failures of an outsider to meet the local goals of communication can be the most illuminating introduction to them (ibid. 3–4); (2) the fieldworker's role as an outsider elicits commentary which is a rich and important source of information regarding the communicative values (ibid. 373–375);[24] and (3) the changing roles of the fieldworker illuminate the different roles the tradition plays in the society (ibid. 52). Without being personally involved, I could never have really understood the power of these short poems. For me, personal experiences have created the basis for my understanding of the poetic idiom as interpersonal communication, and my friendship with some of my regular interlocutors has made it possible to empathize with their emotional self-expression. A tradition in poetic form may also reveal something essential through one's personal experience in poetic excursions. For instance, Caton (1990: 10) describes how his trials to elicit verses himself made him learn more from his own mistakes and their corrections than from hours of recorded examples. My own attempts to compose couplets made me more highly aware of the special cognitive skills required for framing the object and making an image, rather than merely by adding one line to another and creating a rhyme. (See also Caraveli 1985: 282)

Although I was not as young as Charles Briggs[25] at the beginning of my fieldwork, my role as a novice involved very clearly not just my language skills and the knowledge of the tradition, but essentially the lack of fluency in the local modes of communication. Therefore, as described by Briggs (1988: 49), "the sociolinguistic norms placed the responsibility for structuring our interactions in their hands, not mine." Not that people had thought it necessary to introduce me to their ways of communication, but with respect to the mantinádes, and reflecting people's warm response to my curiosity over the tradition, they just ignored any other ways, since for them, the mantinádes represented a mode which is a way to participate in a dialogue and to challenge others to engage in it. One of the significant aspects of my long-term fieldwork has concerned my different, shifting roles from a stranger and novice in the tradition, to an accepted participant in normal conversations, and finally to be included even in the detailed elaboration of themes beyond habitual discourse.

In order for that to happen, such movement involves deep engagement and time. This engagement carries the research dialogue forward in a dual process of enriching the dialogue by the heterophony of conversations and reaching towards understandable wholes and emphases (see also Tapaninen 1996: 16). As described by Bakhtin (1986: 68–69), a single person's "responsive understanding" is part of a dialogue, an internal dialogue, when this is part of a process for appropriating something that has caught the

---

24 For Briggs, the characterization of his involvement and the social criticism exercised by his consultants during the performances were an indispensable means of grasping the features of the subordinated community's self-definition and counter-hegemonic aims channeled through the discourse in the verbal genres in question. (Briggs 1988: 373–375; see also Herzfeld 1985b: 201, 206–207)
25 He was nineteen years old (1988: 49, 52) and I was thirty-five.

person's attention. Bakhtin mentions that some speech genres, such as lyric poetry, are specifically directed towards such responsive understanding further off in time (ibid. 69). This is very true regarding the tradition of the mantinádes, but I see such movement clearly in the formation of the research dialogue: both are based on engagement.[26]

My interpretation of the concept dialogue is therefore essentially connected to the idea of engagement. An exchange of poems in a singing event becomes a dialogue when all participants engage in it by adhering to the chosen theme. Similarly, a conversation becomes a dialogue when the participants are engaged in it by directing their attention to something they are sharing or trying to share in mutual sympathy, although not necessarily agreement, over the subject.

During my time studying the register of mantinádes, the Cretans have taught me that their dialogues can range from very concrete and situated interactions in place and time to lifelong engagement in a process which commands large entities and under favorable conditions creates connections between referents dispersed over a great distance. For this reason, I also interpret that the primary dialogues and the secondary or shadow dialogues (Crapanzano 1992: 205–215) are inherent in the larger ideology of dialogue: each participant in a face-to-face dialogue is also engaged in other internal dialogues which can change the interaction or be changed by it. It can be useful to make a difference between concrete conversational dialogues (primary dialogues) and the processes in which such primary dialogues are "digested" (Bakhtin 1986: 62), as in an ethnographic academic study (secondary dialogues). But I do not think that it is possible to understand either of these without considering that for each participant, a specific dialogue is always internally connected to other dialogues. Since dialogue assumes engagement, this also entails simultaneous interpretation and analysis. While the simultaneous processes of contextualization, interpretation and analysis direct the dialogue during its unfolding, each new conversation is also a potential field for the interpretation and analysis of earlier utterances and dialogues (Bakhtin 1990 [1981]; 1986; Mannheim and Tedlock 1995).

According to this interpretation of the dialogue as engagement, the dialogical methodology does not have to imply that all fieldwork conversations and interviews are dialogues; my own years of fieldwork include many sporadic conversations which I do not regard as being dialogic. This data is equally valid but different from that produced in dialogic conversations and interaction, and creating this in the meeting between people from different cultural backgrounds needs time. In the frame of the research interest of the present study, the sporadic monologues (this refers to the participant interaction, not the internal dialogism of my interlocutors speech as described by Bakhtin, see esp. 1981: 279–285) have been necessary for proportioning the phenomena outlined in the more dialogic meetings. The mere quantity of the scattered casual conversations has clearly contributed to my ability to participate in more demanding dialogues.

---

26 For an essay on the creativity of the process in research, see also Crease 1995.

With the intent of building a dialogic interaction, one of my concrete targets with each potential interlocutor was to meet several times, or even better, to be able to maintain a continuous, interactive relation even at longer intervals. Ironic though it may be, this target was in practice contradictory with another interest: it was important that the first meeting be tape-recorded, since the person would never tell the same stories again, at least he or she would not *perform* them again, and it was this first meeting that was most susceptible for such story telling. However, since the first meeting is indeed a performance in which people tell what they themselves regard as being essential and presume the other will want to hear, opting to meet again after a recorded conversation turned out to be a problem if there were no natural reasons to do so. I often felt that people were disappointed when I wanted to meet them again since at that moment, they felt that they had done their best to tell the entire story. Wasn't I satisfied with that? With people I met outside of the Village, or out of some other network securing a natural continuation, I therefore tried to create possible ties, but often without success. During long-term fieldwork it also becomes evident how many normal prerequisites for friendship shape the opportunities for such continued communication. Furthermore, to lead to a dialogic engagement, the meetings and conversations need to be somehow interesting for both sides. This differs from interviews and situations that are arranged or take place just once.

To illustrate the significance of the time aspect in ethnographic research and particularly the engagement over time, the following concrete example comes to mind. During the early years, I was sometimes told that in the recent past, a man had performed a *kantáda* (serenade) to his future wife. As I was not provided details of how this had taken place, my pre-conceived, vague understanding meant that I thought of this event in terms of Romeo and Juliette: a lone man singing secretly to a woman under her window. In one of our early conversations, Mitsos Stavrakakis had mentioned to me that kantádes were performed with a *paréa*, and although it did not strike me at that moment, the listening of this recorded conversation made me re-introduce the theme in our next conversation. The result is quoted on pages 115–116: the tradition was that the boys always went to sing in a group of four to six persons to a girl; in fact, it was unthinkable to go alone, because it would have been too dangerous in Cretan village society.

By dialogic conversation and interaction, I therefore refer especially to those conversational relations that developed over several encounters and during many conversations, and in some cases this meant over many years. However, these dialogues are also of two kinds; they could be depicted as "dialogic conversations" and "dialogic interaction in conversation." The former grew out of extended, open-ended, yet interview-like, settings and the latter concern the challenges which I encountered during verbal interactions. Dialogic conversations took place with a small number of individuals who were familiar with the mode of long talks concerning their experiences and composition activities, or were able and willing to adapt this, and with whom, through this mutual engagement, it was possible to create a basis for their willingness to contribute to the themes I introduced. This mode was familiar to me from the earlier interviews with Finnish women.

The main part of my experience is constructed of dialogic interaction characterized mainly by the reverse: I had the challenge of grasping what my interlocutor wanted to say. The Cretans' outward-orientated, discursive identity makes it easy to engage them in a conversation but many of them also display a good amount of self-assurance over how and of what to say. This mode of constantly challenging the opponent was something that I was not very familiar with as a mode of communication. While I found this type of communicating to be a most frustrating and a lonely way to learn, it was nonetheless the most instructive and necessary guidance to the very subject of my study: the *raison-d'être* of the mantinádes. While I learned what and how to ask, with all those individuals with whom I was in recurrent interaction, there was nevertheless a responsive, appreciative movement towards taking into consideration my initiatives as well.

Most people first thought that I wanted to talk about mantinádes because I wanted to collect as many poems as possible. But my target concerned the structures and ideals of communication that were intuitively familiar as forms of action to many people, but certainly not familiar topics of conversation. Toward this end, the world which I wished to learn about was entirely oral. By this, I do not mean that people were unable to read and write, but that the organization and aims of conversation were essentially communicative and not directed toward organizing the reality in a logical, hierarchical order. If I wanted to do more than collect poems, I had to grasp first the very foundations of this logic of learning and communication. Instead of listening to what I asked and answering me informatively, most people I met in the beginning challenged me to grasp a point. My general questions were either disregarded or answered with an example, the relationship of which to the whole was left open. A detailed inquiry was highly approved, but for a detailed inquiry, I already had to know a lot! Poor knowledge on the part of the fieldworker led many local respondents to adapt themselves to a simple level of discourse, whereas later, when I was able to show knowledge of minute details of the tradition, I was viewed in conversation nearly as another tradition-bearer.

The basic difficulty with this oral world concerns the high level of referentiality based on (1) the explicit use of local cultural knowledge and (2) the far advanced linguistic codification, say the use of the feminine, masculine and neuter articles to refer to specific but extra-textual entities, as well as (3) the lack of a similar hierarchy of notions which is met in educated Western speech. (Moreover, the Finnish linguistic idiom is organized in a very different way.) Michael Herzfeld writes about the lack of an explicit hierarchical organization of speech (1981: 125–126):

> The lack of any vernacular distinction between the unique instance (or realization) and the underlying principle is constant with: (a) a general tendency in conversation to treat example/paradigm as equivalent to syntagmatic principle: "for example" often precedes a general statement; and (b) the recognition of original authorship in one who uses a familiar mantináda, but in a new and challenging way, so that originality is seen as much in the handling of context as it is in the internal design of the distich.

The former (a) tendency also means that an inquirer wishing to learn an underlying principle will be given only an example, and the overall practice is that the inquirer will not be able to grasp the relation based on that example alone. The latter (b) part of the quote above pertains to the consequences which the consciously perceived lack of closure in the chain of contextualizations of texts and textual elements creates: this is an orientation I will interpret as being improvisation in this study.

Ethical considerations

Nothing can guarantee that the interpretation and analysis of the process and products of human interaction created in conversation, whether dialogic or not, are the same for both or all participants. The balance of power can be very different depending on the community and the subject researched. Although culturally different from Finland, Crete is a part of Greece, a quickly modernizing European country. Many of my interlocutors are much more familiar with the publicity of their own words than I am, and they are all consumers of mass media products. During my fieldwork I often felt that I was myself much too discrete and ethically concerned about not disturbing people or not getting involved in something which would raise expectations of me that I did not feel myself able to fulfill. I could seldom, for example, break the confidential atmosphere of the conversation by taking photographs of my interlocutor – which certainly would rarely have bothered any Cretan. In addition, my attempts at discussing the ethical implications of the use of people's words and names in my work, and my interpretations of the poems, were mainly disregarded as unnecessary talk that was self-evident. All this, of course, neither reduces my responsibility, nor makes me immune to misinterpretations.

I have come to the conclusion that I will present all the composers be using their names in this study. Although this means that I am referring by name to people whose intimacy I wish to protect, in addition to people known to the public, I feel that recognizing their authorship is their inviolate right at the moment they gave me the right to use their names. I also think that the reader will be able to read this study and still respect their privacy, since the focus of this study is not on particular persons, but on the tradition through their contributions. These contributions are personally most valuable to me, and to my capability to write about the tradition, but I could have come to the same conclusions by speaking to other people as well. Just how I came to meet *these* people is the result of coincidences and of chains of human interactions and this does not mean that so many other people would not be worthy of consultation.

For this reason I also do not name the Village I lived in, since the village itself is not the target of my inquiry and any inquirer could have learned as much in many other villages. When the poems presented are not featured as personal compositions or when people have requested anonymity, I refer to them by their first name. Some people whose performances I include in this study remain anonymous because these performances took place before I was actually carrying out the study. I do not think, however, that by including these performances in this study I will dishonor them. Furthermore, in several examples that were narrated to me, the poems are referred to anonymously, in line with the traditional use, and I was unable to pick out the author. I apologize for any annoyance caused by this system.

Data

The interpretations put forward in this study are based on a process-like analysis of the largely incommensurable parts of the fieldwork data both during the fieldwork periods, between, and after these periods. Since the studies and local literature available concerned each a topical or (in time, place, or event) contextually motivated presentation of the tradition, I had to revise each piece of literary information by bringing the theme up during field conversations. Since even the descriptive information is therefore constructed conversationally over a long time, exploiting the principles of dialogic engagement described above, much of it appears without references. Within folklore scholarship, the research is typically based on archived or otherwise carefully documented material, but this type of tradition makes the researcher much more dependent on the personal experiences and on undocumented data. In addition to this, all impulsive communicative performances turn up spontaneously, and thus in situations where recording is hardly foreseen or possible. An improvised performance cannot be reconstructed artificially, as the performance must have meaning, and the meaning arises from the context. As for these spontaneous performances, I therefore have to depend on undocumented, experienced data, which is recorded in the form of field notes afterwards. The poems were often put down to occasional sheets of paper, just as the locals do (today, many Cretans record mantinádes on their mobile phone memory).

However, a substantial amount of information can be obtained through organized and tape-recorded interviews as well as through conversation sessions. Besides the explanations on the composition and the importance, meaning, and uses of the tradition, the interviews provide the recitations of the mantinádes that are most meaningful to the informant, as well as his or her recollections of the situations where mantinádes were sung or recited successfully. Such recitations, recollections and commentary are an important part of the local verbal art. They are essential in understanding the dialogism of the performances, as well as the individual contextualization processes. Due to the nature of the tradition and the dialogic way that it has been possible to learn about it, the recorded conversations form only a small part of my fieldwork experience, but especially those with my key conversant are such in-depth sources, that returning to them has in several cases allowed me to verbalize ideas that have surfaced in many other contexts. As a result, the key conversant form the core source of the examples and points of reference in this dissertation.

The field

Although my objective is to identify the traits of a poetic idiom of a "biologically" definable community and environment that concerns broadly all of Crete, and in practice especially central Crete, this dissertation is not a study of a specific informant, speech community or speech occasion, a "thick corpus" (Honko 2000: 15–17). I am well aware of the problems of trying to address simultaneously the general outlines of the entire register and to describe the locally and individually distinctive practices. I am also aware that by having internalized the tradition in practice mainly in central Crete, which is the center of the contemporary local cultural hegemony, I may unconsciously emphasize those practices that are specific to this region only. Another point is that I have no first-hand experience on the social poetics of the high mountain villages, whose intensely antagonistic male performativity is already comprehensively analyzed by Herzfeld (1985a; also 1985b), and so this is beyond the scope of my study. The reasoning for not limiting the study to regard only the central or lowland areas of Crete is that the primary goal of this work is to discern those characteristics of the poetic register which explain the contemporary perspectives and interest in it. Furthermore, although the island of Crete has (had) many distinctive local cultural forms, the poetic idiom of the mantinádes is emblematically established in the common experience of the entire island. At the level of the experience of individual moments, persons, *parées*, villages, areas and times, the tradition lives a different life at all events. The examples included are, while hopefully representative, each one a unique way of understanding and using the tradition. Thus general observations on mantinádes concern all of Crete (and other Greek areas where rhyming couplets are common). My own experiences of the conversational uses of the poems are situated in the administrative prefecture of Rethimno, central Crete, where most of the casual, daily actions took place as well.

One aspect that the reader of this study may find confusing is the relation of the past and the present. The Cretans' fluid moves between the present and the past confused me for many years during the conversational encounters. The adverb *prohtés*, "before yesterday" is a good example of this: a student of Modern Greek learns the word as an equivalent to "*the day before yesterday*," but the villagers can use it to mean any date in the past – even very remote in time – which is close to the person in relation to his or her own contextualization of that event. For example, specific carnival *gléndia* and other singing and dance events in the village environment were described to me by old people as if they had just taken place very recently, although they dated back thirty years in time. In order to research the factors that contribute to the image of the tradition as expressed and experienced today, I will correspondingly move in a time span that covers contemporary Crete and the experienced, memorized and narrated recent past, since this is the way my interlocutors in Crete have conceptualized their tradition.

Local terminology

I will use both indigenous terminology and my own glosses for certain central phenomena. When my interlocutors use an indigenous term, such as *glén̄di* (feast), or *paréa* (a [musical] get-together), or "theme" (*théma*), I will use these terms. Similarly, I will draw on indigenous terms like "image" (*ikóna*) and *akoúsmata* ("live hearings", live experiences) when these are used even by fewer speakers, but systematically (by those speakers who are willing to dwell on details). The local terms such as theme or image however do *not* point only to one, exhaustive explanation: very much like the mantinádes, their meaning is situationally defined and avoids closure (see also Herzfeld 1985b).

In some cases, as in that of denoting the composition of poems, I will gloss the *vgázo* and other local verbs as to "create" or "compose" (I will give a full description of the local terms in Chapter 6), since the local terms do not translate well into English. I will speak of extemporization or the (textual) improvisation of the extempore composition, which is locally expressed mainly by adding the definition *epí tópou* (on the spot), to the verb *vgázo*.

I will also use concepts such as dialogism and creativity, which are not used indigenously, while discussing the special characteristics of this tradition in relation to other cultures and research. I have tried to make my points clear by resorting to generally conceivable glossing of matters which people in this living tradition discuss in their insider ways or very often, do not need to specify at all. I have nevertheless discussed my use of these terms with several interlocutors I know well. In doing so, I have intentionally drawn their attention to these words and usages to inquire if they accept my interpretations. This interactive method is visible in several of the long stretches of speech that I have enclosed in the present study from the recorded interviews and conversations, and where some of the local experts describe the conversational, self-expressional and artistic impulses behind their poems.

Finally, it is clear that Cretans would not analyze the tradition in the same way as I do here. However, while they would refer to an event by merely quoting a mantináda to someone familiar with the performance of this poem in that particular event, they would not quote this to someone who is not familiar with the event. In such cases, they would rather focus on the point, the mantináda, only after the necessary outlines of the performance situation have been narrated (see Chapter 5). This acknowledgement of the limits of an immediate, spontaneous contextualization (although often contested) and the structural move to a contextualization requiring narrative, rhetorical elaboration is also part of the local discourse on performances.

Outline of the chapters

It was not an easy task to organize the chapters and their contents, since the presentation of the subject matter and the theory necessary for analyzing it were largely products of the analysis themselves. The final organizing principle thus primarily concerns a movement from general to particular: in order to study both the register as the medium for meaning and creativity, and the individual, unique realizations, the study will proceed from shared concerns towards more detailed and specialized topics and opinions. In the chapter on composition, I will introduce views as described mainly by one person and analyze some of her poems. I hope that this method of presentation will illustrate one of my primary concerns: people engaged in mantinádes have an intimate, creative experience of the tradition.

The next chapter introduces the central theoretical conceptions. The basic themes will be the following:

- tradition as a language, a register
- the essential components of performance
- dialogism as a characteristic feature of short, communicative oral poetry
- competence and creativity
- improvisation as an orientation and method of composition in performance
- the double-identity of the register as fixed textual entities and a process

Each tradition forms special characteristics in the society to which it belongs. The third main chapter will therefore start with a short introduction to Crete as the historical, social and cultural setting. The main emphasis in this chapter is placed on introducing the Cretan music, dance and feast traditions, which continue vitally to the present, and of which the mantinádes are an emblematic part. The history, instruments, basic dance forms and the musical form used for improvising mantinádes are introduced, and the festive and recreational singing practices are outlined. I will also explain the topical differences in these traditions and I will describe the traditional forms of singing and entertainment in detail. My reason for this is that the dialogic nature of communication in the *gléndi* (feast) and *paréa* (get-together) is also implicitly present in the contemporary conceptualizing of the tradition and poetry outside of the frames of these events.

The fourth chapter concentrates on the mantinádes as a register, a special poetic language of expression. Here I will present the metrical line, the rhyme and other basic poetic means and the role of the theme as the dialogic basis of conceptualizing and contextualizing poems is introduced. The difference between the actual self-dependent mantinádes and the couplet form as a building block of longer poems is examined briefly.

The fifth chapter focuses more closely on the versatility and on the modes of recited performances. A description of a full array of possible performances will help to show concretely how the poems also form a language of oral expression and thought in everyday life. The roles of the performers and poets in performance will be viewed in relation to gender, as well as to the questions of the means of participation and improvisation. The contemporary written and media arenas will form a separate topic at the end of this chapter.

The sixth chapter studies composition as a metrical, sociolinguistic, imaginary and cognitive practice and skill. I will first discuss how children internalize the tradition and how and when people start to compose. Extracts from interviews with contemporary composers allow the composers' own voices to explain what is meaningful in composition to them. In other words, how does one compose poems and what are the motivations to compose? The analytic frame of my interest is the composition of couplets as structurally and semantically coherent, self-dependent units, and the dialogic nature of these units to the composers. I will then explore the cognitive techniques that are used in introducing new perspectives in the poem-utterances, and finally I will analyze the factors contributing to the possibility of commanding a poetic tradition as a productive language.

In the last, concluding chapter, I will bring together the ideas surfacing from the analysis of the research data and will suggest a frame for a theory of what I will refer to as *dialogic oral poetry*.

II Theoretical frame of interpretation

The present approach to the tradition of the mantinádes concerns the general understanding of the structures of the poetic verbal idiom and the questions of how and where the creativity and meaning is made and experienced in the uses of the tradition. My fieldwork has shown that the local perception focuses simultaneously on each mantináda as a fixed poem, and on the tradition as fluid and productive. Whether old or new, known or unheard, the short poems are seen as *texts* in their own right, clearly bound, self-dependent units as a point of departure. These units are used by people in their self-expression to convey meaning in a process-like, dialogic mediation between other people, performances and poems. To the creators of the mantinádes, the texts provide source material, points of reference and often reasons for composing new texts. Whether extemporized or not, the composition of mantinádes is a process in which parts of the reality are framed through personal fantasy and the expressional potential of the register. The emphasis on acting through the tradition is thus simultaneously on the expressiveness of the textual products, poems, and on the relevance of the individually chosen or created units to human life experience. The theoretical framework presented here wishes to provide a historical and conceptual background for perceiving and discussing these matters.

The two great theoretical movements in folklore of the twentieth century, the Oral-Formulaic Theory and the performance-oriented theories, both attempt to address a previously neglected question of what takes place in oral performance. In the way of shaping their message, most researchers focus on something new, and oppose, or overlook, some points focused on by the previous scholarship. The importance of oral composition and its separate mechanisms with regard to written composition has been established and advanced primarily due to the works of two scholars, Albert Lord in 1960 and Walter Ong in 1982. Both Lord and Ong argued that the end of the oral tradition was marked by the advent of writing and literacy. Once the oral was established, due to these above-mentioned works, it was, however, much easier for others to recover the various forms of interaction between the oral and the written. Very similarly, the recent movements that renegotiate the roles of the text and performance have originated, apart from the historical shortages of the text-centered paradigms in their focus on the *text*, from the extreme focus on the *performance* of the performance-centered paradigms.

As explained by Lauri Honko (1998: 44–51; 2000: 4–17), the folkloristic concept of text has essentially progressed through three stages. Honko refers to the oldest period as "pre-textual," since the interest was not directed to the actual text itself, but on its source-value: the historical, mythological or even artistic content. The focus was directed to the study of the actual texts and their variation especially by the emergence of folklore scholarship as a new academic discipline in the nineteenth century. The new conceptualization of the text provided the basis for the emergence of the historic-geographical method, which was developed by Finnish scholars and widely used by European and American folklorists. The basic concern of this method was the search for the original text, the archetype, which was carried out by studying the variation found in different texts, which were the supposed variants of the archetype. The research in Finland and the Nordic countries followed a scrutinized model of study based on linguistic textual accuracy and on a large corpus of variants, while in the United States, research focused more on the literary value of a text (Fine 1984: 28–30). (Honko 1998: 44–45; 2000: 6) As further described by Honko, what unified the historic-geographical folklorists as well as another contemporaneous school, the anthropological linguists (esp. Boas, Sapir, Malinowski, see Fine 1984: 21–28) who stressed accurate, verbatim transcripts of discourse, was the belief that "cultures could be objectified as texts, and texts were the main object of research" (Honko 2000: 7). (See also Fine 1984: 21–30; Foley 1995b: 603–605)

A third stage of this development was a change in focus from text to performance (Honko 1998: 47–51; 2000: 13–14). The Parry-Lord Oral-Formulaic Theory advanced the move towards the performance paradigm by focusing on the composition in performance and on the interaction between the performer and the audience. The emergence of the sociolinguistics of the Prague School had also shifted the focus from an individual's purely linguistic competence to his or her communicative competence. Beginning in the 1960s, this concern for the use of language and folklore as communicative events was then dynamically developed among linguists, linguistic anthropologists, as well as folklorists. Concrete methodological and theoretical manifests developed first among the approaches referred to as the Ethnopoetics and the Ethnography of speaking.

Ethnopoetics was a project in which especially Dennis Tedlock and Dell Hymes strived to find new, more accurate methods for transcription of the performed Native American texts in order to reveal their paralinguistic features (Tedlock; esp. 1983) and poetic emphasis, which were different from the metrically defined models familiar to the literary audience (esp. Hymes 1981). Although advanced by several scholars, Foley makes the observation that the Ethnography of speaking approach was also personified in the work of Hymes, who required "that scholars pay as close attention to the speaking of folk literature as to what is actually spoken" (Foley 1995b: 609). At the end of the 1970s, performance, in the sense of an emergent event, became a noteworthy paradigm in research. At that time, the focus was especially directed on the covariance of form and meaning and the performer-audience interaction in the performative event. In 1977, the principles underlying this research orientation were explained in the central manifest of the paradigm, Richard Bauman's *Verbal Art as Performance*.[1]

A focus now fixed primarily on the contexts of the emergence and unfolding of performance, and on the communicative interaction in performance, directed the research of textual products to analyze especially those emerging through performance.[2] In some cases, this took the research to the ultimate end of addressing single performances at the expense of recognizing the diachronic elements represented by the textual elements. Therefore, just as several new insights into the interaction of oral and written provided a wider perspective on them as not mutually excluding, but often co-operating, the exclusive focus on performance has led to a theoretical need to reflect in more detail on the dialectics between the textual units and performance.[3]

One major effort to advance this understanding is John Miles Foley's theory of Immanent Art (especially 1991; 1995). Applying the Oral-Formulaic Theory by Milman Parry and Albert Lord, as well as the Ethnopoetics and the performance approach (Foley 1995: 1–28), Foley succeeds in verbalizing many generalities that guide the performance and meaning of the situated words. The basic problem with the Parry-Lord theory was the extreme emphasis on the usefulness of the structures and this was done at the expense of the artistic and poetic ends of the poet. Another problem was caused by the application of the theory of formulas and formulaic systems to all kinds of oral poetry. (E.g. Foley 1995: 3–5) In his work, Foley redirects this focus from the mere usefulness of the structures to an understanding of how structures convey meaning, and offers detailed examples of the varying ways the different poetic registers accomplish this. Later, Foley directed a further focus on the wide variation in the form and mediums of oral poetry traditions and performances, and pointed to the necessity of varied methodological approaches (2002; 2005). Foley's insights concern especially oral *poetry* and his observations are very relevant to all the productive, register-based traditions.

Anna-Leena Siikala remarks that "textualization, identifying a section out of the flow of discourse, is at the core of oral traditions; otherwise they cannot be called traditions at all." (Siikala and Siikala 2005: 58). Moreover, linguistic anthropologists have made an effort to understand the textual units which necessarily make oral traditions, and how they are cut from their contexts and reused in others. The concept of *entextualization* was taken to signify the crystallization of the verbal elements: the process in which a stretch of an utterance becomes separable from its context and reusable in others. That concept was first introduced by Kuipers (1990) and

---

[1] For summaries, see: Bauman and Briggs 1990; Briggs 1988: 5–11; Foley 1995a: 1–28; for history: Fine 1984: 30–56; Foley 1995b: 605–614.

[2] See e.g. Bauman (1984 [1977]: 8–9): "the formal manipulation of linguistic features is secondary to the nature of performance, per se, conceived of and defined as a mode of communication."

[3] For the biases of the performance school, see: Limón & Young 1986; for an overview & new focuses, see Bauman and Briggs 1990; see also Barber 2007: 28–30.

Urban (1991), but among Finnish folklorists, it became known especially through Bauman's and Briggs' article *Poetics and Performance as Critical Perspectives on Language and Social Life* (1990), followed by the book *Natural Histories of Discourse*, edited by Silverstein and Urban (1996).

Like Anna-Leena Siikala in the previously cited study (Siikala & Siikala 2005), most researchers using the concept entextualization have worked with narrative, mythical and ritual traditions. But unlike these, the register-based traditions rely emphatically on the constant new production of texts and on the identification of these texts as individual, personalized utterances. It is therefore important, as Karin Barber suggests (2007: 30–31), to see the process of entextualization extended in two directions: first, towards the basic level of ordinary language acquisition and use – that the formulation, identification and use of "verbal chunks" is an inherent characteristic of all human language use – and second, that the entextualized entities are not frozen but stimulus and stepping stones for further application: improvisation.

The methodological direction of the improvisatory, process-like treatment of the tradition is evident in all earlier studies on mantinádes. Mantinádes, like other similar traditions, have been approached mostly from perspectives other than those used in folklore. As expressed by Lauri Honko (1998: 8), I have often similarly felt that the philologically-oriented studies can offer good insight into the texts without a real focus on their contextualization, whereas anthropologically-oriented works often study the social construction of the utterances without really taking into account the registers behind them. The present *register approach* strives to understand the Cretan arguments, which explicitly value the texts and the textual continuation between the poems performed, by approaching the poetic register of mantinádes from the perspective of the experienced and narrated contextualized events, as a performative, structural and semantic potentiality that is available to the performers and to the composers sharing this tradition.

The register

I wish to emphasize the conceptualization of the tradition of mantinádes as a special *language* of expression. Many previous researchers have commented on the language-likeness of the traditional idioms that allow the new production of verses. Among Finnish folklore research, the idea of poetry as a special language is a well-established phenomenon due to the unifying element of the *kalevala-meter* in all the older oral poetry (e.g. Lönnrot 1919 [1849]; Kuusi 1985). Recent studies of the vast and deep body of archived material also take notice of this language-like potentiality inherent in the tradition. For example, in his dissertation in 1992, Lauri Harvilahti evaluated the applicability of the Formula Theory and its various adaptations to Ingrian lyrical epic poetry. By conducting a close analysis, Harvilahti ends up describing the variety of systems of reproduction in which (1992: 143, translation by the present author) "on the one hand the central semantic contents can be realized by several solutions at the surface level, and on the other, recurrent surface structures varying on their phonological, morphological and syntactic correspondence unite verses, which do not correlate semantically, to wide networks."[4] With the ethnographic study of the Altai oral traditions, Harvilahti further studies the principles of the production of oral poetry in ethnocultural terms (2001; 2003).

A holistic study of one historically well-documented geographical area by Lotte Tarkka (2005; forthcoming) analyzes the intertextuality of the genres among *kalevala-meter* poetry. In this study Tarkka focuses on the potentiality of the register in crossing genre-dependent qualities and shows how singers have built explicit textual references between the genres in their performances. Another scholar, Senni Timonen (2004), offers a series of penetrating analyses of the singers' poetics among the material counted in the earlier research as being lyrical. She also addresses the problems of this scholarly genre in detail with regard to the indigenous performative genres. Despite the distinct research questions posed on the geographically specific or genre-related material in each case, this recent Finnish research is concerned with similar questions of the language-like, register-based identity of the poetry which are outlined in the present study.

One of the durable models used to investigate an oral poetry register from the perspective of its potentiality for performers and composers is represented by *The Singer of Tales* (Lord 1960), a study introducing the Parry-Lord Oral Formulaic Theory. Although Albert Lord holds on to the basic terms *formula* and *theme* as introduced by his teacher, Milman Parry, Lord had describes the poetic idiom used in the composition-in-performance of the South Slavic narrative epic as a comprehensive linguistic, stylistic and performative system (see also Foley 1988: 41–42).

Recently, the concept of *register* has been widely used to denote the special languages of oral performance. This concept was first introduced by the linguist M.A.K. Halliday to differentiate the languages associated with *use*, the situational contexts, from the dialects determined by the *user* (Halliday et al. 1964, Halliday 1978: 31–35, 110–111). Dell Hymes later applied the concept from linguistic use to Ethnopoetics similarly as a definition of the *major speech styles associated with recurrent types of situations*, in distinction to major speech variants (1989: 440). John Miles Foley adopts the term register in oral poetry in the significance of "an

---

[4] Harvilahti finds (1992: 142, translation by the present author) that 1) the verse material can be suitable as a building substance for several poems; 2) The creation of a poem proceeds apart from on a linear level, also on the paradigmatic axis which allows, bearing on the semantic contents, the fitting of alternative elements: words, word groups, verses, even verse groups, to the plot; 3) Formulae and formulaic passages can work as a link between different poetic motives; 4) Formulae can also work in several poems as similar repetitive hierarchic elements which structure the narration. They express, for example, the beginning and ending of an episode, a content or repetition cycle, and give hints of the semantic contents of the poetic text and the emphasis of the plot structure; 5) One can discern multipurpose material, stable semantic units, which are used in particular situations repeated in several poems, and especially formulaic elements conveying the plot that is typical of certain poems or by structurally close poems.

idiomatic version of language that qualifies as a more or less self-contained system of signification specifically because it is the designated and sole vehicle for communication in the act of traditional oral performance" (1995: 15).

Halliday and Foley place special emphasis on the *meanings* encoded into the register and carried by it: a register is recognized by its linguistic and rhetoric features, but essentially defined through the selection of the meanings that are summoned by these linguistic and rhetoric means (Halliday 1978: 111). The code-switching and the use of a register both invite the listeners to enter among these meanings and guide them to be fluently delivered and received (Foley 1995: 15–17, 49–53). Dealing with a variety of oral and oral-derived traditions, as well as contemporary oral and written oral poetry registers, John Miles Foley has turned in his recent research to emphasize register as the key concept in a very similar way as I do in this work (see also Sykäri 2003). During one of his lectures at the Folklore Fellows Summer School in Viena Karelia (June 18, 2007), Foley referred to this register-based approach as the Register Theory.

Since the previously mentioned definitions focus primarily on performance (but see also Foley 2002; 2005 on written oral poetry), it must be mentioned that for the purposes of the present register approach, the scope of the register has to cover more than the oral performance. In this study I refer to register as a comprehensive tool for composition, performance and thought: a special *language* which is recognized and used with its emblematic linguistic and poetic characteristics and means, style and performative devices. The register identity makes the language special not only due to the meanings carried by the register or encoded into the referential expressions, but also through code-switching or the performative atmosphere created by it. This is most evident in the contest registers and events, where the register essentially gives the frame for showing the skills in disciplined extemporizing, very much as it is in the performative dialogue realized by the thematic succession of the mantinádes sung in a singing event (see pp. 106–114).

Often a community uses different registers for different kinds of verbal needs. This is evident, for example, in the ecology of the South Slavic traditions, where the lyric poetry sung by women and the epic poetry sung by men use different registers, with the women using eight-syllable metrical lines, and the men, ten-syllable metrical lines (Foley 1995a: 106; 2005). It has also been demonstrated that dialectal Arab poetry has various metrical formats different in style and contents, used either in different contexts or between different parts of a singing event, as shown in detail e.g. by Caton (1990) and Yaqub (2007).

In the context of the Altai epic and shamanistic incantations, the situation is the same (Harvilahti 2003). Lauri Harvilahti demonstrates, nevertheless, that underlying these registers used in the community there is a cultural basis which he calls an "ethnocultural substrate" (2001, 2003: 89–115). This ethnocultural substrate consists of all the tradition-specific poetic devices and means, and the semantic knowledge of what the poetic expression may be and may tell about. In Crete, such an underlying cultural basis is easily seen in the similarities of the metaphors, formulas and semantic contents of the improvisatory mantinádes and the crystallized, archaic *rizítika* songs, a genre emblematic of western Crete. Another example recognized by several researchers of Greek laments and folk songs is that the same set of poetic images is used in the songs of love and death, which allows a strong emotional expression when the metaphors are placed and referred to in a semantically opposite way (see esp. Alexiou 1974: 120–122; Caraveli-Chaves 1978; Danforth 1982: 74–90; Herzfeld 1981a: 129–130).

A register-based approach also helps to recover those areas between oral and written oral poetry, which until recently have been problematic. John Miles Foley speaks of *written oral poetry* when a poem is composed, transmitted and received by writing, nonetheless composed by using a traditional oral register (2002: 50–53; 2005). It looks as if oral poetic registers that have been deeply rooted in the community have often been employed for such use as well. This poetry referred to as contemporary or local poetry, or as topical verse (see p. 26), describes especially the recent historical events, or refers to social events or behavior (especially those deviating from the normative, see e.g. Tarkka 2005: 47) and in many societies, it is composed by named individuals and is transmitted both/either in written and/or oral form. The style might be close to the idiomatic expression of the register when this is used orally and for traditional themes, in case the poet has adapted the register as his or her "native language" among a living oral poetry (Leino 1975; see Chapter 6). Most probably such verses still remain partly unintelligible for outsiders in the typical, recurrent referents to highly topical insider knowledge. However, often the style is additive and narrative, rather than coherent and poetic, due to it being primarily directed at attracting attention as situated commentary. I will focus on these kinds of longer contemporary compositions in Chapter 4 (see also Leino 1975; Tarkka 2005: 46–47; 329–369).

That notion of written oral poetry suits perfectly in describing several longer narrative poems in Crete. In the case of the short, compact mantinádes we are, however, faced with a larger discussion of when and how the composition takes place, since the *oral* composition does not occur in performance only. This also concerns many of the longer poems. However, orally composed poems are also nowadays normally written down *after* they are composed and can be "announced" through recorded, written or mass media channels. Therefore, there is no single answer to the question of how much writing takes place in the actual composition process when the results are established mainly in a written form (as much as it can be impossible to say how oral or written the actual composition process is in the case of the poets who write poems). Some insights will nonetheless emerge from the poet's own commentary, as well as through the discussions on creativity and competence.

Focus on performance

Performance arena as a frame of experience

In his theory of Immanent Art (1991, 1995), John Miles Foley builds a general theory of how traditional oral poetry works in performance to encode and deliver the message and to guide the reception through the traditional signals. According to Foley's terminology, these signals work as *metonyms* (a part representing the whole) on the levels of phraseology, themes and narrative patterns, referring from the limited scope of what is said to a much larger extra-textual whole (1991: 5–8). These metonyms can be specific, calling forth a certain referred entity, or they can be general. When metonyms are general, by their very presence, they activate the audience to follow the code-switching to the traditional idiom and to the universe of meanings it bears, and to be ready to decode the more specific metonyms. This *traditional referentiality* works, because through the event of performance, and through the use of the register, both the performer and audience are actors in the same mental frame of reference, the *performance arena*. Thus, the use of the register grants immediate entrance to a shifted level of discourse as well as tools to decode the message to anyone sharing the same tradition. The system can work (the performer can encode and the audience can decode the referential signals) with an extraordinary fluency, *communicative economy*, because the connection between the signal and the meaning is agreed upon, having been shaped during centuries and generations in the speech community. (1995: 47–56)

The essential concept for the present study is that of the performance arena as "an experience rather than a designated place or moment" (Foley 1995: 47, footnote 43), a shared mental frame of reference. The short, compact mantinádes have the potential to emerge and be called for in a large variety of situations. Oral poetry, however, has historically been researched much more as texts than as performances. The dynamic permeability of these communicational poem-traditions from festive occasions and singing events to proverbial communication, emotional self-expression and private composition is therefore much less well known. In this study the interest in performance lies especially in viewing how one poetic register comes out in many different kinds of performances, and how, through the introduction of the register, poets and performers also inhabit the performance arena outside of the performance.

Contextualization

In understanding the performance of mantinádes, another essential concept is *contextualization*. The idea of the textual and contextual unity is prominent in Caraveli's analysis (1982) and in Herzfeld's remark concerning the *seamless experience* (1985b: 216). Later, this central idea was explicitly conceptualized as contextualization by Charles Briggs in 1988 (see also

Bauman and Briggs 1990). The term contextualization was first introduced by Cook-Gumperz and Gumperz (1976), and Briggs applies it in his study on the system of conversational genres examined in their contextual realm (1988). In order to research how textual elements are embedded artistically and meaningfully in social interaction, Briggs presents the diversity of the performance practices in the Mexicano genres (northern New Mexico) which are referred to by the locals as belonging to the "talk of the elders of bygone days." These include historical discourse, proverbs, scriptural allusions, jokes, legends, hymns and prayers. All these genres reflect the same, diachronic mentality which carries the ideology and values of solidarity, shared work and human respect. These values are engraved in the words of the ancestors of the community, and they are performed by the contemporary elders especially for the purpose of engaging the young in a critical perception of the present-day cultural and economical hegemony experienced by the community. (Briggs 1988: 359–369) Briggs describes these genres be providing carefully contextualized examples and compares them according to the number of textual and contextual features included. The factors that are characteristic to each genre and that ground the competence needed to perform in them, emerge through these differences.

Briggs builds his analysis on Ethnopoetics and on performance theory. Besides extending these theoretical approaches by dealing with short, conversational genres and romance language material, he is especially concerned of the definition of the concept of context, and the recurrent problems of inclusiveness and false objectivity that are bound to it. Briggs points out that descriptions of context are often falsely determined by the researcher, an outsider to the tradition, as something existing *outside* the actual performance. So instead of integrating the context with the text, the researcher creates a chasm between them. Instead, Briggs emphasizes that the context necessary for understanding a performance is an interpretive framework negotiated between those present in an ongoing process of…

> ….monitoring each other's behaviour for auditory and visual clues as to how the other person(s) is contextualising the discourse. The concept of contextualisation links the study of poetic features and the participants' own interpretive processes in a new way. The study of contextualisation reveals the status of interpretation as an emergent, interpersonal activity that relies on such features not solely for patterning form and content, but also for structuring the process of negotiating a shared frame of reference"(1988: 15). (Briggs 1988: xv–xvi, 2–16)

Strategies of meaning

One focus of the process of contextualization therefore concerns the binding of the textual element to the object and meaning of the utterance in performance and further, as was referred to in connection to my personal experience in the beginning of this study (see also Chapter 5), to the effects it may have on the "real" life. Short, communicative *poetry*, however, has its own special strategies of meaning, and in addition to the interpersonal contextualization taking place in performance, another focus has to be directed on what kinds of elements guide the contextualization of its meaning. Here I am interested in the elements of performance and/or the poem itself. As I will explain later, except on shared, common grounds, the contextualization of a poem-unit can be made from very personal viewpoints. Each person's experience, competence and taste vary, and so poems address very different needs. The contextualization of the meaning of an utterance can also be brought about by varying textual and contextual grounds. This is particularly evident today, when poems have entered the mass media and they are performed interpersonally through mobile phone messages, and when the process of contextualization very often takes place outside face-to-face performances.

In his article 'The Indigenous Theory of Meaning' (1981a), Michael Herzfeld builds a semantic theory of the meaning of a mantináda, drawing on the commentary and examples given to him in conversations with villagers in Rhodes. Reflecting this commentary, the meaning (*simasía*) "resides in the context rather than in the intrinsic features of the song itself, although the notion of context used here may extend to a highly generalized reality" (Herzfeld 1981a: 117). The context of meaning, according to these examples, varies at least between the performative, circumstantial, social, moral and verbal contexts.

According to my own experience, four main categories can be discerned among the points explained in this article. The first of these categories rely on the referentiality of the poem: in such cases, (1) the meaning can be perceived in the *external* contextual relevance of the poem, e.g. the poem sung or recited is relevant to the contextual realm of the ongoing event, or, although out of immediate actuality, the poem is uttered to recall a meaningful event (esp. ibid. 118–120, 127–128); or (2) the meaning is realized by the creative *internal fitting* of a mantináda, in which case the reference becomes visible through textual manipulation. Textual manipulation often but not exclusively refers to the formulaic or morphological changes of an existing poem or to the repetition of a part of an earlier poem in the extempore creation of a new one (ibid. 123, 126–128, 136, 139). The meaning can also be entitled (3) to the *continuation* (*sinéhia*) between the mantinádes performed competitively / in a singing event; thus, in this case, the meaning is intertextual and resides between the poems (ibid. 120, 123, 139). The meaning can lie (4) in the "affirmation of an eternal verity" (ibid. 120), or in the "recognizable truth (stated by the song) which the singer and his audience have drawn from their own shared experience" (ibid. 121). This means that the argument of the poem is (or can be in certain circumstances) generally relevant to human life in this cultural setting (ibid. 122–123).

This article was a good basis for my own perception in the field: it helped me balance the implicitly expressed statements with those that were made explicit in the conversations. I will discuss these cases in more detail in the fifth chapter (participation, improvisation and meaning), and suggest some reformulations based on evidence emerging during the intervening time of Herzfeld's fieldwork (in the 1970s[5]) and mine (1997–2009). The basic observation, however, remains very much the same: the evaluation of meaning can be based on several alternative or parallel factors. These factors vary from purely performative ideals – the continuation in the verbal dialogue – to the meaning entitled to the relevance and inventiveness of the reference(s) made, to the meaning perceived in textual representativeness and/or creativity. Nevertheless, a particular emphasis has to be assigned to the role of the *text* in each of these cases – even the performative contextualization of a poem is identified on textual grounds, on the match between the chosen theme and the poem discussing it.

Dialogism

Dialogism is a prominent element in the Greek verbal expression and I propose that one of the reasons why mantinádes have always been popular, and have become even more today, is that they are pointedly a dialogic register as much outside a concrete communicational frame as they are within it. Dialogism is also one of the core concepts in Briggs' work on the conversational Mexicano genres (1988; see above) and in this study, he analyzes the dialogic elements of concrete communicative and narrative interchange. As Briggs states, performance in all the genres he examines is always dialogic by nature, and in every performance, both contextual and textual components are present to a varying degree, depending on the genre. The contextual means change apart from their quantity, in quality, when moving from the more conversational genres towards genres where narrativity takes more room. Comparing different genres, Briggs finds a continuum between contextual and textual emphasis, and their interplay in performance, involving diverse external and internal dialogical methods. These dialogical methods span from (1) the actual turn-taking in performance to (2) the ongoing control of the performer on the audience responses of whether the message is understood, and accordingly, shaping both the form and content, to (3) the structural (internal) dialogism of the performance features in the creation of the textual element. Briggs speaks about *external dialogism* when referring to the actual turn-taking and the performer-audience co-operation in performance, and of *internal* dialogism when referring to the dialogism realized through textual means, for example reported speech, in the more narrative genres he examines. (1988: 354–356) Both forms of dialogism, the actual performative turn-taking and the internal dialogic formation of the text, are also relevant in the present context.

Briggs also recurrently refers to the dialectal relationships of the past and the present, which is the multifunctional basis of performance in all the genres counting as the "words of the elders of the bygone days." In most cases, these dialectal relationships are produced performatively. For

---

5 Between December 1973 and July 1974 in Rhodes and 1974–1978 in Crete (1981a: 140: footnotes 1 and 2)

example, they can be produced through tying elements which weave a quotation (the past) into the performance context (the present), although specific signs also exist for this purpose.

For building such analogies, the metrical, productive registers typically work very metonymically and referentially, as explained above with regard to Foley's theory on performance and Herzfeld's theory on meaning. In the short form and functionally language-like register of mantinádes, I propose that this referentiality is directly based on the exploitation of the *dialogic orientation* of speech and language, as claimed by Bakhtin (1981):

> (The speaker's) orientation toward the listener is an orientation toward a specific conceptual horizon, toward the specific world of the listener (282);
>
> The word in language is half someone else's. It becomes "one's own" only when the speaker populates it with his own intention, his own accent, when he appropriates the word, adapting it to his own semantic and expressive intention. Prior to this moment of appropriation, the word does not exist in a neutral and impersonal language (it is not, after all, out of a dictionary that the speaker gets his words!), but rather it exists in other people's mouths, in other people's contexts, serving other people's intentions: it's from there that one must take the word, and make it one's own. (1981: 283)

What has emerged from my study is an interpretation that the speaker's conscious revisiting of the previous or earlier poems, expressions and speech acts, sets the scene for a third form of dialogue, a dialogue dramatized through references.

Creativity and competence

To understand the expressive potentiality of the registers and genres of verbal art, the focus on competence is a central phenomenon. Despite the historical distinction in how competence is understood (see below), most collectors and researchers of folklore opt to choose informants who are the best singers, tellers or ritual specialists. During fieldwork, the local people themselves are eager to direct the inquirer to a specialist, as my experience in Crete has also made very evident. This means that locals and scholars alike agree that by listening and talking to competent performers who are recognized as experts by the community, an outsider can best receive the knowledge that the community regards as essential, and superior.

During the twentieth century, the perception of the individual changed dramatically. While the individual competence recognized by communities was always appreciated by selecting informants who could give the most representative texts, during the earlier text-centered research paradigm, this individual capacity was mainly regarded as being a linguistic and mnemonic skill to hand down pieces of tradition. When the textual body was regarded an autonomous and anonymous heritage of the *folk*, then the extra-textual individual or collective meanings, the embedding of the textual elements into the context, and the interaction evolving in performance were not of much concern.

By applying the new field of sociolinguistics that became influential in anthropology and folklore studies at the same time, Hymes altered the interpretation of the notion of linguistic competence towards a more inclusive, performative idea of *communicative competence* (Hymes 1974: 75; in Briggs 1988: 5–6). In the 1980s, the anthropologists Michael Herzfeld and Charles Briggs, scholars with vast experience among the short, communicative traditions, both underlined that the interactive communicative competence is what the *performers themselves are concerned with* (Briggs 1988: 3–4, 6–7; Herzfeld 1981a: 116; 1985b). A competent performer, as shown by Briggs with regard to the Mexicano genres of "the talk of the elders of the bygone days", invariably creates a unique synthesis of both the contextual and textual components under the agreed-upon guidelines of the tradition. (1988: 352–358)

> Competence thus emerges from an intertextual process of reaching back into past performances, selecting a particular set of elements, and interpreting their meaning. It also entails a critical reading of the ongoing social interaction and perhaps other dimensions of modern society as well. As the two come together in performance, both are transformed. Certain elements of antes [past] have come to be associated with new meanings, just as particular elements of ahora [today] are now seen in different light (1988: 357).

The models discussed above on how competence and meaning are conveyed and perceived in performance are also fundamental for this work. The concept of competence focuses on the public, shared practices of the community and on the possibility of seeing the shared aesthetic and communicative values as inherent and expressed in the performances of the given genre. Yet in Crete, the performances seemed on the one hand to highlight the inventiveness and surprise, and on the other, the internal aesthetics, to a degree which called for closer examination of the nature of this competence. Therefore, apart from the experience of how the poetic expression emerged in performance, I also felt the same poetic language to be meaningful in other, inwardly turned ways. For instance, poems were recited meditatively, especially by old people. What overwhelmed me when I first met those inside the living tradition was their continuous presence in the performance arena, as well as their easy access to it, and sometimes their quick, unexplained moves. Without any necessary frames, their poetic expressions could range anywhere from a serious life story or stated idea, to a proverbial communication, to an example of poetic perfection according to the individual taste, or to a metrical, textual or contextual game. Some people could recite the same poem over and over again, because it has meaning – some invent new ones without hesitating to experiment *whether* they have meaning.

Similarly, it did not quite fit my assumption of the communicative format that many composers in fact expressed to me that they valued equally, or even more, the moment when the poem is formed in their mind, when it "comes up," often when they are alone, than the moment they bring out a poem in performance. The compositional poetic inventiveness and its capability to serve as a medium of ideas and feelings are clearly stated as being one of the most important facets of the mantinádes tradition. These perceptions in Crete made me notice that poetic expression plays a very profound role in a person's individual way of working mentally.

For this reason, I also apply the more flexible notion of creativity to my analyses of the mantinádes uses. Although creativity is a contested concept, two more reasons to elaborate on it emerge directly from my field experience. The perception constantly surfacing during my fieldwork was that people who participate in this tradition do so because it gives them an option to express their individual creativity in their everyday life. Individuals compose, recite or think through poems especially because it is a creative way to communicate, to express oneself, to recollect past moments or to understand something that has happened. My interpretation is that creativity is a value in itself for these people and that it is the grounds for all different kinds of individual experiences of meaningfulness in a performance or a poem, or the process of composition.[6] Creativity emerges in different ways in each situation and person, but the notion is faithful to the Cretan idea of mantinádes as a tradition whose manifestations are always *new, surprising and valuable* (this is how Margaret Boden (2004 [1990]: 1) explains the meaning of the word creativity; see below). Another reason is that by understanding these different ways in which creativity is experienced and focused on by people, we are better able to understand the transformations taking place today when poetry is brought from oral communities and performances and transferred to the written medium and to the mass media.

The research on creativity discusses predominantly two basic oppositions: first, whether creativity is or should be recognized as an end-product, namely in something new that can be permanently added to the domain of this creativity, or in the process itself (of a performance, improvisation, scientific work, etc.); and, second, whether creativity is a subjective phenomenon or something that needs social confirmation. What is widely agreed is that the contemporary Western idea of creativity is mainly connected to innovation, to the newness of ideas and products, which are produced by exceptional, innovative individuals and which remain permanently in use. People in Western societies are accustomed to focusing on the results of the creativity and view them as *works*: products which can be used, art that can be enjoyed, songs that can be listened to, or books which can be read. The original creator has made this work and he or she is creative.

---

6 When trying to find relevant literature on creativity in the winter 2007–2008, I was astonished (see also Ingold and Hallam 2007: 1–2), to find that hundreds of titles were available on creativity in the areas of business and teaching and nearly none among cultural studies. Creativity and improvisation have arisen as meaningful topics in the anthropological research (see also Cerwonka and Malkki 2007) only at the very same time I was looking at how to conceptualize my Cretan impressions (but see also e.g. Bronner 1992; Sawyer 1997).

With this kind of recognized individual creativity as a starting point for his research, the psychologist Mihaly Csikszentmihalyi (1996: 1, 24), however, denies that creativity resides in the mind of the person only. In what he refers to as the Systems Approach, he shows that the work of a talented individual is always a process which is connected to the symbolic area, the *domain* in which the person works, as well as to the *field*, the society or in-group which is able to evaluate and acknowledge what is creative. Thus, to produce something creative, in addition to his or her personal qualities, a person has to be in the right place at a right moment (historical, economical, social opportunity; receptiveness of the field; luck). However, as Csikszentmihalyi observes (ibid. 47), very few of us realize these moments, and yet fewer can act when realizing a good opportunity: to act when the right moment comes, one has to be extremely well-equipped in this special domain. Two qualities therefore especially characterize the individuals who are recognized for their creativity: they have without exception a deep desire for the activity they are doing for its own sake and (therefore) they are ready to invest a vast amount of time and work into it. The personal talent, or aptitude, and the ability to see things from different, alternative perspectives, which is often behind a moment of discovery, can be fruitful only when these two prerequisites are fulfilled. (Csikszentmihalyi 1996)

Studies on performance creativity come to the very same conclusion about the qualities that make performers and performances creative: deep devotion and years of hard work give the experience the performers need to have to improvise, the readiness to act in changing situations and the expertise to react to the cooperators' contributions. Although there is (normally) no end-product in performance that remains, as Csikszentmihalyi & Rich (1997: 63) point out, the difference is mainly that the time of the process is minimal with regard to the produce-focused creativity: the tripartite connection of the person, domain and field works very much the same way.

The anthropologists Tim Ingold and Elizabeth Hallam elaborate on the historical meaning of the concept creativity in their introduction to the recent volume on *Creativity and Cultural Improvisation* (2007). They argue that looking at creativity as innovation is to read the process backwards. As they show, similarly as do many contributors to the book, the linking of creativity exclusively to innovation is historically a very recent phenomenon and in most cultures other than Western culture, people still focus on the improvisatory process. Keith Sawyer (1997: 2) similarly argued that it may be far more common for performance to feature the location of the perception of creativity than the end-products.

Whether or not improvisation is *real* creativity is a question raised in a detailed analysis by Tim Ingold (2007: 45–52). By contrasting further the approaches to creativity as an eternal re-combination of existing elements into new entities – as if all the components were there ready to select – and the idea that the process itself is creative, Ingold refers to Henri Bergson's example: "the artist's invention is inseparable from the progress of his work" (ibid. 47). Ingold thus concludes that "the movement of consciousness, in the painter's work, is creative in bringing forth the idea it embodies; it does not merely give outward expression to a conception that has sprung ready-formed to his mind." This means that creativity locates essentially in how people find and make their ways through a process.

Csikszentmihalyi, while choosing the target of his psychological research among individuals who are widely recognized for their creativity, notices that there are fields in which what he refers to as *personal creativity* can exist: poetry is essentially one of them. The same aspect of creativity as something new and meaningful to an individual, although not undiscovered by others before this person, makes the cognitive psychologist Margaret Boden distinguish between psychological creativity and historical creativity (2004 [1990]: 2). While stating that creativity means new, surprising and valuable, she continues that all these definitions can have several meanings. The two definitions of new, three definitions of surprising and the unending diversity of the valuable, are significant for the present purposes. Therefore, apart from that something can occur for the first time in the history of mankind, it can be newly discovered by an individual, as well as be surprising according to the personal experience and valuable with very different, even changing criteria. (ibid. 1–10)

Conceptualizing improvisation

The idea of improvisation is strongly connected to the previously discussed themes of register and performance. Although the concept was already presented in the previous discussion on creativity as well, contextualizing the concept of improvisation in the context of folklore research requires further discussion about the conceptions of authorship and aesthetics in traditional oral poetry performance and composition. This type of discussion has been absent from mainstream research probably because by the time researchers started applying their new contextualizing insights to the study of performance, metrical oral traditions were rarely if ever thought of as a current field of study. As a result, scholarly efforts were directed, as previously mentioned, essentially towards narrative and mythical traditions and towards defining poetic elements other than the metrical. In the literally oriented research of oral poetry texts, improvisation as a term has a long history of association with something individual and artistic in a literary sense, therefore controversial to the idea of folk culture and recurrent items of folklore.[7] This attitude of improvisation as creating "often unsubstantiated images of creativity, spontaneity and novelty" as Honko states (1998: 53–54), is current even in very recent research. On the other hand, in the case of individually produced topical verse, especially when appearing in print, literary criticism has applied the aesthetics of imperfection that is typical of musical improvisation. I will introduce this background by providing a short historical account and then view how improvisation is understood in

---

7 Fernandez (2005: 98–99) refers to another evident reason for the dislike of improvisation in academic research: although improvisation has played a significant role in the successful adaptation of human beings to new conditions, the development of organized, established structures underlies the humankind's progress to a remarkable degree.

music. I will then turn to perspectives given by previous researchers focusing on mantinádes and discuss the problems of the different kinds of metrical registers and singing cultures. Finally, I will suggest how the concept of improvisation can be applied in these contexts of oral poetry.

Perceptions of improvisation among folklore scholarship

The early collectors of Finnish folk poems in the seventeenth and eighteenth centuries expressed their particular admiration towards improvising folk poets, who "can on the spur of the moment make up and sing songs of any subject" (Cajanus 1697, in Kuusi 1985: 96–97). As noticed by Heikki Laitinen (2006: 44–45), this admiration starts, although in a reverse mode, as early as in 1583, when Jacobus Finno in his foreword to a hymn book depicts how the devil itself helps the singer to find words to ever new songs. Porthan, one of the major contributors to the Finnish folk poetry collections in the eighteenth century, describes in detail how new verses are created continuously, "although only few of them are spread outside the home parish of the creator or last longer than the lifetime of the composer or his contemporaries – since new poems all the time push the old out of their way – unless the pen of a person who can write notes them down or, much more seldom, they are given to be printed" (Porthan 1983 [1766–68], in Laitinen 2006: 44–45, translation by the present author). As noticed by Laitinen (2006: 44), Lönnrot describes practically and in a way corresponding to any contemporary improviser's perception, the requirements for being able to improvise: listening to others, learning a profound repertoire, and engagement in constant practice.

Such views of oral poetry traditions are essentially based on treating a living singing culture as a whole. In Finland, the perception of folk songs as belonging to separate genres, especially to epic and lyric, developed during the early nineteenth century and became established with the publication of Lönnrot's *Kalevala* in 1835 and his *Kanteletar*[8] in 1840. The result was that the folklore scholarship began to emphasize the role of the epic. This is because epic poetry, as characteristically more stable, fitted better the paradigmatically formed research questions and the new text-critical methods. The few divergent contributions on the more associative and improvisatory lyric poetry were disregarded in the mainstream of theorizing in the field. (Timonen 2004: 11–12)

Although some of the divergent voices, like that of the Estonian folklorist Oskar Loorits (see below), advocated the study of *whole songs as performed* rather than partial items serving the purposes of the historic-geographical method, the mainstream of the research had adapted the ideology of defining the history of the supposed original songs, the archetypes. Along with this ideology, researchers logically disregarded such qualities as spontaneity and individuality in performance, not to speak of conscious, deliberate

---

8   A collection of lyric folk songs

composition. Although one of the main strategies of the emerging folkloristic scholarship was to show that the oral was different from the literary, this distinction also concerned a strict gap between the anonymous, collective and individual, the artistic. This connection is clearly woven into the widely influential rhetoric of Jakobson's and Bogatyrev's early definitions of *langue* and *parole* as reflecting the essential difference between folklore and literature (1980 [1929]: 10; boldface in the original):

> The role of the performer of a folklore work should not, under any circumstances, be identified with that of either the reader or with that of the reciter of a literary work, much less that of the author. Considered from the viewpoint of the performer of a folklore work, these [folklore] works represent a fact of **langue**; that is, an extrapersonal, given fact already independent of the performer, although admitting of manipulation and the introduction of new poetic and ordinary material. But for the author of a literary work, this [literary] work appears to be a fact of **parole**; it is not given **a priori**, but is dependent upon an individual realization.

Furthermore, the commentary given by Albert Lord after the publication of *The Singer of Tales* (1960) also clearly reflects this attitude. A careful reading of this study shows that he had understood the skilful composition in the local epic register not just as a replacement of formulas, but as a fully developed method of using a poetic idiom, a register, very much like the ethnomusicologist Samuel Baud-Bovy presents the improvisation of mantinádes in his dissertation (1936). In *The Singer of Tales*, Lord refers to improvisation as "not a bad term for the process, but it too must be modified by the restrictions of the particular style" (1960: 5). Later, Lord expressed a much more negative perception of the improvisation. He makes the following distinction between the concepts of composition-in-performance and improvisation in discussing the applicability of the Oral-Formulaic Theory to the short, stanzaic, lyric Latvian dainas (1989: 42–43):

> The traditional singer uses the traditional formulas and themes, compositional devices, whose techniques, together with certain basic patterns, the singer has learned from listening to other singers. Improvisation involves making up a song on the spur of the moment, creating a song ex tempore, and applies properly to non-traditional material and methods. Neither the Serbo-Croatian epics nor the songs of Homer were improvised. These two methods of composition also contrast in that the formulas and themes used in composition-in-performance are traditional, whereas those in improvisation are more frequently new. The traditional formulas and themes have the depth of many years and generations of singers behind them. The improviser is using material which is often thought up on the spur of the moment.

Lord neither specifies what kind of poetry exactly he means by improvisation, nor does he specify what kind of material he regards as *new*. I had the opportunity to discuss this with John Miles Foley, a former student of Albert Lord, who verified Lord's negative attitude and also that Lord never makes explicit what he means by the notion (interview in Helsinki,

November 16, 2006). From the perspective of Finnish folklore studies, it seems evident that his negative arguments were enhanced by the reluctance of philology-oriented research to see folk poetry as such a flexible element in the hands of creative individuals. Even though Lord wished to introduce the *performance-in-composition* as an organized, traditional method of oral composition, and the usefulness of the formulas for producing the narrative under the pressure of performance was a real concern to him rather than the artistic creativity, his theory was at the time at least in Finland, interpreted indeed as artistic "improvisation."

This is made explicit by Matti Kuusi (1985: 85–99) when he analyzes the improvisatory proverb commentary of Anni Lehtonen, a talented female singer of *kalevala-meter* poetry, whose repertoire is documented to an unusual extent. In that text, Kuusi describes the paradigmatic conceptions concerning the idea of a rigid text and the research of archetypes and shows willingness to revise "the a priori conception of a good singer of *kalevala-meter* poetry as a passive, faithful maintainer" (1985: 98).

> In Finland, we have adopted a skeptical attitude towards the model of explanation of the folk poetry as created by Albert B. Lord on the basis of fieldwork conducted in Yugoslavia: the singer creates while performing, makes up, as a master of traditional composition technique, the poem anew each time. The academic school notwithstanding, we have concluded as Romantic illusion the descriptions of Ericus Cajanus, Juslenius, Mennander, Porthan, Lönnrot, Europaeus, Polén, ect., of singers of poems who – as Cajanus expressed the matter in his dissertation in 1697 – "can on the spur of the moment make up and sing songs on any subject." (Kuusi 1985: 96–97; translation by the present author)

> The notions "poem," "original form" and "variant" do not make sense in the oral traditions, argues Albert B. Lord; the fact that they seem logical and necessary to us is because we live in a society of the written word. Therefore we scientifically try to render static a phenomenon, which by nature is *fluid*. (Kuusi 1985: 97; translation by the present author)

Lord often explicitly refers to the singer of tales as a creative individual (1960, passim) and I assume that Lord's thesis was interpreted as placing the individual too much on the side of *parole*, the individual realization, at the expense of merely manipulating the existing songs. Lord, indeed, defended himself in 1975 by stating the following:

> On the other hand, the poet does not "improvise", that is to say, he does not make up consciously entirely new lines or entirely new passages. Just as a story teller, when he retells a story, will sometimes use the same sentences, or sentences very like the ones he has used before, so the singer in his story telling in verse will use lines he has used before, or lines like them. Neither of them consciously concerns himself or is even aware of whether he is using the same or slightly different or quite different phrases. Both of them are telling stories and are concentrating on that. What I am describing is that special kind of composition in verse

that does not seek newness or originality that is not afraid of using the old expressions – a special kind of "improvisation", if you will, but not improvising out of whole cloth. In my attempts in the past to combat the idea of a fixed text that was memorized, I have apparently given the impression that not only is the text different at each singing by a given singer (which is true, of course), but that it is *radically* different, entirely improvised. This is not true. South Slavic oral epic is not, nor, to the best of my knowledge, is any oral traditional epic, the result of "free improvisation." (Lord 1975: 16–17)

Lord elaborates carefully that when Parry, and later Lord himself, spoke of oral poetry while creating the Oral-Formulaic Theory, what they meant was the oral-traditional *narrative* song (Lord 1989: 42). The Oral-Formulaic Theory was thus formed on the basis of one epic subgenre in the Serbo-Croatian tradition, and the multitude of forms, techniques, functions and aesthetics of oral poetry was not explicitly included in the scope of the theory. Nevertheless, due to the immense popularity of the work, its emphasis on the *usefulness* of the formulas and formulaic structures later became problematic in two ways: the formulaic structures were implicitly adopted as a general model to explain all oral poetry, and the aspect of usefulness shifted the focus away from, among other things, the fact that these structures essentially carry extra-textual meaning. (Foley 1988: xi, 109–111, et passim; Foley 1991, 1995) Therefore, even those researchers who were faced with different kinds of poetry registers which were not oriented towards telling a story remained captives of this model. For example, Jeff Opland, who claimed that *free* improvisation was indeed the mode of composition in the register of South African praise poetry, entangled himself in the debate on the aspect of usefulness rather than showing the structure of that register and the possibilities of improvisation typical of it (Opland 1985: 152–193). Improvisation, as verified by the early collectors, is essentially a disciplined activity in which the conventional, recognizable elements are consciously taken as the starting point for creativity. This perception of improvisation will be discussed below·

Improvisation in music

Improvisation as a form of performance is most typically connected to the jazz and folk music traditions (also modern dance and theater), which forms a useful analogue. For example, Hamilton (2007: 192) observes that, "improvisation is a near-universal tendency in music and needs no defence." Reflecting on the above-mentioned problems that were related to folklore studies, improvisation is considered to be *free* or *new* mainly in the very limited category of free jazz. In the predominant jazz tradition, as well as in Eastern musical traditions and in the folk music traditions in general, improvisation is regarded as a disciplined, a conversational process which each participating musician contributes to by creatively elaborating on the chosen and shared rhythmic and melodic patterns. In free jazz, "playing out" means that the musician who improvises can completely abandon the basic rhythm and melodic patterns, whereas "playing in," a feature typical of the predominant jazz tradition, Eastern musical traditions and folk music in general, means that the improviser explores, analyzes and varies the rhythmic and melodic patterns and themes within the conventions of the selected musical form or genre. Although a performer can temporarily withdraw from the others or intentionally play against or break the patterns, there is always an intense contact existing between the participants. A fundamental part of this improvisation is the co-operation by performers in the reciprocal challenges in the melodic and rhythmic formulas (which is often described as *conversation*; see e.g. Berliner 1997). In this sense, improvisation means that music and musical genres are understood as languages constituted of rhythmic and melodic elements which can be freely united within the guidelines and the "grammar" of the register. Therefore, although separate units of the outcome are not played/sung for the first time, the performance as a whole is unique, created in that form only at that one time. In brief, improvisation is creation in process, the course of which is determined by the participants in a living situation. (See e.g. Berliner 1994; Lortat-Jacob 1987; Nettl 1998)

In his philosophical book on the aesthetics of music (2007), Andy Hamilton calls this the *aesthetics of process*. The common aesthetic code of Western musical tradition is that of composed music, of a perfected, ready-made product, and as Hamilton shows, this is the opposite to the logic of the process in improvisation. Hamilton calls this as *aesthetics of perfection*. From this perspective, improvisation is regarded as imperfection: full of faults and repetition.[9] This means that the aesthetic code of perfection is that of the product. So, the original composer is the creator, and the performing musicians can show their talent in their virtuosity of handling their instruments and in their creative interpretation of the compositions, much like the reciter of a literary poem would. The textual or notated starting point is, however, a fixed entity – a work.

Both aesthetic codes, process and perfection, deeply determine personal artistic expectations and experiences. It seems that it is indeed extremely difficult for most musicians trained in the Classical Western musical tradition to change the code and "play without scores." Similarly, it is likewise extremely difficult for a person brought up and trained or self-taught within an improvisatory folk music tradition to enjoy playing a piece with no room for improvisation.[10] This rough dichotomy clearly points to that, the personal talent and aptitude notwithstanding, the question of

---

9 Cf. to what Csikszentmihalyi & Rich (1997: 51) write: For instance, since music in many senses is ephemeral, an aesthetic of jazz as an imperfect art (Gioia, 1988) has developed, which tolerates "mistakes" as minor blemishes to be expected when improvisers take risks and explore new musical territory.

10 Since 1999, I have observed and discussed the experiences of my husband, who as a professional percussionist was first self-taught as a child, later studied ethnic percussions through acoustic learning for four years, continuing on to classical percussions and to rhythm analysis. His experience in performing and teaching ethnic Eastern percussions and rhythms both in Crete and in Finland suggests a striking dichotomy in these aesthetics.

improvisation concerns the aesthetic code, and correspondingly, what the performer has *learned to think possible*.[11]

Improvisation and metrical registers

On the basis of the musical analogue, improvisation can be characterized as a creative, process-like and as the unpremeditated use of register in a performance. With verbal registers, the task of defining improvisation is somewhat more complicated than with music: are we dealing only with the formation of distinctly new textual entities, or does creative adaptation of the existing material count as improvisation as well?

Opinions approving only the former definition exist, as well as those approving both. The twofold nature of the notion improvisation is expressed by Yorgos Amaryanakis, a Cretan-born Greek musicologist, who pointed out (1988: 328) that with regard to mantinádes, improvisation can signify either the extempore composition of a new text, which in that form has not been known before, or else a new, situationally motivated chain of already existing poems, resulting in a new "song." Herzfeld (1985a: 141) has correspondingly stated that the originality in a performance can be acknowledged on the grounds of a new text as well as on creatively fitting an existing poem-unit to a particular situation, which results in a new meaningful connection. Both these researchers therefore underline the attitude and aim of eliciting a situated meaning at the very moment of performing.

On the other hand, ethnomusicologist Samuel Baud-Bovy, who describes the versatile tradition of mantinádes, uses the term improvisation when he conducts a comprehensive structural study of the linguistic and poetic components and of the aids of creating extemporized, contextually motivated new textual units (Baud-Bovy 1936: 313–369). Thus, Baud-Bovy talks about improvisation as an instantaneous form of composition at the time of the performance, in line with the regular use of the term in connection with contest poetry. Researchers of the Hispanic verse singing traditions, as well as the Basque *bertsolaritza* poets and researchers (Armistead & Zuleika 2005; Garcia et al. 2001), use the concept *improvised oral poetry* to denote forms of poetry composed on the spot in communicational exchange of verses within the frames of an organized singing event. In a verbal contest, these verses are composed reciprocally on the spur of the moment, according to the selected theme, tune, meter and rhyme pattern, and offering proof of immediate textual composition is regarded as essential.

---

11 In Crete I met students with no earlier music education who were learning the rhythmic phrases and patterns as a language and improvising from the very beginning, because that was how music was introduced to them. On the other hand, I know several contemporary Cretan musicians who have taught themselves by listening to audio records, or have learned with a teacher without using notes, but do not "put a note above what is received," e.g. improvise; their learning process has focused solely on playing fixed melodies.

The twofold conceptualization treats improvisation as a sociolinguistic skill to create meaning spontaneously during a performance, which does not necessarily require producing an original text. With regard to the traditional performance of the *kalevala-meter* poetry, Oskar Loorits expressed the following opinion in a manuscript completed in 1942 (1964: 188, translation by the present author):

> The share of improvisation in the performance of our folk poems should not in any case be understated, because it is there indeed where enormous differences of level can be discerned in the "greatness" of individual singers, in their artistic maturity and taste, their mental qualifications and inclinations, their skill to adapt and orientate themselves in different situations as well as their intellectual potential to captivate the audience and carry it away to sing and put its soul to the verses. Thus the function of improvisation is not so much the composition of new verses, but the skill to adapt and combine the verse material, the exploitation and combination of all kinds of common verses in the performance, which normally is constructed completely from traditional ingredients, but as a whole is unique and transforms and changes each time.

I think that this attitude also reflects well the deep sigh which I received as a response to a question I posed to a group of men outside a *kafenío* in Lasithi (see photo on page 42); I asked them whether there had been many *mantinadolóyi* in this village in the old days, and one of the men replied: "In the old days, we were all *mantinadolóyi*." Rather than claiming that everyone used to create new poems, which would be the primarily meaning of the word,[12] he meant, in my interpretation, that within a living and collectively shared singing culture realized in recurrent occasions, several members of the community were able to apply the flexible formulae and the patterns of the register and were able to individually contribute to the emerging performative dialogues. I also interpret that such improvisational orientation characterizes the communicative performances of many elderly people in Crete even today.

A narrower interpretation expressed by Baud-Bovy, which nevertheless reflects the clear distinction perceived by several traditional singers in Crete and elsewhere,[13] conceptualizes improvisation essentially as producing a new textual entity ex tempore, "on the spot." This meaning is unambiguous with regard to several registers which are used in genres such as singing contests or mocking songs, in which contextual elements are bound to the immediate textual structure. This distinction is made on the basis of the special cognitive skills required from the performer to transform his or her

---

12 Although the ending *-logos* might also mean "collector," this interpretation of the word *mantinadológos* was rejected by Maria Lioudaki in her defense of the local terminology already in the 1930s (Papadakis M. M. 1992).
13 See e.g. the distinctions made by Larin Paraske in the beginning of the twentieth century between the situations in which certain songs should be sung as they are, and situations in which one can insert elements of one´s own, and in the latter case, those between combining existing material and creating new songs (Timonen 2004: 274–276).

situational associations and fantasy into a text in the flash of lightning. The Sardinian performer and scholar Paulu Zedda (2009) analyzes this skill as an extended capability of using the working memory, distinguishing it from the capacity provided by a good long-term memory, which enables the adoption of a vast amount of memorized poems.

It is common in Crete for people to separate the skill to extemporize[14] in a situation as a special talent in a composers or a singer, and in some areas and communities, competent performers are or have been expected to command immediate textual improvisation. In most areas and communities, however, a singer's repertoire includes mostly selected, already existing poems or personally composed, previously unpublished poems. In the singing events, as well as in many other communicative situations, spontaneity can also be demonstrated in the creative adopting of the poem to the event. Because poems are so short, this can be paralleled to the practice of matching an existing formula to the whole of a longer, improvised poem. As for the past *traditional* improvised oral singing events in the Hispanic areas, there are similar references to ready-made verses having been used in these events (e.g. Christian 2005; Fernandez 2005: 107–113).

Verbal improvisation can therefore be conceptualized in broader or narrower terms, but does it in any way differ from the concept of composition-in-performance? In the Oral-Formulaic Theory, the oral method of composing of a narrative epic song was referred to as *composition-in-performance* by Albert Lord. Composition-in-performance explains the process of individual, context-sensitive verbal rendering of an epic or other narrative where the plot and motives and themes are familiar to the composer and his or her audience. The process of oral composition contains wide variation in the aesthetic and situational decisions and in the placement of universally applicable traditional material, but it also contains new images and lines created by the performer (Lord 1960; Harvilahti 1992; 2004). The singer himself, however, maintains that he is delivering a traditional song, even word for word (although this "word" is not a lexicographic word, but a flexible unit of expression; see Foley 2002: 11–21; 2005: 67–68).

With regard to the metrical registers, we are therefore clearly faced with very different kinds of singing traditions and song materials, as well as the singers' indigenous genre- and situation-specific orientations and practices. In each case, skillful singers use the register to render a performance which is a unique, whole entity. I suggest that a difference can and should be conceptualized between the concepts of composition-in-performance and improvisation. However, this difference, contrary to what Lord has maintained above,[15] does not emerge in how formulaic or traditional this register is,

---

14 The Greek verb *aftoshediázo*, "self-plan," can be used in speech, but more often ex tempore composition is expressed in other ways: *vgázi/teriázi epi tópou* (he or she creates on the spot); *vgázi/sou ta lei kat'efthían* (he or she tells it to you straight/immediately).

15 For example, concerning the Latvian traditions, as cited by Lord (1989: 44), the short lyric *dainas* (which, although unrhymed, have been much like mantinádes) are found through computer analysis to be as *formulaic* as the traditional long narrative epics (Vikis-Freibergs & Freibergs 1978: 338).

but rather in one or several of the following points: (1) verse narratives (and many other genres where oral composition takes place) are produced during a performance under the authority of a *single person*; (2) the focus is on a *known plot or familiar material*, from the authority of which the performer consciously draws; and (3) the performer views that he or she is acting towards delivering a piece of the shared tradition. Quite contrary to this is the orientation of the improviser: (1) the performer feels that he or she is using the register as a tool for *saying or singing something of his or her own*, and (2) that the entity produced in that situation is *new, unique*. The performance is characteristically (3) *reciprocal*, or carried on by *turn-taking*. I therefore interpret that with regard to the oral composition in a performance in general, improvisation is essentially a particular orientation, determined by the performer's conscious, deliberate acts towards rendering an individual utterance. Although this terminological difference primarily concerns how people orientate towards the register and how they define their actions, this self-definition seems to be significant, for example, in the reception of the written-down performances either as the "right" performances or as part of the reserve (see Lord 1960: 124–138 and discussions in Chapters 5 and 6).

To conclude, if we adopt a wider perspective to a tradition such as the mantinádes, we need to examine the idea of improvisation from both perspectives mentioned above. First, we need to explore improvisation as a general orientation towards performance, of reacting to a text or context by an individual, spontaneous verbal act. This type of improvisation can be achieved by applying an existing text, and for the sake of clarity, I will specify it as *contextual improvisation*. Second, we can examine improvisation as a method of using the register for the creation of new textual units during a performance, which in turn can be specified as extemporization or, correspondingly, as *textual improvisation*.

Poems are, of course, also used in other modes in many circumstances. For example, there is a stable, ritual character to the mantinádes sung to initiate a celebration or a get-together meal, or to the mantinádes sung by women to honor and advise the bride and groom while preparing them for their wedding. The role of these mantinádes is to enhance the feeling of the feast and solidarity; they focus on shared traditions as the qualifiers of social ties. In addition, improvisation is not an exclusive orientation of the singing events, as will be indicated in the following chapter. Few people are capable of extemporizing verses entirely spontaneously, and in many Cretan communities other principles are stated as fundamental, instead. Furthermore, in discussions on composition, ex tempore composition is only a minor category. Composition is a separate theme, which stretches far beyond the communicational ex tempore situations (see Chapter 6).

Poems as text and process: the double-identity

In music, the melodic and rhythmic stretches that are shaped during collective improvisation within a performance may become *works* in themselves – units which adopt a fixed form and remain in the repertoire. (In addition to being a feature of the actual performance, improvisation is often used as a creative, communicative method for *finding the form* of a final, more fixed product as well.)[16] During a verse singing event in Crete, old poems are sung and they can be slightly altered for the current purposes, and completely new poems are also composed ex tempore. Many new, ex tempore compositions reflect the moment at hand and may be forgotten later on, but they may also remain a way of recollecting the event by those present. Some poems gain a universal status as examples of poetic and semantic excellence, worth remembering and/or reusable in other contexts. This process of *entextualization* differs from a musical performance and from verse singing that contains several lines, because every new poem composed on the spot is easily detachable, transferable and re-applicable by *anyone* who hears it and finds it useful and significant – not only by the performers themselves, who are able to use the register productively, but also by people who cannot create poems by themselves. Since these short, textual entities have clearly bound semantic contents, they are also directed and interpreted as personal utterances. These qualities that are inherent in the mantinádes lower the threshold of regarding the texts as works.

Improvisation, as explained above, enhances the aesthetics of being in an evolving process within a performance – within an interpersonal, dialogic process. Cretans, however, unanimously underline the *autonomous* character of a single mantináda. This becomes evident in the following description by Yorgos Sifakis (2004; 041110a), provided during a discussion on what a good poem is:

> Since a good mantináda, eh.., I will give you a simple definition, which is however very substantial, as well. This description is not made by me, but by an old woman from Anoya, when she was asked what a good mantináda is like. And she says, with her way of thinking: A good mantináda, she says, *must raise your hair*. When you hear it, something penetrates you; really this has happened to me, too, when I hear a very good mantináda, it hits like a current, an electric current.
>
> (V): *But can this happen when you hear only the mantináda or more when you hear also the story behind it, the event?*
>
> (Y): Yes, the event as well, but as I told you a while ago…
>
> (V): *That means that through its words, a mantináda has to be so good, that even when you don't know what the other has thought…*

---

16 This view was presented in several presentations in the seminar on improvisation held by the Graduate School of Ethnomusicological Studies and Dance in Kallio-Kuninkaala, November 2–3, 2006.

> (Y): *Certainly*! Because, on the same theme, there are many mantinádes! One is simple, another loses somewhere, yet another, let's say, has a word which is not Cretan...

This means that in Crete, there is an explicitly stated, parallel interest towards poems as texts, and these are thought of as end-products in their own right. This double-identity of mantinádes denotes that poems simultaneously are "monuments" and "stepping stones," in other words, individual texts and particular moments as well as a way of being in an on-going process.

While the texts are appreciated by locals, a literary mind from outside the tradition often reads them in a very different way. The reason for the lack of laudatory statements on the "personal" folk poetry among the literary sources lies inherently in the unfamiliarity with this double-logic: poems are seen as texts through the aesthetics of perfection, only like an "autonomous" literary product.[17] Excellent, beautiful poetry which works as well in print as it does in performance, is made orally, and poems that are aesthetically and semantically coherent, and therefore reusable, are also especially appreciated and remembered in oral communities. It is only in this sense that the crystallized forms considered to be folk poetry and that last from generation to generation can be singled out during the passing of time. But much of the individually composed oral poetry is creative as communication, self-expression and play *within* various personal and social dialogic processes. In a traditional oral poetry culture, people focus on the process, and even contextualize the products as belonging to a kind of on-going process. As has been argued above by John Miles Foley, these products are laden with referents to a wider, shared traditional knowledge; they reflect a wide net of textual and contextual moments of communication in the community and are also enjoyed as parts of it.

---

17 I put the qualifier "autonomous" in brackets since, the time-aspect of the production, reception and reaction notwithstanding, how far, in the end, are written texts from this? Quality is as much or as little guaranteed by the medium in both cases, and texts and contexts are given both shared and personal meanings in several external and internal dialogic processes. In the light of the Cretan tradition, I think that Jakobson's and Bogatyrev's early adaptation of de Saussure's definitions *langue* and *parole*, which they defined as "a collection of necessary conventions adopted by a social body to permit the exercise of that faculty [language] among individuals" and "the individual, particular speech act" (1980 [1929]: 4), can refer to the interplay between shared traditions and their shaping into individual utterances in both literature and productive oral poetry alike. While these researchers noticed the significant relationship within folklore between "the work of art and its objectification" (ibid. 9), or "tradition and improvisation" in oral poetry (ibid. 17) as *langue* and *parole*, they essentially used these terms to qualify the difference between folklore (as *langue*) and literature (as *parole*).

III Crete and traditional performance contexts

Crete as historical, social and cultural setting

Crete is a Greek island of 8,259 km² (3,189 m²) and approximately 650,000 inhabitants today. Geographically, two mountain chains divide Crete into areas with very different natural circumstances. Likewise, the history, sources of livelihood and cultural conditions of these areas have differed significantly. The western and central parts, except for the high mountain ranges, have water and greenery, whereas the eastern and southern parts are dry and rocky. The major towns Iraklio (population of approximately 120,000 inhabitants today), Hania (50,000) and Rethimno (35,000), lie on the North coast. Tourism is an important source of income in Crete: apart from the largest towns and their immediate surroundings, which have all come to be remarkable tourist resorts, Crete's coastline as well as the inland areas are thickly dotted by villages offering tourist activities and facilities.

In ancient times, Crete was a part of the Greek world and was the center of the Minoan culture. Later, Crete belonged to the Roman Empire and then to the Byzantine Empire. Due to the abundance of natural resources and the strategically attractive location of the island, Crete has a long history of occupations, insurrections and battles for freedom. Crete was occupied by the Arabs from 827 to 961, the Venetians from 1211 to 1669, and the Ottoman Turks from 1669 to 1897; then it became autonomous for fifteen years, before finally being united with the Greek State in 1913. During the Second World War, Crete underwent German invasion, and Cretan resistance led to the Germans burning many villages to the ground.

During the Venetian occupation, the intellectual and literary artistry of Crete flourished (see Panayotakis 1990; Holton 1991), while peasants struggled under intolerably heavy oppressive conditions. Little information is available concerning the cultural conditions of the peasant population in this period, or from the times following the Ottoman capture and occupation of the island. During the Ottoman period, an abundance of Turkish words were introduced into the vocabulary of everyday life, as was the case in Greece and in the Balkans in general. The contemporary local presentation of history emphasizes the religious chasm, and the Ottoman reign is treated as the "dark years of oppression of the Christian population" (e.g. Detorakis

1990: 271–437). From the beginning of the Ottoman reign, however, many orthodox Cretans converted to the Muslim faith (and were later called Turko-Cretans), and some informative interpretations on the complexity of this fact have lately been presented by Molly Greene (2000). The main point is that the majority of the Muslim Cretans were ethnically Cretan and not Turkish by origin. As is still recalled by some whose grandparents had witnessed the times before and during the population exchange (see below), Christian and Muslim Cretans led their everyday lives mainly in friendship, and any excessive acts of violence were committed by separate, criminal individuals (051102).

At the end of the Ottoman occupation, in 1897, a significant population exchange took place. More than half of the Muslim Turko-Cretans, especially from the rural areas, immediately left for Asia Minor. Meanwhile, the town areas, especially Iraklio, received minor waves of Greek Christian refugees from Asia Minor[1]. This movement culminated in the enforced population exchange occurring at the end of the Greco-Turkish wars in 1922–1923, when all the remaining Muslim population (around 33,000 people), mainly residing in towns, was resettled in Turkey. The basis of this contract was faith; Turko-Cretans were ethnically Cretans for the most part and did not, for example, speak Turkish. Crete in turn received Greek Christian refugees (33,900) from Asia Minor. (Detorakis 1990: 458–459, 466–467) The result of this exchange was that small town areas, especially the principal town of Iraklio, experienced a radical change in population and a tremendous cultural impact brought about by the urban population from the cities of Asia Minor. In the long run, this also had an impact on the development of Cretan music, even though there was little cultural interchange between the rural and urban population at that time owing to the very different life conditions (Zaïmákis 2001: 110–136). In general, the cultural conditions did not change much in the rural areas, which included the vast majority of Crete and the Cretans (around 85%).

Crete has always been primarily an agricultural island, with pastoralism featuring as the second most important source of livelihood. The anthropologist Michael Herzfeld points out that in contrast to other rural Greek communities, Cretan shepherds have enjoyed a much higher status in society than the Cretan farmers (Herzfeld 1985a: 22). Furthermore, Cretan mountain guerrillas were famous fighters in the Greek War of Independence (starting in 1821), but later Crete, especially the mountain areas, have shown great reluctance towards the centripetal forces of the Greek State. In fact, the Cretan shepherds and the mountain population are well-known in Greece for stubbornly holding on to their independence, local values and unlawful customs. As Herzfeld states, the harshness of the Turkish occupation was posed as an explanation for many idiosyncratic ways of behavior, like animal raiding, vendettas and keeping guns. (Herzfeld 1985a: 19–33.)

---

1 The total population in Crete counted 72,353 Turko-Cretans and 206,812 Christians in 1881, and correspondingly 33,496 / 270,047 in 1900 (Detorakis 1990: 458–459).

In rural Crete, the primary cultural differences correspondingly occur between the pastoral population of the mountains and the agricultural and fishing populations of the lowlands. In eastern Crete, the settling of refugees from Asia Minor brought a different, somewhat more liberal culture, especially in regard to the place of women in the community[2]. During the past ten or twenty years, economic benefits and changing lifestyle have alleviated the tensions in Crete and helped reduce the animal raiding[3] and vendettas even in the upper Milopotamos area; yet in this area the aggressive potential is kept alive by the unchanged social structures.[4] In addition to the study by Herzfeld (1985a), who specifically addresses the local structures of animal raiding taking place in this area, the Greek anthropologist Aris Tsantiropoulos has recently (2004) published a comprehensive study on the social structures that maintain the vendetta.[5]

In central Crete, special attention has to be paid to the high mountain village Anoya, which boasts a superior cultural capital and today forms a municipality by itself. The number of musicians and *mantinadolóyi* (mantináda-composers) produced by Anoya is high, but the village has also imposed a cultural hegemony over the entire island. Local traditions in some parts of Crete have suffered from this hegemony, and it is also criticized for this reason.

In the past, the vendettas and animal raiding also concerned the department of Hania, the Lefka Ori mountain area, but several people have told me that since the number of people killed in vendettas in Hania became too high, the shepherds managed to obtain a mutual contract of putting an end to the hostilities and ceasing the raids. Several resident populations in Crete and on other islands (e.g. Naxos, Kos), as well as those overseas, are said to have been created due to people fleeing from the communities after committing deadly acts or for fear of retaliation to the whole patrilineal surname group. Although it is chiefly the people in the mountain villages – thus, only a part of the Cretan communities – who are characterized by fearless violence, and rebellious, idiosyncratic and illegal customs, these characteristics are attributed to all Cretans in colloquial references elsewhere in Greece.

The Village where I lived during my principal fieldwork periods is located in the valley of Milopotamos, in a distance of only about twenty

---

2 Both virilocality and uxirolocality are found in the Greek world, with many related cultural and social consequences. Virilocalism associated with pastoralism can encourage a patriarchal model, as in the Cretan highlands, whereas the basin of the Aegean sea is known for its uxirolocality and generally more equal gender model (see Loizos & Papataxiarchis 1991: 8–10, and the articles in their book).
3 A small article in the local newspaper *Rethymniótika Néa* in October 2000 states that crime has declined in Crete during the first nine months of the year, in relation to the previous year. The crimes presented in numbers are: robberies, thefts, car thefts, car accidents, and animal thefts. Animal thefts have reduced in number of cases from 79 to 56, and in number of animals from 2,023 to 1,400.
4 On April 7, 2010 the daily paper *Elefterotipía* reported the news of manslaughter committed in the village of Zoniana; because there was an immediate fear of more victims among the major patrigroups involved, powerful police forces were stationed in the village.
5 For an account of this research in English, see also Tsantiropoulos 2009.

A village surrounded by olive groves in the Milopotamos valley. Photo by the author, September 2007.

five kilometers (fifteen miles) from the zone of the high mountain villages. The life in this village, however, has no symbolic affinity and, as far as I know, no literal affinity with the upper villages (Anoya notwithstanding). My experiences of the "wild" villages of Milopotamos therefore rest on the criticism advanced by my own Village and by the other lowland villages and can thereby only amount to stereotypic images. In my Village, for example, raiding is only witnessed through the role of the victim: the contemporary raiders coming from the upper villages raid animals in powerful, modern jeeps, each year stealing an economically significant number of heard.

Rural depopulation is sharp in several districts of Crete and old people remain isolated in villages falling into decay; Milopotamos, however, is also distinguished for maintaining healthy age structures in many of its villages, as it is in my own. In the Village, this is possible since traditional occupations such as herding and coal burning are combined to work and enterprises in the nearby commercial center, towns and tourist resorts.

Until the end of the 1970s, pastoralism and farming (primarily olive oil, olives, wine and grapes, but also a significant number of other products, such as fruit) were the main occupations on the fertile island. Crete therefore never experienced the devastating emigration waves that many of the small Greek islands suffered.[6] After the Second World War, the rural de-population drove people to the local urbanizing centers and to the city of Athens. From the beginning of the 1980s, the tourism which had started to develop in

---

6 For anthropological studies, see e.g. Just 2000, and Kavouras 1991.

the 1960s, quickly grew into an important business throughout the island, affecting the economic, social and cultural structures. Tourism provided women work outside the home, and many shepherds and villagers quickly become rich through land sale. However, professional food production still keeps many villages alive, and large flocks of sheep and goats are seen and heard everywhere outside the urban areas. Part-time production, especially growing olives, is a normal part of life for most families. This also means that supplementary income is commonly acquired outside the official economy. Although the grey economy and corruption are deeply rooted in the Greek society in general, the part-time food production in Crete provides a significant supplement to the families' livelihood. Towns are small and the countryside is near, and as most of the townsfolk are citizens of the first- or the second-generation, contact with the village of origin are often actively maintained.

The woman's place in Cretan society has become increasingly more liberated during the last decades of the twentieth century, even though in many families, especially in the pastoral villages, patriarchal norms are still clearly obeyed. The realities of rural village communities, where the spheres of daily life of women and men were highly separated, are still valid. The social life in the towns and tourist areas is, of course, different. Yet changes in conceptions have been overwhelmingly rapid. It was unheard of, for example, until very recently, that a bride would be pregnant at her wedding; in October 2009, I discussed with a friend who had attended three such wedding feasts that year. Nevertheless, villages and areas still vary with regard to social and cultural concepts, since the conditions of life until the last decades of the twentieth century have been very locally confined.

Even though social changes and the privatization of life have progressed rapidly, especially during the last two decades of the twentieth century, daily life is characteristically comprised of intertwined rural and urban factors (see also Just 2000: 20–28[7]). In many areas of life, the uncritical accepting of the "modern" is overwhelming, like the degree to which the traditional healthy "Cretan diet" has given way to the commercial low-nutritious and high-fat food products even in the countryside. Television provides role models in appearance, interests and behavior, but in a village environment, for example, marriages can still be negotiated through a matchmaker.

One phenomenon of "modernism" which has amounted to a *kinonikó mastíyio*, social backlash (as described in the daily newspaper *Rethimniótika Néa* in October 23, 2009) are the high death rates from car accidents, which have been augmented by speeding during the twenty-first century.[8] Driving under the influence of alcohol is also common, particularly among young

---

7 For a comprehensive description of a small Greek island's social life and structures, and an eye to the recent change, see Roger Just's book: *A Greek Island Cosmos* (2000) on Meganisi, based on fieldwork during 1977–1980, but completed after a short stay on the island in 1994.
8 In 2010, only the Easter traffic (26.3. – 5.4.) in Greece caused 414 car accidents of which 28 were fatal, 42 were serious, and 344 were light; resulting in 31 deaths, 50 serious injuries and 475 light injuries (*Elefterotipía* April 6, 2010 www.enet.gr).

men, and speeding is the primary reason for deaths and injuries on the roads. Since long mourning periods are still maintained in the villages, these deaths not only cause suffering for individuals and families, but injure the community socially. When close relatives die, people dress in black for one year (widows and widowers often for the rest of their life) and they withdraw from all social enjoyment for that time, but when people suffer an untimely death, the whole village dresses in black. In such circumstances, a *gléndi* or a get-together for singing is completely out of the question. This sad phenomenon and its far-reaching social and cultural consequences became all the more noteworthy during the years of my fieldwork, and it finally also occurred in the Village in 2009.

However rapid, if unevenly proceeding changes the social reality and traditions undergo, the Cretans' respect of local values is nevertheless very evident. A good example of this cultural self-esteem is the way they maintain their musical and verbal traditions, as well as the Cretan dialect. Even if the lexical richness of the dialect has diminished considerably, the morphological and syntactical varieties and the phonological idioms are very clearly heard in the villages even today. According to Kimmo Granqvist (1998: 10), the Cretan dialect has been highly valued among its speakers, unlike some other Greek dialects. When I first begun my fieldwork (1997), many Cretans proudly argued that expressions and words vary enormously, even from village to village. This is often true, for instance, in the naming of (old) objects of peasant life. As for the differences in morphological and syntactical variants and the basic vocabulary, the main distributional differences are between the western on one side, to the eastern and central idioms on the other (Kontosopoulos 1988). The same pattern can be seen in other cultural traits as well, like the western tradition of the sung *rizítika* and that of the instrumental music and improvised mantinádes in the rest of Crete (see below).

Cretan music, dance and song

Cretan dance music serves as an important vehicle for singing mantinádes.[9] Other than the *rizítika* songs of western Crete (see below), the calendar songs, and a small number of other songs performed vocally without instrumental accompaniment, most Cretan music consists of instrumental dance music. The tradition of playing wind instruments has died out quite completely; these instruments (reed pipes; bagpipes in Lasithi) were found in the pastoral mountainous areas in the past.

Dance music, however, has survived to this day to be performed at all major feasts and the lyrics are almost without exception mantinádes. The poetic text can either be fixed to a certain melody, or the musical form can support extempore singing and verse making. The latter concerns especially

---

9 As sources for information about Cretan dance music, I have used the following primary sources and bibliography: 991202, 041110, 051102; 050906, 060823, Amaryanakis 1988: 327–328; Diktakis 1999; Kaloyanides 1975; Williams 2003.

The workshop of Antonis Stefanakis in Zaros. Instrument construction is one of the current artisan trades in Crete. Stefanákis constructs all kinds of stringed instruments. Visible here are two laoúta, two bouzoukis, and a laoúto (hanging on the wall); situated on the table are half-made liras.

Antonis Stefanakis still also makes reed pipes (called the habióli or thiambóli, depending on the region) and he is one of the last in Crete to play this pastoral instrument.

Cretan dances are chiefly line dances and they are performed by modest steps. The first dancer, however, is able to show his talent in imaginative and physically demanding variation. One of the well-known Cretan dancers, Stamatis Papadakis, performing with the dance group of the historical and ethnographic association of Rethimno in 1971. Photo private collection of Manolis Tzirakis.

the *kondiliés,* a musical genre that can be danced to, but is chiefly related to the improvisatory performance and the free singing style, *himatikó* ("loose"). *Kondiliés* are intended especially for informal singing in a *paréa* and have been extremely popular in eastern and central Crete. *Kondiliés,* like all Cretan dance music, is performed in 2/4 time (the *sirtá* is also in 4/4). Of the asymmetrical rhythms, which are popular on the mainland and largely in the Balkans, the *kalamatianós* (7/8) has been common earlier, but this is rarely performed today.

From the great wealth of local dance music forms, only five forms are commonly performed today. Of these, the *kastrinós* and *pentozáli*, which are instrumental, and the *soústa*, which has fixed lyrics, have established musical forms. The *kondiliés* and *haniótikos sirtós*, which can serve as a vehicle for verbal expression with mantinádes, were instead developed zealously by many local musicians during the early twentieth century. Both dance music forms consist of melodic formulas that offer the creative musician an opportunity to improvise by creating new variations as these formulas are repeated many times (for details, see Kaloyanides 1975: 139–150).

With the exception of the *soústa*, all these local dance forms are line dances.[10] The *haniótikos sirtós* is the most popular dance in the feasts today, as everyone knows the basic steps. The *kondiliés* (or *siganó pentozáli*) is

---

10 A comprehensive description of Cretan dances is available in Tsouhlarakis 2000; see also Nikolakakis 2008.

The soústa is one of the few traditional forms of pair dances in Crete. In the 1950s, new international dances were also introduced, such as the tango. As told to me by Katerina Kornarou in 2001 (010422), her father, a violinist in the region of Merambello, did not like to play these modern dances that brought the couplets in close contact, and when he performed them, he sent his young daughters home. Photo private collection of Manolis Tzirakis.

A traditional Cretan marriage in central Crete: a procession leading the bride to the church. Photo private collection of Manolis Tzirakis.

danced only at weddings as the bride's dance, *horós tis nífis*; this is the first dance after the wedding ceremony when mantinádes are traditionally sung to her. As mentioned above, the main importance of this musical form is to serve as a vehicle for improvisatory singing.

The main instruments played in Crete today are the lira (*líra*, a fretless bowed lute with three metal strings), the laoúto (also *laghoúto*; a large long-necked[11] fretted, plucked lute, with a pear-shaped body), the violin, the mandolin and the guitar.[12] The laoúto and the violin appear to be the oldest melodic instruments. They were introduced to the urban areas during the period of the Venetian occupation (1211–1669), and they are mentioned in the Cretan literary documents from the sixteenth and seventeenth centuries. The laoúto and later, the mandolin, have been used especially for singing in the informal *parées* and for the *kantádes* (serenades). Some assume that mantinádes might have come as a "parcel" to Crete during the Venetian times (Kiriakidis 1978: 218–221), which can be interpreted etymologically from the most probable origin of the word mantináda < "mattinata", (= a morning song, a serenade-type vocal song).

The violin has been played since the Venetian times in eastern and western Crete and it remained the principal solo instrument in dance music in these areas until the latter half of the twentieth century. In eastern Crete, the violin was accompanied especially by the mandolin and by a small double-membrane drum, the *dauláki*, and in the western area, the violin was accompanied by the laoúto. The violin was an expensive instrument since it had to be made by a master and was often ordered from Italy; thus, the new instrument that was introduced to the island during the eighteenth century from Asia Minor, the lira,[13] quickly became popular particularly in the central and rural parts of the islands. The benefit of the lira was that it could be made cheaply from local wood by skilful craftsmen and even by the musicians themselves. Before the twentieth century, the lira was played alone with the accompaniment of tiny bells attached to the bow. In central Crete, the lira was later accompanied in the *gléndi* by the mandolin, and especially after the 1930s, by the laoúto. In the *gléndi*, the lira-player or violinist is responsible for melodic elaboration and variation, and mainly either he, or the *pasadóros*, who is the accompanying laoúto- or mandolin-player, also serves as the main singer, alternating between the vocal and instrumental sections.

During the first half of the twentieth century, many talented local musicians enriched the traditional Cretan styles by introducing new influences. The Ottoman occupation in Crete came to an end and the Orthodox Greek refugees from Asia Minor, who replaced the Muslim Cretan population, were mostly from urban, intercultural towns and regions. These refugees brought with them a strong musical tradition that enriched the local music

---

11 Not to be confused with *oúti* (ud), the short-necked Arabic lute, which is also played in Crete and Greece, but very rarely.

12 For the instruments and their history, see: Amaryanakis 1988: 329–330; Anoyanakis 1972; Nikolakakis 2007; Papadakis 1989; Tsouhlarakis 2004 and also his web-site: www.tsouchlarakis.com.

13 The pear-shaped ("Cretan") lira, which underwent an evolutionary process through various forms in the first half of the twentieth century, is played in the southern Aegean islands: in Crete, Kasos and Karpathos. The first mentions of this type of an instrument called the lira by Greeks date back to the tenth century from Asia Minor. It is known to have been played in Crete since the eighteenth century, but how and when it entered this area are unknown. (Anoyanakis 1991: 259–275).

The lira and two laoúta in the 1950s. Thanasis Skordalos on the lira, on the left, Yannis Markoyannakis on the laoúto, on the right, Yannis Bernidakis (Baksevanis) on the laoúto. Dancers: Manolis Yoryoulakis, Stamatis Papadakis, Thodoris Skordalos and G. Angouridakis. Photo private collection of Manolis Tzirakis.

during the musically fertile middle-war period. Moreover, the local and expatriated musicians co-operated extensively.

During this middle-war period, the *ziyiá* (pair) of one lira and one or two laoúta, which was formed in central Crete, became the emblematic ensemble that is today widely identified as "Cretan music". The laoúto was now used especially for rhythmical accompaniment, but when there are two laoúta in the *ziyiá*, the one of them may play melodically, which used to be more common before, especially in western Crete. During the following decades, Cretan musical expression continued to flourish and many of the musicians also became well known internationally.

Meanwhile, a political "purification" campaign had interpreted the violin as being a "foreign, non-native instrument" in Crete. With this erroneous interpretation by Simon Karas, the director of the folk music programs at the national Greek radio, the use of the violin in performing Cretan music was banned in all radio programs in 1955.[14] Karas had later admitted his error, but the ban was never officially lifted. This ban, and the simultaneous electronization of the lira-laoúto ensemble, which now made it suitable to perform on stage with loudspeakers, made the lira superior and this also advanced the cultural hegemony of central Crete throughout the entire island. Several violinists in western Crete continued their tradition in this difficult situation, but in eastern Crete, this caused the acoustically performing generation of violinists to withdraw from the *gléndi* during the 1970s.

---

14 The full history is narrated in Papadakis 1989: 42–47, see also Tsouhlarákis 2004.

The far western and eastern parts of Crete reflect clear differences in their styles of playing the violin. The performance practices in eastern Crete were markedly bound to the social, improvised communication in the local society. In the most popular local dance form, the *angaliastós*, it was the dancers who improvised mantinádes, one by one to each dancer who responded in kind (this practice is unknown elsewhere on the island). The break-up of the traditional acoustic performance setting and the loss of the repertoire arranged for violin resulted in a rapid disappearance of this rich musical and verbal tradition.

Rizítika songs of the western Crete

In the mountainous rural areas of western Crete, in the prefecture of Hania, the main form of entertainment has been and still is the singing of slow, crystallized narrative songs called *rizítika*. Although different in form, the long coexistence of these songs with the mantinádes is evident in their shared formulas and metaphors. *Rizítika* songs contain nearly all the themes of the folk songs of the other Greek areas. The oldest layer refers to the Byzantine epic poem hero, Digenes Akrites.[15] Other layers can be distinguished as referring to the periods of the Venetian (1211–1669) and Ottoman (1669–1897) occupations, and the latest songs refer to the historical events of the twentieth century.

These songs are short (averaging only ten lines), mainly composed in the *dekapentasíllavo* meter, but unrhymed and extremely crystallized in their form and poetics. They are performed vocally by a male voice and by a chorus that repeats the verses to a slow, free rhythm, without musical instruments. Both the first singer and the chorus produce vocal decorations and repetitions of the verses, and the performance of a song takes a long time. The *rizítika* songs are divided into two categories: table songs (*tis távlas*) and journey songs (*tis strátas*). Table songs are still popular and can be sung around the table at any festive occasion or informal *paréa*, with food, wine and *rakí*.

In a *gléndi*, the shorter and merrier mantinádes are often sung at the beginning of the event, and at the end of each song. Today, mantinádes connected to the *rizítika* performances are mainly traditional, in line with the reason for the festive occasion. Until the 1970s, however, mantinádes were also intensively improvised reciprocally at the beginning of a feast to get started, or in middle of the feast. In these areas, dance music and instruments were and are played only for dancing during the evening of a marriage as well as during other major feasts; entertainment during get-togethers and shared festive meals is carried out by singing *rizítika* songs.

Today the journey songs are rarely sung in a natural context,[16] but in the past, these songs were sung while walking to other villages (especially when

---

[15] The acritic poem came to Crete between 961–1210, where one of the surviving manuscripts of the poem was written down (S. Alexíou 1969).
[16] But even today, if collectively on the road, a *Sfakianós* (Sfakia is the southern part of the prefecture of Hania) hardly keeps quiet, which I was able to witness once when in Anópoli

fetching the bride) or to fields, or during a night-time serenade, *kantáda*,[17] near the house of an adored girl. On these occasions, the *rizítika* could also be accompanied by musical instruments. All the verses were sung and repeated two or three times, making one song last long, even as long as one hour. (060504; 060712; Amaryanakis 1988: 323–324; see also Beaton 1980: 160–161; Kaloyanides 1975: 25–27; Magrini 2000)

Even though the *rizítika* songs are currently known in other parts of the island, due to concert performances, music clubs featuring live music, and the access to recorded material, the natural performance of the *rizítika* takes place mainly in the villages of the original area in the prefecture of Hania. Contrary to the situation elsewhere in Crete, in the *rizítika* area, where the basic instrument for folk songs is the human voice, musical instruments are rarely played. Kapsomenos (1979: 21–22) also remarks that the main production of new historical songs (that can take the form of a *rizítiko* song or a *ríma*) falls in the same region, where the tradition of narrative song is strong.

Shared performance arena, the gléndi

The traditional gléndi

The main collective entertainment in the village communities consists of the annual and seasonal celebrations as well as the life-cycle celebrations. The Greek word *gléndi* can signify all kinds of merriment, but in the village use, it refers particularly to the entertainment related to major feast days – in Greece, these include primarily the village saint's day, the carnival, as well as celebrations of marriage and baptism. The *gléndi* takes place in the evening of the feast day after the ritual acts and religious ceremonies have been conducted, in some cases also on the eve of the feast day. The social significance of these events as performance arenas was enhanced because all members of the community took part in the festivities, and to participate, friends and relatives travelled on foot and by donkeys from other villages. These festivities were therefore an important, and unique, opportunity for young, unmarried people to see each other, because in the Cretan society, the activities of the unmarried girls were almost exclusively conducted in the home environments. This meant that the *gléndi* was the main event and context in which women could publicly sing mantinádes and where poetic confrontations took place between men and women.

The village saint's festivals first conduct major religious services during the previous evening and then early in the morning of the feast day. The morning service of the feast day ends at the breaking of the sweet

---

on a Sunday afternoon without a bus connection to get back to Rethimno. I was taken in a private bus bringing the priest and relatives of the groom from Anopoli to the bride's village, Vrisses, for a wedding. After the first turnabouts, the Sfakian priest came in front, and rizítika songs were sung throughout the trip by him and the driver.

17 Mantinádes were sung in other areas during these kantádes.

Until the 1970s, donkeys were the main means of transportation between the mountain villages. Here, the company of the groom travels to the village of the bride. Radamanthis Androulakis is on the lira. Photo private collection of Manolis Tzirakis.

The morning service of the paniyíri of Saint George (April 23rd) in Asi Gonia, 1997. Photo by the author.

church bread and/or consuming another food associated with that day. The celebration then culminates in the *glέndi* that evening. A traditional wedding feast went on for several days and consisted of a wide repertoire of mantinádes. Besides being sung within the frame of the evening *glέndi*, mantinádes were also sung at various moments of preparation as well as before and after the wedding ceremony. Still today, in some of the more populous villages, the women sing traditional mantinádes when they prepare the bride and the groom for their marriage. In the Hania district, men also sing rizítika songs at various points in the preparations. Such ritual mantinádes (in Hania rizítika) are still most often sung in the metaphorical game, when the escort of the groom comes to take the bride to the church. During former times, it took hours or days for the procession to make its way from the village of the groom to the village of the bride, and singing was the natural pastime.

Dance is the central element of the *glέndi*: all communities hire musicians for the dance, although the get-togethers (for these, see below) normally related to it can be conducted by singing only. The traditional format of a *glέndi* in the village square was thus the following: The musicians were placed in the center, sitting in traditional peasant chairs, which were half-turned towards each other. The dance began, and the dancers formed a circle around the musicians. The people sitting and standing also formed a circle around the dancers. As people recollecting the past *glέndia* always emphasize, this was an arrangement that placed people near each other.

Musicians in their traditional performance position. Yannis Markoyannakis on the laoúto, and Yerasimos Stamatoyanakis on the lira. Photo private collection of Manolis Tzirakis.

The famous Cretan dancer Stamatis Papadakis leads the bride, her daughter, to the first dances. Photo private collection of Manolis Tzirakis.

The dance began following the ritual order that was specific to the feast, and the first mantinádes sung thus depended on the reason for the festivity and these were predominantly traditional. In central and western Crete, the musicians were primarily responsible for the singing. In these areas, the singing during the dance could be carried on exclusively by the musicians, but in many areas, other local performers, who were known for their good voices and repertoires, little by little gathered tightly behind them.

Later at night, if a break occurred in the dancing and, especially after the dancing came to an end, it was the turn of the paréa of the village singers to start improvising mantinádes. During the feast, men had consumed a fair amount of wine and *rakí*,[18] thus gaining in spirit, and the late night exchange of mantinádes easily introduced more personal, competitive forms between two or more villagers.

The gléndi and the dances in eastern Crete

The significant difference between the practices in eastern Crete and those of the central and western areas was that during several local dances in the *gléndi*, the dancers in eastern Crete improvised the mantinádes[19] while dancing. Dances were also organized outside the big feasts, even on every Sunday in the villages where there were girls of a marriageable age. This was described to me by the violinist Vangelis Vardakis (051102) from

---

18 Strong home-made brandy distilled of grapes.
19 The word mantináda is written as mantiniáda, and pronounced as "mantinyáda", throughout the eastern Crete.

Ierapetra in a way that was identical to the account of Maria Lioudaki in the foreword of her collection of mantinádes (1936): beginning in the morning, young men went around the village and asked the girls' parents' permission for the girls to participate. During the afternoon, the dance was organized in a spacious house, on a square, in the courtyard of a church, or in the shade of a big tree near a well. The girls went there with their mothers, but it was mainly the young who danced. Maria Lioudaki writes (1936: i): "In these dances the young boy in love always found an opportunity to declare with mantinádes to the loved one his love or pain, sorrow or joy, even anger to the unfaithful." I referred earlier to that the division of themes in Lioudaki's collection reflects the themes recurrent in the singing among such dances; they may be seen to reflect particularly the world of this young, unmarried youth.

In eastern Crete, the *angaliastós* was always the first dance to start the *gléndi*. This "embracing" dance was especially liked because it allowed a closer physical touch between the participants than did the other dances. Here a girl who was placed at the beginning of the line (which was alternating between girls and boys) initiated the singing. She would improvise a mantináda for each participant, who had to respond in kind, then leave her place to the next, and a full round was danced in this way.

I asked my informant Vangelis Vardakis why the role of the woman in the performance was so important in eastern Crete. He responded that even if the woman's place in the society was not free in this district, the ability to perform and improvise during a social occasion, by singing and dancing, was regarded as being an important exhibition of a woman's suitability for upholding the social relationship as a wife and a member of the household. Nevertheless, Vardakis had also inquired from his teacher why a woman had always started the singing in this improvisatory dance. His teacher answered: "because women have a much better command of words" (051102).

The gléndi in the rizítika area of western Crete

Thus far, I have described the rizítika songs as the main ritual entertainment in the commensal feast, wedding processions and get-togethers of this area. As I have also referred to, in these areas, the *rízes* (roots) of the Lefká Ori, the musical instruments, were rarely played, and musicians were called in from the coastal areas only to major festivities that included dance. This was especially true for the wedding *gléndi*.

The singing of the rizítika, which took place in all the other stages of the festivities, was regularly interspersed by mantinádes, and competent performers also dueled by performing mantinádes. During the dance in the *gléndi*, it seems that it was common in most areas that whereas the musicians started the singing of mantinádes for the dance, the audience was urged to participate and to sing in the succession (Diktakis 1999). The significance that the mantinádes have had in the flirtation and teasing between young people within the frame of these festive occasions is documented from this area equally as from the other areas (060504; 060712).

Poetic confrontations

In mountainous pastoral Crete, as in the tribal Arab cultures (see esp. Caton 1990), the poetic verbal duel has been a socially established form of quarrel and negotiation. Michael Herzfeld (1985a: 144) observes that: "In a community where manhood requires a constant exhibition of performative skill, the clever mantináda can reduce an opponent symbolically without giving him the chance to respond in any other domain." In such high mountain villages, the performative code of speech acts could thus be very demanding. Furthermore, in these pastoral communities with distinct, patrilineal subgroups, the boundaries of the groups are continuously shaped in social communication. As a consequence, these communities have also cultivated the poetic duel to a very different degree than the lowland peasant and fishing communities.

However, engaging in a serious rivalry or exchanging contentious tones with one's fellow villager is present in all areas in the recollections of these shared performance events: although poetic duels could take place on many occasions, wedding festivities seem to have served as particularly favorable settings for them. The explanation is evident: these festivities, while celebrating the new unity of the couple and two kin groups, have also provided a social basis of measuring other existing relations and of scrutinizing the forming of possible future ties. The latter reason seems to be significant with regard to the most recurrent stories and recollections; that the young boys and girls were able to see each other was not only an innocent pleasure between them, but a critical moment for the whole collective.

These duels could be a domain of competitive and offensive male discourse, either during the dance, or predominantly, during other personal confrontations taking place within the frames of the social atmosphere of the *gléndi* (see e.g. Herzfeld 1985b). Many stories are still told of the shame of singing old, hackneyed mantinádes, and especially of the conflicts between the eager candidates for a son-in-law and the father who rejects him contemptuously.[20]

The following example was narrated by Despina Papadaki, 2001 (010329) about her grandfather:

V: *Yes, because some have written that it was difficult for a girl to tell her feelings to a boy, or the boy...*

R: /But they did not tell their feelings...

D: /In the dance one could say a mantináda... My grandfather, to tell you a very old [story]... My grandfather, someone loved his daughter, my mother's sister, my mother has told this history to us... And he takes this girl, whom someone wanted to abduct, and he goes to a wedding,

---

20 For descriptions of verbal duels, see Herzfeld 1985a: 142–146, with an extended discussion in Herzfeld 1985b, and for a parallel tradition in the village of Olimbos in Karpathos, see Caraveli 1985 and Kavouras 1991.

to the dance, my grandfather takes his daughter's hand and dances with her, my grandfather first and his daughter after... How would he leave someone else to take her hand, he took and danced with her, and they sat down after. There was the same [candidate for] son-in-law who had said that he will abduct her. But he was...the last one in the village, let's say. My grandfather was prospering, with the s*alvári*, he was a captain. And he says:

> *Yi-aide pio áhristo kormí / ksanígi na se klépsi*
> *Tahiá ke to touféki mou / sto béti tou tha péksi*

> Look what a useless body / is looking to abduct you
> Quickly also my rifle / to his breast will be fired

Think now, and he [the boy] didn't say anything, that is, that he [the grandfather] had said such a mantináda! That he had said that the boy was useless! So the boy became frightened, since he was...he said that he will kill me, if I make a move to oppose, he will kill me! Mihalákis, Captain Mihalis. To tell him such a mantináda; and it was told to us by my mother. Just like that, he said it in a paréa and no one talked. That is, if bloodshed would be created, fifteen-twenty people can get killed. For one mantináda!

Duels could also take the form of a teasing discourse between two performers. Many adult informants recall that in the *gléndi*, the exchange of such *antikristés*, reciprocal mantinádes, was a pervasive form of performance between a woman and a man particularly in the first part of the twentieth century, and several informants now over seventy years old remember these from their youth (for contemporary *antikristés*, see pp. 189–190).

The following example was narrated by Agapi Moshovaki in a conversation in 2001 (010329): Agapi explains the following history from her youth, directing her words especially to a local girl present in the interview situation, because the exchange of poems had taken place between her and this girl's uncle. The event took place when Agapi had gone to a *gléndi* in another village with her father, and the uncle of this girl had been there, too:

> And he was unmarried as well as I, too... and we were singing now there and I say one mantináda:

> *Den tóne thélo áshimo / kaliá ftohó ke kálli*
> *Yatí t'ambelohórafa / de férnoun tin angáli*

> I don't want him to be ugly / better a poor and handsome
> Because the vineyards / don't bring along embraces

> And your uncle said to my father, he says uncle Nikolaki, if I say a mantináda will there be a misunderstanding? No, my father answered him, by no means, and he looked me at my eyes and he says me:

Agápa ploúsio ki áshimo / pará ftohó ke kálli
Yatí otan piná kanís / den tou mirízi-i-angáli!

Love rich and ugly / rather than poor and handsome
Because when one is hungry / the embrace has no fragrance!

Transformations of the gléndi

During the 1970s, most of the weddings or baptismal *gléndia* were transferred from the village squares to special permanent or seasonal commercial centers of entertainment, known as the *kéndra* (sing. *kéndro*). These were built first in the urbanizing centers after the Second World War, and starting in the 1970s, they begin to appear throughout the whole island along with the (politically launched) reinvigorating wave of interest towards the endemic musical tradition (Kapsomenos 1987: 15).

Today, the festivities and *gléndi* may still take place in a village-square setting, but this happens less and less frequently. The village saint festivals, the *paniyíria*, and the celebration of marriages that in Crete today command a large audience, from one to three thousand guests, are often transferred from village squares to the *kéndra*. In the Village where I stayed, the baptismal feasts, which typically host about 300 guests, are organized in the village square or, during the winter, in the village society building more often than in a *kéndro*. The Village still has one marriage every two or three years as well; these festivities can take place in the village square when the number of guests is reduced to around one thousand, which the square seats.

The organization of these festivities in the village is a collective effort, in which reciprocity and a sense of solidarity is shared among the relatives, co-villagers and the friends involved.[21] The main joint preparations carried out before the feast day concern the slaughtering of the lambs by the men, and the preparation of the cold appetizers by the women. Wine, *rakí*, meat, and appetizers are often provided by the family and relatives even when the wedding *gléndi* is held in a *kéndro*. In a village wedding, the day before the wedding is busy and culminates in the *antigámou* held in the bride's village. This festive dinner is organized that evening for all the helpers and for those not able to be present at the actual feast. The day of the feast starts early. First, fires are built for the large pots in which the *piláfi*, the traditional, obligatory rice dish is cooked in meat stock (the first meat course is boiled lamb, prepared beforehand) by certain experienced women of the village. Then, the rest of the meat is often taken to be roasted in the oven of the local bakery. Next, bread, salads, services of cold appetizers are prepared and stored. And finally, the tables are set and the feast area is decorated. After the ceremonies, when the meal is served, another round of helping hands is at work: a thousand or so guests are now served three courses. The entire group is ready again for portioning out the food and the young men carry

---

21 The following description is based on my own involvement in the preparations and *gléndia* in the Village in 2004–2007.

it to the tables. Only after the last watermelons are cut for dessert is it time for the team to relax and participate in the *gléndi*, in which the musicians are now ready to start the dance (musicians can start their program by more lyrical repertoire while people finish their dinner). This is why it is easy to understand that the atmosphere in the village *gléndi* is so special and why the dance normally lasts until early morning hours even today.

During the summer season, well-known Cretan musicians participate in the *paniyíria* in the different villages nearly every day, either in the open air *kéndra*, or in the village square. In the latter case, the village society or the local athletic society can organize the event and the profits from the food and drinks sold provide the necessary income for the society's activities. Active villages have good organization teams and regular feasts, and these are advertised by posters that are put up all around the municipality. Some parts of the preparation of the food can be very similar to that of the wedding, although today, most *paniyíria* have fixed portions of meat and French fries, and canned soft drinks, even *krasí tis paréas*, a cheap wine packed into one liter carton packages; the people line up and pay for these in a serving place on the side.

The musical and singing activities in these contemporary festivities are left to the professional musicians, and the creative audience participation takes place mainly through dance. The dances are booked with and paid to the head musician for a family or *paréa* on behalf of one of its member. Each group then takes turns in dancing when announced. The musicians sing traditional verses, or verses from their own repertoire, which may contain their own compositions, but most often consist of mantinádes written by a *mantinadológos*, a mantináda-poet. This also used to be the case in earlier times; it is generally regarded that musical and verbal creativity are different and that rarely both are present in one person.

During the late hours and after warming up through the consuming of alcohol and enjoying the social atmosphere, just like in the traditional village environment, a *paréa* may take up a dialogue in the mantinádes. Often, when the *gléndi* starts to break up, and the large audience has dispersed, a *paréa* of those mostly involved (for example, the bride's male relatives, the groom, the father, or the godparent) gathers in front of the musicians and they are given the microphone to sing. Audience participation in singing the mantinádes is also a very popular part of the late-hour performances in the music clubs in town during the winter season, although at least the performing musicians' opinion is that these performances completely differ from those taking place in the village environment.

The society has changed considerably during the last three decades, and since participation in the wedding, baptismal and village saint feast *gléntia* concerns each person often several times a year, a critical local attitude is also apparent. Participation in several successive and sometimes even parallel weddings is costly, because a *fákelo*, an envelope with money, is given or sent on each occasion. Participation is ethically compulsory, because not showing up would be dishonoring the couple and their relatives. There has been an abrupt shift of the feasts from the village squares, where musicians played acoustically and sat in the middle of the space, to the setting where

Posters advertizing musical performances in kéndra, similar to those informing of the paniyíria during the summer season. Rethimno, September 2009. Photo by the author.

Performance taking place in a baptismal celebration in the local village association's hall. The group consists of two laoúta, a mandolin, a lira, and in this occasion (due to the presence of my husband) percussions, which are sometimes added to the group today, although they do not make part of the traditional combinations in central Crete. Milopotamos, 2004. Photos by the author.

Crete and traditional performance contexts

The father of the baptized son leads the close relatives to the first sirtós dance.

Towards the end of the gléndi, when the dance is over, the close relatives and friends gather to perform mantinádes in front of the musicians.

musicians are up on a bandstand and the music is mediated electronically through amplifiers. The modern star culture, revolving around the big-name musicians and the use of powerful amplifiers without professionals in sound engineering, often culminate in high noise levels. For this reason, many adults avoid the contemporary *gléndia* which take place in the *kéndra*. The consumption of the alcohol has also become much more extreme when the wine-drinking in many cases (but not all) has been exchanged for the competitive emptying of whiskey bottles (see also Caraveli 1985). This is one of the reasons why many critical voices point out that a person's individuality when performing and improvising was traditionally displayed in disciplined, virtuous ways. In the modern Cretan society, instead, the interpretations of individuality can be quite egocentric in nature (see also Dawe 1996 and 1999).

Casual singing events

Until recently, the informal gatherings of a *paréa*, a circle of (male) friends or relatives, took place regularly in a *kafenío* or village square. Even further back in history, these participants took turns hosting the gatherings in their houses of a village. These encounters were the most common arena for singing verses. All my informants testify that in the lively village communities, a *paréa* was formed even for the slightest reason. Although the Second

A paréa in Ierapetra in the early 1960s, Manolis Englezakis on the violin. Photo by courtesy of Vangelis Vardakis.

World War and the following social change had already reduced collective traditions, the sharpest increase in the privatization of the habits in Crete has advanced since the beginning of the 1980s. This is when television became a permanent fixture in every *kafenío* and living room, and the owning of cars became a common occurrence, allowing people to move during their free time and consequently to also choose their entertainment outside their living environment. In short, commercial entertainment has since replaced much of the self-made collective local culture. As a result, the role of a musical *paréa* is now clearly that of an optional pastime, whereas until the 1980s, it was the only way of casual entertainment among men and an important arena for social discourse. As the *mantinadológos*, Aristidis Heretis from the Anoya village defined, although everyone currently longs for these *parées,* "no one takes the leading role and makes it happen" (fieldnotes October 28, 2005).

A clear decrease in collective traditions had become evident even during the last ten years of my own fieldwork. In the Village, during the summer, the generation of teenagers ten years ago still gathered to barbeque, sing, and play nearly every evening at a spot a little outside the village. As young adults, this generation is now occupied with work and studies outside the village, and the change of lifestyle is most poignant among the youth. As a consequence, these occasions are extremely rare.

Today, however, traditional musical *parées* do take place between those most dedicated to Cretan music and song. During feasts, or due to a personal reason for a festivity, people gather together to perform privately. For example, parées are still formed by male relatives for singing on the night of a wedding. In towns, there are taverns and *mezedopolía*[22], which encourage people to perform. A musical *paréa* is most likely to gather around at least one instrument, the mandolin, laoúto, lira or violin, but a lack of an instrument is not a definite obstacle. In a paréa, mantinádes are sung in turns by fluent singers, or in more casual get-togethers, by all present one-by-one in a circle. A good way to become familiar with contemporary singing in parées in *mezedopolía* and *kéndra* is to visit Yorgos Sifakis' web pages: http://www.youtube.com/simisakogiorgis.

The most common way of such informal singing, with the musical form *kondiliés*, is the following: a singer begins and sings the first *dekapentasíllavo* (fifteen-syllable) line, and the *paréa* repeats it (during this time, the singer has the opportunity to think of the second line when extemporizing verses). The singer then sings the second line, whereupon the next singer takes up his turn immediately. The second line is thus not repeated. During the performance, digressions of various lengths are inserted, and lines may be parted to cover two or more musical cycles; the dipartite, or tripartite, structure is a rule when singing to the *sirtós* tune.[23]

---

22 Small, intimate, traditional-style places that serve mezé-plates and traditional drinks: carafes of wine, *rakí* (a home-maid brandy) and ouzo. These are very popular among young adults and students as well; the number of these places in the old town of Rethimno grew significantly at the turn of the twenty-first century.
23 For a full variety in the forms of singing, see Kaloyanides 1975.

A contemporary paréa in Rethimno in November 3rd, 2007. Antonis Pavlakis on the lira, Yannis Apostolakis (left) and Yannis Markoyannis (right) on the laoúto. Photo by courtesy of Yorgos Sifakis.

The following transcription shows one example of singing with *kondiliés*.[24] The participants are Nikiforos Aerakis (N.A), Aristidis Heretis (Yalaftis; Y) and Yannis Aerakis (Poloyannis; P). The transcriptions are organized in three columns from left to right: first, the singer's text, second, the chorus repeats, and third, the intervening audience exclamations. The poetic text of the mantináda that is formed appears in boldface.

P: *Aides, de me pirázi pos pernoun / i hróni ke miséne*
       Aides, **I don't mind how they pass / the years and (that) they go by**
                                                        Yásou Yanni!
                                                        Hi Yanni!

                 'Opa, ta hrónia ke miséne
                 Opa, the years and they go by
     De me pirázi pos pernoún / ta hrónia ke miséne
     I don't mind how they pass / the years and (that) they go by
                      I hróni ke miséne
                      The years and they go by
     Tou érotá mas skéftome / to télos pio tha [?]éne
     I think of our love / and how that will end
                                                 Yásou Yanni!
                                                 Hi Yanni!

---

24 The audio material for this exchange, provided to me by Yorgos Sifakis, is available on line as a companion to my article *Dialogues in Rhymes. The Performative Contexts of Cretan Mantinádes* in the journal *Oral Tradition* 24, Number 1 (Sykäri 2009). The article covers an earlier version of the present chapter and parts of Chapter 5.

N.A: *Aftós kopeliá mou*
 The one, my girl

 Yásou Arhonda!
 Hi Noble one!

Aftós pou den agápise / ésto ke mian iméra
The one who didn't love / be it just for one day
 Ópa, ésto ke mian iméra
 'Opa, be it just for one day
 Aftós pou den agápise / ésto ke mian iméra
 The one who didn't love / be it just for one day
Ésto ka mian iméra i---
Be it just for one day, ---
'Inta tha pi pos ékame / ónte thá 'rthoun ta yéra
What will he say he did / when old age comes?

 Yásou Yalafti!
 Hi Yalafti!

Y: *Ófou éla ki éla kerá mou*
 'Ofou, éla ki éla, my lady
 Ospou na íme zontanós / de tha to batoniári
 As long as I'm living / it will not give up

 Yásou síndekne Yanni!
 Hello co-sponsor, Yanni!

 'Opa de tha to batoniári
 'Opa, it will not give up
I héra mou na to kratí / ts' agapis to doksári
My hand to hold / the bow of the love

P: *Lemoniá mou, i----*
 My lemon tree, ---
 'Ine polí pou kánoune / keró ke de 'gapoúne
 Many are those who live / a long while without loving
 'Ine poli pou kánoune / keró ke de 'gapoúne
 Many are those who live / a long while without loving
Keró ke de 'gapoúne
A long time without loving
K'egó mian óra tou sevdá / va háso ti lipoúme
And I one hour of love / to miss that ('s what) I regret

N.A: */Kopeliá mou ématha egó-- ke monahós / ke de paraponioúme*
 / My girl, I learned also to be alone / and I don't complain
 Ématha egó ki'amonahós / ke de paraponioúme
 I learned also to be alone / and I don't complain
 Ématha egó ki'amonahós / ke de paraponioúme
 I learned also to be alone / and I don't complain
Ke- mayirévgo ke dipnó- / ke théto ke kimoúme
And I cook and eat dinner / and I lay down and I sleep

P: *Esí 'soune pou moú 'leges*
 It was you who told me
 Esí 'soune pou moú 'leges / 'gápa me mi fováse
 It was you who told me / love me, don't be afraid
 Esí 'soune pou moú 'leges / 'gápa me mi fováse
 It was you who told me / love me, don't be afraid

>   *Kopeliá mou ke---*
>   My girl, ke---
>   *K' edá misévgis ke mou les / pápse na mou thimáse*
>   **And here you leave and tell me / stop thinking of me**
>
> Y: *'Efaga méli k' ékousa*
>   I ate honey and felt
>   (music passage)
>   *'Efaga méli k'ékousa / sta híli ti sfakáda*
>   **I ate honey and felt / on my lips a bitter taste**
>
>   *Aidés*
>   *'Ela kerá, kerá mou, yatí—*
>   Éla lady, my lady, because--
>   *aidés sta híli ti sfakáda ya de-*
>   aides on my lips a bitter taste because it-
>   *Ya de me táyises esí / paliá mou filenáda*
>   **Because it was not you who fed me / my old girl friend**

During such performances of a *paréa*, the poems sung are thematically linked to each other so that they form a thematic dialogue. This example deals with the theme of love and the speakers dwell on the aspects of a relationship from different perspectives.

The next longer exchange of mantinádes provides an example of how changes in theme take place during the performance. This live recording was tape-recorded by Yorgos Sifakis and features a late night performance towards the end of a baptism *gléndi* held in a village named Alfa.[25] In order to concentrate on the development and changes of subject, I present only the poetic texts here (repetitions and exclamations are in line with the previous example). The main part of this performance is an improvised exchange between the singers Yorgos Sifakis (Si) and Yorgos Saris (Sa). Later, three other feast guests (P3, P4, and P5) participate as well. The singers start by referring to the reason for the feast and particularly to the joy of the father and his male relatives for having a son after three daughters (Sifakis makes special reference to the recipe "inherited" from the father-in-law, who also had three daughters and one son). Later, some references are made with regard to the famous lira-player Moundakis, who was born in this village, as well as to another local lira-player, named Dandolos, who died prematurely. A line is added to depict the changes of themes, and a dotted line indicates a transition between the themes.

> Si *Dákri harás ekílise / Yóryi sto mágouló sou*
>   *'Opos pothis sou évhome / na dis ton anipsió sou*
>
>   A tear rolled down / Yóryi on your cheek
>   As you desire I wish you / to see your nephew [grow up]
>
> Sa *Apó keró perímene / ti méra ya na stáksi*
>   *Kíno to dákri tsi harás / poú 'ha kerous filáksi*

---

[25] I received this recording only very recently, in September 2010, and was therefore not able to analyze it further in the present study.

For a long time it waited / the day to drop
That tear of joy / I had put by a long while

Si *Papadimítri pés to mou / ke 'sí to mistikó sou*
    An píres prika sintayí / apó ton petheró sou?

    – Tris kopeliés k'enan yo!

    Papadimítri, tell me that / tell me your secret
    Did you receive the dowry, the receipt / from your father-in-law?

    – Three daughters and one son!

Sa *Na min to pis to mistikó / de prépi na katéne*
    Apoú borí ki-apáno tou / etsá grikó ke léne!

    Do not tell the secret / they don't have to know
    The one who's able makes it / that's what I hear people say!

Si *Evrádiase ke símero / pia méra de vradiázi*
    Ma i kalí paréa mas / ómorfa diaskedázi

    The night fell also today / which day would not grow night
    But our great company / marvelously celebrates
    ………………..
Sa *Pia níhta de tha vri to fos / pia méra to skotádi*
    O tapinós o prótos érondas / den toú 'fike simadi

    Which night will not reach light / which day the darkness
    The innocent first love / to whom it didn't leave its stamp?

Si *Pios alonévi me hioniá / pios spérni kalokéri*
    Pios íne pou to lismoná / to próto tou to téri?

    Who threshes with the snow / who sows during the summer
    Who is the one who forgets / his first mate?

Sa [*Pios íde hioni…*]
    Pios íde kápsa me voriá / ke hióni me to nóto
    Ke pios ekselismonísene / ton éronda ton próto?

    Who saw the snow..
    Who saw heat with north wind / and the snow with that from south
    And who has forgotten / the first beloved?

Si *Énas megálos érotas / poté de lismoniéte*
    Ke kínos pou ton éhase / tha zi na tiranniéte

    A great love / will never be forgotten
    And the one who lost it / will live being torn

Sa *Próti m' agápi k' éronda / elpída ki'oniró mou*
    Ftáni kontó i-anámnisi / na zíso ton keró mou?

    My first love and passion / my desire and my dream
    Should a memory be enough / to go on living my life?

    ———————

Si *Nótos esí, voriás egó / antítheta fisoúme*
    Ke móno stin apanemiá / borí n' agapithoúme

    You are South, I am North / we blow in the opposing directions
    And only at the time of no wind at all / we can fall in love

Sa *Nótos esí, voriás egó / antítheti anémi*
    To prágma pou zesténo 'gó / kánis esí ke trémi

    You are South, I am North / the opposite winds
    The thing that I heat / you make to shiver
    ....

Si *Sto mesostráti tsi harás / me vríke kategída*
    ke stégnoksá 'po ti fotiá / pou m' ánapse i-elpída

    At the midway of the joy / I was found by a storm
    And I dried of the fire / which was lit by the hope

Sa *S' éna spiliári skotinó / tou pónou ksehasméno*
    'Ine keró ts' elpídas mou / to lípsano thaméno

    In a dark cave / of pain, abandoned
    A long time my hope's / remains lay buried

    ———————

Sa *'Ekama fíllo ke fteró / stsi yitoniá tis páli*
    Ki-ómos aftí den ékame(ne) / ton kópo na prováli

    I was searching around / at her neighborhood again
    However she wasn't / bothered to show up

    ———————

Si *'Ine-i kardiá mou símero / sa foundoméno ródo*
    I meraklídes tis Alfás / smíksan ke tou Tripódo

    My heart is today / like a rose in bloom
    The merry-masters of the Alfa / met, as well as those of Tripodo

    ———————

Sa *Pérasa, ksanapérasa / apó ti yitoniá sou*
    'Ehis kakés yitónisses / ke vríkes ton belá sou

I passed and passed again / by your neighborhood
You have bad female neighbors / and you got in trouble

Si   *Ta mátia sou íne thálassa / tsi omorfiás pou léne*
     Ki-apáno tous polés kardiés / navayisménes pléne

     Your eyes are the sea / of beauty, as they say
     And on them many hearts / shipwrecked sail

Sa   *Taksídepsa sti thálassa / sto blávo to matio sou*
     [E]naváyisa k' ída kardiés / hiliádes sto vithó sou

     I was faring at sea / in the deep blue of your eyes
     I shipwrecked and saw hearts / thousands, in your depths

Si   *Stou érota sou to yaló / thélo na navayíso*
     Ke de me gniázi sti steriá / na mi ksanayiríso

     At the seashore of your love / I want to be shipwrecked
     And I don't mind if to land / I will never return

P3   (*'Onte th' akoúso tsoutsoudió*)
     'Onte th' akoúso mourmourió / ke tiganioú tsoudía
     Ke tou bukalioú kakárisma / kámo kalí kardía

     (When I hear the hissing of roasting)
     When I hear the murmur / and the frying pan's hissing
     And the bottle's clucking / I have a good heart

Si   *Den eksanastelióthike / tétia paréa páli*
     Den prolavéni to krasí / na béni sto bukáli

     It has never gathered / such company before
     The wine doesn't have time / to enter the bottle

P3   *Dialégo tsi prosehtiká / tsi fílous ápou káno*
     Ap' ti knisára tsi pernó / ke stin kardiá tsi váno

     I select carefully / the friends that I make
     I pass them through the fumes[26] / and enclose them in my heart

Sa   *'Opios ki-an kámi sti zoí / filiés ke ti glendísi*
     Me ligostá parápona / tha fíyi na ti 'físi

     Whoever makes in life / friendships and celebrates it [life]
     With few complaints / will leave it behind

....

---

26 Fumes from meat grilled on coals.

Si   *Ksípna Moundáki meraklí / Dándole palikari*
      Na ton apothavmásete / apópse to lirári

      Wake up, Moundaki, merry-master / Dandole, brave man
      You should all admire / this evening the lira-player!

Sa   *Síko apó ti mávri yis / Dándole palikári*
      Paraponiári liratzí / ke piáse to doksári

      Rise up from the black earth / Dandole brave man
      Suffering lira-player / and pick up the bow!

P4   *Sti strata tou ksehorismoú / pou s' édiokse makriá mou*
      Símadia ya to yirismó / na vál:is kopeliá mou

      On the way of separation / which threw you far from me
      Signs for the return / you should lay, my girl

Sa   *Horísame ki-o yis t'alloú / parápono den éhi*
      'Opos ki-apoú tsi dio kianís / to lógo den katéhi

      We separated and one to the other / does not have complaints
      As well as either of the two / doesn't grasp the reason [of the separation]

Si   *O horismós sou m' ánikse / pliyí osán t' alóni*
      K' ída tin perifánia mou / sa vítsa na zevlóni

      Separation from you opened me / a wound as big as the threshing ground
      And I saw my pride / to bend like a twig

Sa   *Pliyí p' aníyi o horismós / o hrónos den ti yéni*
      Ki-as pagoudiá sto diáva tou / ki-as fénete klisméni

      The wound opened by separation / time will not cure it
      Even if it calms down on the way / even if it looks closed

P5   *Pliyí p' aníyi o horismós / me mayikó votáni*
      Ke me megáli ipomoní / ísos borí na yáni

      The wound opened by separation / with a magic herb
      And with great patience / maybe can be cured

Si   *'Opou ki-an páo skéftome / pos th' apomínis móni*
      Ke sa mahéri kofteró / i sképsi me pligóni

      Wherever I go I think / that you will be left alone
      And like a sharp knife / the thought wounds me

Sa   *'Opou ki-an íse mi skeftís / pos íse amonahí sou*
      Yatí 'his síntrofo pistó / ti sképsi mou mazí sou

Wherever you are, don't think / that you are all alone
Since you have as devoted companion / my thought with you

P3 *Moú 'takse i Míra mou hares / ma edá metanioméni*
(?)

My Fate promised me joys / but here, regretful
(?)

Sa *Hrónia psarévo ya na vró / hará sti thálassá sou*
Míra, ke pánta vásana / sérno ap' ta nerá sou

For years I fish to find / joy in your sea
Fate, and always sorrows / I pull from your waters

P3 *Vásana ki-álla vásana / mi m'arnithís ke dós mou*
Mi m'arnithís mikroúla mou / ke yínou síntrofós mou

Sorrows and other sorrows / don't deny me but give me
Don't deny me my little girl / but become my partner

Si *Thálassa íne i hares / ma den katého bánio*
Ki-as káno is ta vásana / ton próto kapetánio

The joys are a sea / but I don't know to swim
Even if I act in the sorrows / as the first captain

P3 *Harés ki-an éhi i zoí / egó hará den ída*
Yati éhas' áp' tin arhí / ts'agápis tin elpída

Even if life has joys / I never saw a joy
Since I lost in the beginning / the hope of love

P3 *Na mázeva ta dákria / p' apó kopéli kléo*
Thá' ha dikí mou thálassa / mésa na bo na pléo

Had I collected the tears / that I cry from early age
I'd have my own sea / to go in to swim

Si *Alfá mou ómorfo horió / pou vgánis meraklídes*
Ke san ton Veryanókosti / oréous liratzídes

Alfa, my beautiful village / who make merry-masters
And like the Veryanokosti / splendid lira-players

Sa *Mésa ts' angáles sou-éthapses / megálous liratzídes*
Ke-óso na stékis tha yenás / Alfá mou meraklídes

> In your arms you buried / great lira-players
> And as long as you stand up you'll give birth / Alfa, to merry-masters

---

Si *Mia pétra mes' ti héra mou / na sfíkso tha throulísi*
    Ma kléo ónte tha ti dó / ke de tha mou milísi

> A stone in my hand / if I press, it will be broken
> But [even if] I cry until I'll see her / she won't speak to me

Sa *Pétra na sfíkso tha yení / ammos ke to katého*
    Ma stou sevdá ti dínami / n' antistathó den ého

> If I press a stone it will become / sand and I know that
> But the power of love / I don't have [means] to resist

P3 *Haráki ná' ne rizimió / na kátso tha voulísi*
    Ki-állos na bi stis thálassas / ton páto tha porísi

> On a firm mountain top / should I sit it will collapse
> And another who'd sink - of the sea - / - to the bottom, he will walk

Si *S' éna haráki státhika / ke toú 'pa ton kaïmó mou*
    Hília kommátia eyínike / áp' ton paráponó mou

> On a mountain top I stood / and I told it my worries
> Thousand pieces it became / of my grievances

Sa *S' éna haráki ekoúmbisa / ki élega ton kaïmó mou*
    Ki-ída metá ke kséserne / ston anastenagmó mou

> I leaned against a mountain top / and I told my worries
> And I saw later it to draw back / on my sign of despair

This exchange of poems shows how the themes are developed according to those taken up by the singers. On this occasion, Sifakis, an experienced singer and a guest from outside of the village, inserts mantinádes at regular intervals to honor the village and the paréa, which the other performer(s) either take up or pass by in developing the previously initiated theme. As most mantinádes are extemporized by the performers, some semantic inconsistence is also evident.

The singers emphasize the significance of all singers' adherence to the theme: whatever the theme introduced by the first singer, one's poems communicate about this theme until the theme is exhausted, and only then a new theme will be introduced. When there are several singers, as in the first example above, the developing of a theme will be more exhaustive than when there are only two performers, as in the second example, who compete in taking turns. A new theme can be developed in the natural chain of poems sung. The singers, however, also point out that the capability to introduce new, stimulating themes is an appreciated skill in a *mantinadológos* (991202; 041110a; 060823).

Sometimes a theme can also be changed on purpose by making a point of it, as in the following extemporized examples, which were recalled by Yorgos Sifakis in his *mezedopolío* the Mesostráti in Rethimno, 2004 (041110a). He sung the first poem in a *paréa* after many poems sung about Charos, death:

Den íne fengarólousto / to apopsinó to vrádi
Ma epá na stamatísoume / ta lóya ya ton 'Adi

This evening is not / illuminated by moonlight
And here we'll stop / the words about the Hades

In the next poem, he wanted to disperse the *paréa* because it was already late:

'Omorfi íne i vradiá / ma piós tha dayandísi
Ohtó i óra to proí / aúrio na ksipnísi

The night is beautiful / but who's the one capable
At eight o' clock the morning / tomorrow to wake up?

Each singer has his personal repertoire and style, and in addition to his extemporized and personally composed earlier poems, the singer's basic repertoire consists of memorized poems that he likes and that he has inherited, for example, from his father and grandfather. Between known participants, each person's repertoire is familiar to the others, and when a good, new composition is presented, others will know to lift their eyebrows in admiration. As further remarked by Mitsos Stavrakakis (060823), even in the old times, one could not really know if such a new poem was improvised on the spot, or merely presented for the first time. He said that he himself often holds onto a new poem for a moment until he can surprise others with it; during a singing occasion, he would not even introduce the suitable theme himself, but wait for someone else to do that.

It is noteworthy that in Crete, these singing events do not necessarily show explicitly antagonistic tension between the singers; the events can be generally characterized as co-operative occasions, although featuring "healthy" rivalry which enhances the creative contribution in composition and performance. Nonetheless, just like among many cultures where poetic dueling is a popular dramatic performance on stage, the audience enjoys the intense atmosphere of rivalry, and they can urge performers to compete with each other (041110b; 060823).

Kantáda

Thirty years ago, the *parées* still gathered to perform night-time serenades, *kantádes*, near the house of an admired girl. The following description given by Mitsos Stavrakakis explains how these *kantádes* were carried out (060823). This description also provides a good image of these times and the communication that occurred in Cretan village life.

(M) A *kantáda* at those times, in my years [the 60s, 70s], had the meaning, which meaning, that I liked some girl in the next village; there were no, there were no mobile phones, no telephones – the only way, the only way to make her understand something, was to go down to her lane, you know, the lira-player playing, and I sing a few mantinádes, to make her anticipate something.

(V) *But you did this always as a group? There was always a group; you didn't go alone?*

(M) Not alone, never alone. That was also a little dangerous to go alone…since if she had a brother, he'd ask what is he seeking near our house!

(V) *(Among a group) It was also difficult to know who is the one interested in the girl…*

(M) Eh, Yes, you are picked on when you go alone.

(V) *So, always a group?*

(M) Always a group, four to five persons. Three, four, five, sometimes six.

(V) *And you had then always an instrument with you?*

(M) It was usually the mandolin, or lira, mandolin and lira, or one of the two… and, mostly from the group, from the 5–6 people, it was one or two interested (in the girl), so one helped the another!

(V) *Was it always a certain girl, or would you go just like that, a trip to the next village…?*

(M) No, let me tell you something, we went, let's say, to the *paniyiri* to the next village. There, you saw at the dance a beautiful girl – Ah, this one is beautiful! Or, you saw her for the first time, because normally, they do not go around, during those years, the girls did not go around. Well, you saw her in the *paniyiri*, in a wedding, in a baptism, etc. Eh, when you saw her that way in the feast, whose is she, you ask! She's the one's who lives there, fine. Eh, in a certain moment, then, let's go to make a *kantáda* there! After, of course, some glances had preceded, some glances had been exchanged.

(V) *Ah, there had to be…*

(M) Yes, she had to give you the right to start to get engaged in the matter. And that took place with eye contact!

A *kantáda* can also have another meaning: until recent decades, during the late hours of any *gléndi,* a singing *paréa* might start going around the village from house to house. Food and drinks were served to them, and a chicken might even have been cooked for a soup to refresh the singers' throats that were tired from singing. In the Village, up until ten to fifteen years ago, the singing *parées* were formed to visit the homes of the celebrating heroes of the day during name days, when traditionally a banquet is organized at home for friends, relatives and passers-by.

IV The poetic language

Origins of the metrical structure and the emergence of the mantináda

The metrical structure of a mantináda is based on a fifteen-syllable line that in Modern Greek is normally referred to as *dekapentasíllavo* (= of fifteen syllables) or today rarely, *politikós stíhos* (= the common verse). This verse form is by far the most common meter in Greek folk poetry, as well as in the early literature and art poetry in the Modern Greek language. The verse is based on a syllabic, iambic line, and the natural word stress can fall freely on any even syllable (second, fourth, sixth, or eighth), except in the beginning of the half-lines, where an uneven syllable (the first or the ninth) can be stressed. A line contains two half-lines and the mid-line caesura is always clearly marked. The first half-line contains eight syllables with an obligatory stress either on the sixth or the eighth syllable, and the second half-line contains seven syllables with an obligatory stress on the fourteenth syllable:

Yí-nou ston kám-bo le-mo-niá / ki e-gó sta ó- ri hió-ni
1, 2,   3,   **4,**   5, 6, 7, **8** / 9, **10**, 11, **12**, 13, **14,** 15

Na lió-no na po-tí-zon-de / i   dro-se-rí   sou kló-ni
1, **2,** 3, 4, 5, **6,** 7,   8   / 9,10, 11,**12**, 13, **14,** 15

May you become a lemon-tree on the plain / and I snow on the mountains
So that I can melt and let be watered / the cool branches of yours

Two *dekapentasíllavo* lines form a couplet when the end-rhyme joins them together, and when independent, this unit is called a mantináda in Crete. One of the most common rhymed verse forms is exactly the same form, written as a *quatrain* in four verses, and thus with the rhyme pattern a,b,c,b. In Crete, couplets are also conceptualized and sometimes written in four lines, and it seems that the difference is explained by historical reasons only.

The fifteen-syllable *dekapentasíllavo* line became established during the Byzantine years as a dominant verse form in Greek folk poetry, as well as in the early vernacular literature, but its origins, whether oral or learned, have not been confirmed unambiguously. In Ancient Greek, the meter was based on the alternations of long and short syllables, but already in the beginning of the Christian era, during a long and complicated process, this started to be displaced by an accentual meter. Alexiou & Holton (1976: 22–23) regard the fifteen-syllable line to be either derived from the Latin *versus quardratus triumphalis* (the rhythmic insults hurled at a triumphator by Roman soldiers), or from the octosyllable and heptasyllable used at the level of popular poetry. The latter case is supported by Alexiou & Holton and is based on the fact that the "fifteen syllable is not exclusive to Greek but a common and natural rhythm for folk poetry based on meter" (1976: 25). They situate the development of the *dekapentasíllavo* line somewhere between the sixth and ninth centuries, which means that neither case can definitely be attested due to a lack of evidence for this actual vital period of formation, before the year 900 (Alexiou & Holton 1976: 23).[1]

The verse form is normally referred to in Greek as *dekapentasíllavo* (= of fifteen syllables), or more rarely as *politikós stíhos*. The Greek adjective *politikós* is used here to mean *kinós* (of common use), which prevailed during the Byzantine era and is still used in certain expressions (e.g. *politikós gámos* = civil marriage), and not in its modern meaning of "political." The verse form is explained (Alexiou & Holton 1976; Beaton 1989: 94) to have been named in this way, contemptuously, by the Byzantine authors from the twelfth century onwards presumably because of its popular nature. Why then the Western researchers have used the term "political verse," which is a misleading translation, does not become clear from the above bibliography. In this work, I refer to the metrical line by its common Greek name *dekapentasíllavo*.

Crete was ruled by Venetians between 1211 and 1669 and, having been influenced during that period by the Western European literature models, experienced a literary high season from the fifteenth to the seventeenth centuries. Crete was already an important cultural center in the thirteenth century, and a way to the West for the fleeing intellectuals of Constantinople after the Ottoman capture of the City in 1453 (Holton 1991: 3–4). The Cretan Renaissance is described by Holton (1991: 15) as being…

> …the result of an extraordinary cross-fertilisation of cultures that took place in a society that, by the sixteenth century, had developed a homogeneous character of its own, neither Greek nor Italian, but Cretan. The literature and art of 16th and 17th century Crete owed much to the models of the Italian Renaissance, but they have a distinct quality of their own. Cretan Renaissance literature is not Italian literature translated into Greek, for it was also nourished by a native literary, and folk, tradition which sprang from the Byzantine roots.

---

1 For an overview of the problem and bibliography, see Alexiou & Holton 1976: 22–34; also Beaton 1980: 75–78; 1989: 94–97.

This meeting of the East and West in Crete in the period of Venetian rule had an important impact on the development of Modern Greek art and literature (Holton 1991: 16).

The Western European literature model introduced the use of end-rhyme that had never systematically been used by the ancient Greeks, or in the literary forms of the Byzantine Empire. As for Greek folk songs other than these rhyming couplets, end-rhyme is rarely encountered. It is uncertain whether the couplet form in Crete predates the use of end-rhyme. While an occasional unit of meaning consisting of two lines may occur, there was no systematic use of it before the introduction of rhyme. (Beaton 1980: 149) The origin of the name mantináda is thought to be derived from the Italian *mattinata*,[2] a morning song (a serenade-type vocal composition), which strengthens Kiriakidis' (1978: 218–221) suggestion that the rhyming couplet form came to the island with the Venetians as one parcel.

The first systematic use of rhyme is found in the late fourteenth century in the poetry of the Cretan Stefanos Sahlikis, and according to David Holton (1991: 12), the emergence of the couplet form as the standard may well have been due to Sahlikis. Beaton supposes that the literary poet, having read the foreign originals, first composed poems in rhyming couplets and in the vernacular that conformed to the new Western literary tastes. The recitation or singing of these written poems subsequently introduced the form to the folk poetry as well. (Beaton 1980: 149–150)

By 1500 at the latest, the couplet form had become standardized in Crete. The manuscript of "Vienne" is dated somewhere between the fifteenth and sixteenth centuries (Pernot 1931), and the love-poems it contains generally take the form of rhyming couplets (although unrhymed couplets and triplets also exist).

While written in the vernacular, the literary works of the Cretan School also acquired a powerful means of expression by adopting the themes, metaphors and formulas of the folk poetry traditions. Possibly due to these familiar elements, the literary works then easily entered the popular culture. The most significant work, *Erotókritos* of Vizenzos Kornaros, a romantic narrative poem of 10,010 lines written in rhyming couplets around the year 1600,[3] is popular even today. According to the local oral history, the whole *Erotókritos* book is often said to have been memorized by heart by the illiterate Cretan shepherds. The work has been read by singing, and long sections of the text were and are still sung as a song to special *erotókritos*-melodies.

> Mitsos Stavrakakis, 1999 (991202):
>
> (M): Determining role, of course, here has played Kornaros with the *Erotókritos*. It's very significant. The *Erotókritos* has played a catalytic role! That (work) has put a stamp on the soul, on the mentality of the Cretan. That is, there was no shepherd who in his sack did not have (the

---

2 I have not found any scientific research that offers an analysis of the name or its origins.
3 Literary critics have published extensively on this work, and on the others of the Cretan School. For an overview of the work and the genre, see Holton 1991: 205–237.

book). My father's brother knew by heart the whole work! I never forget that image by the fire, in the village, of my father holding the *Erotókritos*, and reading it by singing! And we were sitting, all the daughters who did not go to the *kafenío*, and the two young boys, us. Six people, my mother, and my father read singing. Like the serials on the television now, which are interrupted, tomorrow again! And we had the anxiety for what happened, because we were small children.

V: *Did that take place in all the families?*

M: In really many. By singing.

V: *That has put in Crete the framework for the appreciation of the poetic word?*

M: Yes, just like the sculpture of Aphrodite, our aesthetics have been influenced by these things. When I form an opinion about a woman, how do I form that? We have these sculptures in our mind for the right analogies. Or, for the man, the Adonis. The same works for us with the word, the *Erotókritos* has played the role of the sculptures, like *Homer*, as well. But here in Crete, the *Erotókritos*."

Kostoula Papadoyanni, 2004 (040727)

K: *(Referring to her youth and learning the tradition)*: What was positive then is that I read the *Erotókritos*, since I had a lot of time. I was eighteen, no family, no school, I read the *Erotókritos*. That was the most significant: that was the beginning. To begin with, it was really difficult to *read* it since I had heard it many times sung.

V: *Did someone in your family sing it?*

K: Everyone in the family sung it. And if some pieces came from the radio, humming with it was the mother, grandmother, father, whoever was present. Thus it was a big problem, when I first tried to read the book – I couldn't read, I was singing! The melody was so strong – and I couldn't go on quickly. After a couple of days, I managed it.

Many verse couplets from this work are adopted as they are, or little changed as a mantináda, and the principal people, the loving couple Aretousa and Erotokritos, have entered the folk metaphors especially in wedding songs. Parts of the text belong to the contemporary repertoire of some musicians in their performances and recordings. The importance of this work in forming the poetic aesthetics and romantic focus of the poetic expression in Crete seems to be profound indeed.

Couplets have a special place in Greek folk poetry, distinguished from the rest of the tradition by their structure and versatile character. By the early nineteenth century, according to Beaton (1980: 149), couplets are found in all Greek-speaking areas in towns and on islands, but were unknown on the rural mainland, where the association of the rhyme with Westerners and with literature was taken "as proof of sexual deviancy," followed by a contemptuous dismissal. During the twentieth century, couplets have been an active tradition, especially on the Dodecanese Islands, and they are still featured on the southern islands of Crete, Kasos and Karpathos. During a short trip to the island of Naxos in July 2005, people referred to some people living in the village of Apiranthos, who were supposedly of Cretan origin, who "talked with mantinádes" (fieldnotes July 22, 2005). As the manuscript of Vienne (Pernot 1931) shows, the rhyming couplet model spread to several southern islands in the fifteenth and sixteenth centuries; their use on these islands does not mean that they are of Cretan origin. My friends from the island of Kos claim that several old people, if served a few glasses of wine, can still recite mantinádes for hours and some also compose new poems. On these islands, the poems are known by the name mantináda, and in Cyprus, where the tradition has also been strong, by the name *tshiáttisma* (see also Filippidis 1987–89). Among the Greek population of the Asia Minor coast, the couplets referred to as *amanédes* (sing. *amanés*) were sung in a special, melismatic and plaintive way.[4] Referring to Kiriakidis (1978), Beaton (1980: 148) lists some other names used for the rhyming couplets in the different parts of Greece: *patináda* (Hios) and *kotsáki* (Cyclades).

Poetic form and means

Each word in Modern Greek has an accent and this accent distinguishes minimal pairs (e.g. *nómos* = law, *nomós* = prefecture). The accent in Greek may fall on any of the last three syllables and it is marked in the written language. In poetry, the stress in natural words therefore needs to conform to the metrical pattern, and this reduces the choice and placement of the words. On the other hand, this demand entails that the meter is the same in both recited and sung verses, which allows an easy transition between the different kinds of performances and speech acts.

The ethnomusicologist Samuel Baud-Bovy has examined in detail the rhythms of the different metrical lines in Greek folk poetry in his doctoral dissertation "La chanson populaire Grecque du Dodécanèse" (1936). Baud-Bovy examines the rhythm of the poetic *dekapentasíllavo* line when sung, and then of the same poetic line as recited according to the accent rules of spoken Greek (1936: 34).

According to Baud-Bovy, the principal accents of the *dekapentasíllavo* line fall in a song on the following syllables: 2 (or 1), 6, 10 (or 9) and 14, and secondary on syllables: 4, 8, 12 (in lullabies, as an exception, on 15). The line consists of two half-lines, which are eight-syllables and seven-syllables, and these are balanced musically, rhythmically and sometimes melodically. When singing, the second half-line, which is shorter by one syllable, is made equivalent in length to the first half-line mainly by prolonging the second last (always accented) syllable, by a pause, or by prolonging the last syllable (only in lullabies).

---

4 Konstantinos Romeos (1952–5: 281) remarks in his article on the distich songs of Pontos that the popularity of the *improvisation* of these distiches follows the distribution of the lira as a musical instrument (Crete, Cyprus, the Dodecanese and Pontos). Romeos was most probably influenced by the interpretations of Karas, as noted in Chapters 1 and 3 – so this may refer to the lira, but also to the violin, which in some of these areas was played exclusively and in many other areas much earlier.

When the poetic text is recited, according to the analysis based both on narrative songs and couplets, the stress falls on the syllables in the following numbers out of the total of 260:
2 (and 1) = 209; **6** = 164; **10** (and 9) = 201; **14** = 260; and **4** = 150; **8** = 125; **12** = 89.

Baud-Bovy concludes that there is a perfect fit between the poetic and sung line, and formulates the following stress rules: 1) the stress falls always on a paired syllable; 2) the fourteenth syllable is always stressed; 3) the first and the ninth syllables may be stressed; 4) stressing of any other syllable is extremely exceptional, except in the improvisation of couplets. (Baud-Bovy 1936: 58–62)

Thus, the first half-line of a *dekapentasíllavo* line contains eight syllables, with an obligatory stress on either the sixth or eighth syllable, and the second half-line contains seven syllables, with an obligatory stress on the penultimate, the fourteenth syllable. Otherwise, the stress may fall on any even syllable, except in the beginning of the half-lines, where it can fall on the first syllable. This stress pattern is simultaneously sufficiently uniform (musical) for an immediate recognition of the meter and is very flexible for building a variety of rhythmical and sound patterns. The fact that the metrical pattern is identical both when sung and recited (the natural word stress has to conform to the metrical pattern) makes the line a real passe-par-tout in the Greek world.

The separation of the half-lines by a caesura is so clear that even if the verse is *semantically* conceived as a fifteen-syllable line (which corresponds to the full semantic unit ending of the rhyme word), mantinádes are *structurally* conceived as being formed of four parts. As I mentioned earlier, they are therefore semantically and structurally exactly the same as what is referred to as quatrains in many cultures. With regard to the mantinádes passed on to us from former times, it seems that the closely related sentence constituents did not easily cross the caesura. Today, this is not a strict rule and this may be where writing has played a role. However, most examples of enjambment (between the half-lines; there is never enjambment between whole *dekapentasíllavo* lines) which I know (and appear in the present study) are featured in extemporized poems, which may mean that the quick, extemporized composition has always been more susceptible to enjambment between the half-lines, very much like it is for other exceptions in the metrics and rhyme. Perhaps perfect balance is such a superior factor for remembering and for the aesthetics that the poems having closely related sentence constituents that crossed the caesura have merely been dropped off in the course of the time. For an example, let us examine the following *mantináda*:

> *Skífto sti vrísi ya neró / m'aftí me mia sterévgi*
> *intá 'kama stzi Míras mou / kakó ke me pedévgi*
>
> (Kostas Kontoyannis)

> I bow to the spring for water, / but it runs dry at once
> <u>What did I do to my Fate / bad,</u> and she mocks me
> (=what bad did I do to my Fate, and she mocks me)

The first line presents an actual situation, and the caesura divides the two clauses. The second line comments on what has happened by posing a question, and the word "bad" that belongs to the first clause, is situated in the beginning of the second half-line.

It could still be said that while a researcher may have to count syllables, a mantináda-poet, or standard Cretan, or even any well-informed Greek, surely does not. Baud-Bovy writes (1936: 340, translation from French my own):

> I have never met a singer who had been conscious of how many syllables a verse is composed of. When the listeners hear a false verse, they notice straight away the incorrectness, but can't tell the reason, whether it is a badly placed caesura, or lack or excess of syllables. They just remark that "the song doesn't match" (*den tairiázei to tragoúdi*).

My experience is exactly the same as expressed by Baud-Bovy, even if people in Crete are currently well aware of the definition of the poetic meter. A metrically failing couplet is said "not to fit/match" or "not to be a mantináda". The musical-metrical pattern of the *dekapentasíllavo* is so natural to the Greek language that it is quite automatically recognized by any Greek.[5]

The end rhyme binds two *dekapentasíllavo* lines together and makes the couplet form. The rhyme is often complete (the last syllable and the vowel of the penultimate syllable are the same), but indigenously there is no great discrimination of an incomplete rhyme, an assonance (when the consonant of the last syllables are not the same). Rhyming concerns not the graphically but phonologically identical syllables, but sometimes, especially when quickly extemporizing verses, the composer may content himself by using assonance. Baud-Bovy finds[6] the Greek folk song's attitude towards rhyme to be careless (1936: 342), and for example, he points to the familiar case of the rhyme words repeating the possessive pronoun *mou* (my) or *sou* (your) at the end of the lines. In my own conversations with Cretan composers, rhyme is always noticed as one of the primary characteristics of a mantináda. But it is also stated often, even by those mainly writing their verses, that the semantic weight of the message always overcomes the focus on perfect rhyme.

Building the end rhyme nevertheless requires special attention, and a poor or non-existing rhyme is normally regarded as a failure of the mantináda. According to Baud-Bovy (1936: 342–347), traditional formulaic pairs of rhyme words are a good aid for the improviser. Nevertheless, contemporary poets do not admit to consciously using such ready-made formulaic pairs,

---

[5] Professor Alexis Politis told me (personal communication, June 26, 2004) that as a university student, his professor had warned the students not to enter the *dekapentasíllavo* rhythm unconsciously in writing.

[6] Baud-Bovy is a French-speaker, and the question of what end-rhyme means is much more delicate in the French language and poetry than in many other languages, especially English (see e.g. Scott 1988: 11–13).

although many of them do say that at least in extemporization one has to formulate in one's mind the rhyme words first. The situation of managing to get only two verses to rhyme together is of course quite different from that of the improvisation in some languages where a group of several lines has to conform to the same rhyme pattern. For instance, the Basque *bertsolaritza*-poets learn by heart "families" of rhymes in order to be able, within the frames of the selected rhyme, which covers eight or ten lines, to select the best words for the meaning intended (Garcia et ali 2001: 93–101). I will examine rhyming in more detail in the sixth chapter, in connection to composition.

Besides these basic metrical rules concerning stressing and rhyme, there has to be good acoustical balance between the vowels and consonants in the poem. Most often this concerns avoiding hiatus in the word boundary (the meeting of two vowels that are stressed or otherwise clearly separated into two different syllables). Just as in dialectal speech itself, apocope (elision of the terminal vowel of the word) and aphaeresis (elision of the beginning vowel of the word) are widely used in mantinádes, and various fillers can also be added for this acoustical effect. When the two vowels encountered at the word boundary can be pronounced as one syllable (synizesis), they are also counted as one. In quick composition, nevertheless, it seems a rather frequent practice to fulfill the meter by also pronouncing both vowels, when needed. During the composition process, a competent poet can use the addition or deletion of syllables as an issue of personal decision that is informed by one's sense of style and by the intended meaning or nuance. Different strategies produce very different acoustical patterns, which an experienced poet can adopt to his advance (see Chapter 6; also Holton 1991: 11–12). The ways of rendering the dialectal poetic expression correctly into written form are analyzed extensively in the articles and books of the local philologer and *mantinadológos* Mihalis Kafkalas, as explained in Chapter 1.[7]

In adapting and dividing the poetic text to the musical rhythm and cycles in a sung performance, many types of digressions and refrains are used, as was shown in the previous chapter. The digressions are used not only for metrical purposes, but particularly for personal variation (see Caraveli Chaves 1978) and performative goals: performers and audience both focus on the ongoing mode of action, the performance.

The mantinádes that remain in the local repertoire and are cited again and again, are often in addition to their semantic significance, also acoustically harmonious and well balanced. The most important rule of organizing the components of a couplet is indeed the balance. This balance takes place both structurally and semantically between lines, between half-lines and sometimes even between the halves of a half-line. By citing examples, Baud-Bovy carries out an extended analysis of the possibilities of grammatically constructing verses: how lines and half-lines are organized as constituent parts of a sentence, and how half-lines are balanced internally.

---

7 For poetic means, see Kafkalas 1992; also Kafkalas 1996: 21–24, Psaras 1996: 46; Holton 1991: 11–12.

Correspondingly, he then analyzes the balance of the semantic structures. (Baud-Bovy 1936: 313–336) In conversation, the effectiveness of a poem is normally also attributed to the roles between the verses: the second verse should be stronger than the first.

The syntax of the Greek language with the nominative, accusative, genitive and vocative cases allows great freedom that is fully exploited in the uncountable variety of syntactical structures. Moreover, the feminine, neuter and masculine articles are used extensively to refer to implicit meanings, many of which have to be intuitively known from the general Greek language use or from the dialectal forms. The Cretan dialect allows many morphological transformations in the stress or the length of the word because of the dialectal forms, parallel variants and diverse diminutive forms that add or reduce the number of syllables. A typical example is the word *déndro*, a tree, which can be used when needed to fit the metrical pattern, whereas the dialectal form *dendrí,* where the stress falls on the last syllable, is preferred when possible.[8] During a performance, a verbal play may be based on minor syntactical and morphological alterations to known verses, showing the dexterity of the poet particularly in how he or she can change the meaning with just little variation in the form. Furthermore, as described by Herzfeld (1981a: 126–127, 133; 1985a: 142–143; 1985b: 203), a part of a previous line may be repeated in reciprocal verses to create a contrast with the previously stated meaning, just as performing a known mantináda creatively in a new occasion is a full license to recognize the *authorship* of the verses.

What renders the poetic expression in a rhyming couplet form distinctively a *Cretan* mantináda – a significance always emphasized by the Cretans themselves? Most significant indeed is the use of the Cretan dialect, which marks the language on all its meaningful levels: phonological, morphological, syntactical, and lexical. Of these, the phonological idiom is still very clearly heard in the everyday language in the villages, and according to Granqvist (1998: 10–11), it is the best preserved level from the standardization that started in the early 1950s, along with the major social changes. Crete has long been a self-dependent entity, and unlike some other Greek dialects, the Cretan dialect has been highly valued among its speakers (Granqvist 1998: 10). As the poetic traditions are also particularly appreciated and alive even today, the idiomatic dialect and expression is preserved in the poetic language. According to Mihalis Kafkalas (1996: 15–16), a pure Cretan *mantináda* avoids the use of common language when local expressions are available, as well as foreign words, new or artificial words, slang, idiomatic expressions of other Greek dialects or of a very narrow local distribution, words that are without poetical value and archaisms that are no longer familiar. This manifesto, although given by him to the composers of mantinádes in literary contexts, corresponds well to the "purely" oral mantinádes. To conclude: the dialectal words and structures convey expressive accuracy and color as well as syntactic variance and thereby help the poets to avoid flat expressions.

---

8 For a detailed description of dialectal forms with reference to contemporary mantinádes, see Kafkalas 1992.

In any verbal tradition, the oral poet employs a resource of traditional words, metaphors, formulas and patterns according to his or her competence, which can be linguistic, poetic, as well as communicative. The longer Modern Greek lyric and epic folksong material is typically formulaic. Analyses based on the Oral-Formulaic Theory have been carried out by Sifakis (1988; in Greek), and in English, briefly by Beaton (1980: 35–57; see however critics in Sifakis 1988: 144–146) and by Anna Caraveli-Chaves (1978). Mantinádes share the same metrical line with the rest of the Modern Greek tradition and thus many of the formulas as well. The characteristic rules of the register, however, must be derived with an emphasis very different from those of the longer poetic forms. The distinguishing compact structure of the couplet makes the essential forming of the phraseology and the significance more dependent on the morphological and syntactical micro-cosmos. Humor, sharpness and punning are important, and a change of style is easily realized when the performance situation allows it: for example, romantic stereotypes can be used for ironic, amusing effect that is contrasting to the original poetic nuance (see the example in Herzfeld 1985a: 142–144, quoted in Chapter 5).

For the improviser of mantinádes, as "auxiliary mediums," Baud-Bovy includes the following: rhyme-clichés, couples of expression, stereotypic epithets and half-lines passe-par-tout. He notices that it is not possible to undertake a similar task as executed by Milman Parry (1928a) with Homeric poetry, to examine exhaustively the formulaic epithets in the flexible, versatile mantinádes, but Baud-Bovy lists many typical examples. According to him, the most common unit for a formula is a half-line, and normally the first half-line, because rhyming determines the construction of the second half-line. (Baud-Bovy 1936: 340–364) Preceding the later emphases of John Miles Foley (1988: 110–111; 1991; 1995) with regard to the Oral-Formulaic Theory, Baud-Bovy observes that the technical analysis brings about the problem of shading the aesthetic values that are often present in many couplets, and that after showing the importance of the stereotypical epithets, their artistic value should be demonstrated as well (Baud-Bovy 1936: 365).

As might be typical of the productive registers, the basic vocabulary does not differ very much from the spoken idiom, but the register leans heavily on shared idiomatic expressions, metaphors and metonyms. The lyric images and metaphors are most often taken from nature, and they are shared with other Greek folk poetry genres. Based on published song material, Petropoulos has listed a comprehensive selection of these metaphors in his doctoral thesis entitled *La comparaison dans la chanson populaire grecque* (1954). Like the world over, the symbols for human feelings, moods and destiny are the sun, moon, flowers, birds, and natural phenomena. In the reduced length of a mantináda, metaphors must also be short and clear, often just one word, like the example of the partridge for referring to a girl at a marriageable age (thus "hunted" by boys; see Chapter 6). Especially in sentimental verses, the first verse typically contains a metaphor from nature and the second line links it to personal experience.

Thematic contents

Mantinádes cover a wide variety of typical performance situations, styles and topics in their thematic contents and context of use. Asking people about whether mantinádes are divided into categories most obviously prompts the reply that there are mantinádes for each situation in life. The categories of *erotikés* (erotic), *pirahtikés* (teasing), *satirikés* (satiric, or generally, making fun of the target), and *filosofikés* (philosophic) mantinádes may be generally identified to describe the style, but such definitions are not clear-cut or exhaustive, especially regarding the process of composition or the context of use.

However, when inquiring about someone's favorite mantinádes, or asking for an explanation on which particular mantináda is deemed to be good, the request is turned into an immediate counter question: *on which theme?* This is because theme as an indigenous category is clearly connected to the way in which singing events are conceptualized. In festive or recreational singing events, the singing is organized according to (1) themes typical of the situation, e.g. greetings, songs to the bride and groom, etc., and (2) themes "opened" and evolving along with the progress of the singing event. Any subject can arise as a theme for the exchange of poems in song, although quite often this pertains to matters relevant to human emotional life (love, separation, loneliness, etc.). Any straying from the agreed theme – whether conventional, random or purposely chosen by one of the participants – can be strictly criticized[9]. Although mantinádes are thus a register freely generating new texts and themes, the meaning of the performance of a particular poem is evaluated with regard to how it contributes to the theme at hand. This has already been discussed in the chapter on singing; here, I will introduce the categories of style, those referred to above, as well as discuss the local attitudes towards the idea of theme with regard to the written collections.

The impact of the vernacular romantic literature, especially *Erotókritos*, on the poetic standards has already been referred to. The "Vienne" manuscript (Pernot 1931) contains material originally from the Dodecanese islands and Crete mainly in the form of short rhymed or unrhymed couplets, and it focuses solely on love and courting. Correspondingly, the strongest urge towards self-expression through mantinádes is today unambiguously invested in erotic and emotional messages, and in various aspects of love and relationships, which are the most common subjects in a singing event, as has been mentioned in the previous chapter. In traditional patriarchal Cretan village communities, a mantináda was not only a cherished way to express oneself but, as described earlier (p. 23) by Mitsos Stavrakakis, the *only* possible way to communicate these subjects.

Another significant motive for singing or reciting mantinádes in the closely-knit village communities was to comment on the everyday occurrences of the village life, and to tease, satirize, or even mock the opponent.

---

9 For an example, see Caraveli 1982.

The *pirahtiká* (or *pismatiká*), the "teasing-songs," contain the body of the more conversational mantinádes uttered and composed to remark on interpersonal tensions, especially between women and men. According to older people, this used to be very common in the villages during the first half of the twentieth century, but it could still occasionally take place. Even today, when a female and male poet meet, such erotic and teasing motives may contribute to a dramatic performance even when there is no relevance to it in real life (examples will follow in Chapter 6). Due to the way these poems are performed, they are referred to as *antikristés*, reciprocal mantinádes.

The first example of the *pirahtiká* dates back to the sixteenth century (Pernot 1931: 58) and presents an exchange of arguments between a girl and a boy; the following example is recollected by one of my informants and refers to the 1990s.

"*I-agápi próti étihe / períssia n'agapáte*
ke-op' agapísi déftero / tis prótis den thimáte"

O nios apoloyíthike, tis kóris sintihéni:

"*Oses thoroún ta mátia mou / pistévis óti agapó tes?*
es' íse fos ke mátia mou / tes perissés yeló tes,
es' íse ke ta mátia mou / es' íse ke to fos mou
ke séna thélo na thoró par' ánthropon tou kósmou"

The first loved one happened / to be loved very much
And when one loves a second time / the first will be forgotten

The youth defended himself and answered to the maiden:

"All those whom I see with my eyes / do you think I love them?
You are my light and my eyes / the rest I make a fool of
You are both my eyes / and you are my light
And I want to see you more / than anyone in the world"

Another example was recounted by Kostas Kontoyannis in 1999 (991124)

Yes, there are teasing (*piráhtikes*) *mantinádes*, but it is more the women who say them to the men and the reverse. It still takes place; much more, of course, it happened in the old days, but it still takes place, like when one boy said to a girl who didn't want him:

Sa m' arnithís agápi mou / ínta tharís pos káno
'Ena tsikáli fayitó / trógo na min potháno

When you reject me my dear / what do you think I'll do?
A large pot of food / I eat in order not to die

The girl answered to him (he was slightly fat, too):

Ta máthia sou ín' san t' avgá / ke kóli sou varélia
ke-ótan prováli̇s ke se dó / kserénome sta yélia

Your eyes are like eggs / and your bums like barrels
And when you appear and I see you / I fall over with laughter

A wide body of mantinádes, more or less seriously stating a philosophical conception of life, can be described as *philosophiká*. The following poems are created by Aristidis Heretis, who is well known for his imaginative images and satirical tones. As a *mantinadológos,* he is often depicted by other contemporary poets as being closest to the traditional village expressive style. (1999, 991123 and an interview in the magazine *Kondiliés*, number 10, August–September 2007):

'Opios 'gapá alithiná / vásana de fováte
Móno ta stróni páploma / ke théti ke kimáte

The one who really loves / is not afraid of worries
He just makes them a quilt / and lays down and sleeps

Péte mou énan áthropo / pou ta 'hi lísi óla
Etsá den tá' lisa ki-egó / ma de me gniázi kióla

Mention to me one human being / who has solved everything
So neither did I solve all things / but nor do I worry of that

Hílies forés sti sképsi mou / se váno ke se vgáno
Ná 'se kalá pou moú 'dokes / douliá na tine káno

A thousand times in my mind / I put you in and take you out
Be well you who gave me / work to be engaged in

Other poems that were cited to me by Yorgos Sifakis as examples of qualitative superiority in 2004 (041110) are:

Na anaválli̇s ti hará / ftáni éna dákri móno
K' éna potámi dákria / den pnígoun énan póno

To displace the joy / only one tear is enough
And a river-full of tears / does not choke one pain
                                        (of unknown origin)

Dendrí pou de sou méllete / na fas ap' ton karpó tou
Mi kimithis ston ískio tou / ke páris ton kaïmó tou

The tree, of which you are not going to / eat any fruit
Don't sleep under its shade / and take yours its longing
            (entitled to Stelis Kalomiris in Papirakis 2004: 16)

A traditional, very stable body of fixed mantinádes is still used extensively in greetings and felicitations. The following is one of the best known greetings:

Hília kalós orísate / hília ke dió hiliádes
O kámbos me ta loúlouda / ke me tsi prasinádes

Thousand (times) welcome / thousand and two thousands
The plain with the flowers / and with all its greens

Like many such greetings, wishes and toasts, mantinádes *tou gámou* are also usually traditional and rather fixed in form; these wedding songs are sung by women while they prepare the bride and groom and by the musicians outside of the church, and later to begin the dance.

In printed Cretan collections (e.g. Droudakis 1982; Lioudaki 1936; Pavlakis 1994), the large variety of mantinádes is organized in many more detailed thematic categories. The mantinádes in Lioudaki's collection (1936) are categorized into the following main- and subcategories:

(1) *Praises for the beloved girl*: Beauty, Slenderness and grace, Carriage, Face (subdivided into: General, Fair, Dark-skinned, Rose-red, Mouth and tongue), Neck, Hair, Feet.
(2) *Praises for the beloved boy*;
(3) *Old loves*;
(4) *Praises and the power of eyes*;
(5) *The worries and pain of love*: Secret love, Visible love, Crazy love, Eternal love, Dreams, Sacrifices, Greetings and welcoming, Oaths, Wishes, Hopes and hopelessness, Suspicions, Worries, Fires, Sighs, Tears, Pains, Patience and impatience, Anxiety and rejection
(6) *Curses*: General, To the beloved girl or boy, To mother-in-law, To enemies
(7) *Fate and Fortune*
(8) *Consolation*
(9) *Passions*
(10) *Separation*
(11) *Complaints*
(12) *Kisses*
(13) *Obstinacies*
(14) *Jealousy and infidelities*
(15) *Aphorisms*
(16) *Teasing*
(17) *Humor*

(18) Miscellaneous: *Out of the beloved's house, At get-togethers, In the dance*: (subdivided into: To the lira-player and to his lira, To the dancers, Teasing to the dancers);
(19) *Forty-mantiniáda* (a play in get-togethers or dance in which numbers from 1 to 40, or up to 100, are given to the singer who answers with a mantináda containing this number; local eastern Cretan varieties).

These themes especially illustrate the mantinádes *sung* in the dances and village festivities, and thus they demonstrate the emphasis on the shared repertoire.

As I have noted earlier, these classifications in collections can be criticized for neglecting to recognize the village usage of contextually defined meaning. However, all the authors of the above-mentioned major collections are Cretans who come from a village background. Although they are also teachers and/or scholars, and literary objectives are evident in their work, the question of themes has still another significant aspect in the present context. When Cretans themselves read these collections, the poems are not seen as being representatives of performances, but as a poetic reserve: existing poems in their exact textual forms are in a very real meaning viewed as a shared "pool of tradition" (Honko 1998) from which individuals can draw for their situated, improvised and personal needs. Furthermore, from an indigenous point of view, the thematic classification in the collections reflects the primary importance of the thematic connection in performance: theme is the cognitive category of the situated contributions in a sung dialogue, and in many cases, correspondingly, the identification of something (an event, discourse, poem, etc.) as a theme is the primary impulse for composition (as will be shown in Chapter 6).

I discussed this subject in 1999 with Mitsos Stavrakakis (991202), inquiring as to why he uses classifications in the publications of his own poems. At first he hesitatingly sympathized with the idea of a literary practice that obviously motivated my question, but then he begun to object to this explanation:

> "*They also exist in life*. These that deal with erotic love are erotic, the other that are of separation adopt the theme of separation. About the loneliness…about the freedom then…here I have put the categories, you can as well…here, for example, about the desire, because three mantinádes have the word desire, I say this category is that of desire, but in here you can also find the erotic, whatever. It's a little bit technical, it's for, I don't know, literary use. (…). *But when you say* a mantináda and the other laughs, it is a *satire* that tells: your face is like that of a pig…it's not *erotic*. If you put it in the category of humorous, you call it satirical, sarcastic, or something like that. Compulsory you put it into one of the categories; there are erotic, humorous, then there are philosophical. *But by themselves they go into categories*.

To understand how a theme is recognized, and to observe the phenomenon in later examples, it is important to recognize Stavrakakis' words: "*because three mantinádes have the word desire, I say this category is that of desire.*" This description suggests that the notion of a theme can be a concrete, lexical center of associations.

When I interviewed the primary school children and one young adult who is actively performing music and mantinádes in the Village in October 1999 (991913/1 and 991013/2), they all told me that they were learning mantinádes in written collections rather than from family members or even in the *gléndi*, as was customary some decades ago. The children regarded memorizing poems as a self-evident, natural prerequisite for having as much material as possible for taking part in the thematically proceeding, improvised singing events, familiar to them from the older boys' recreation. When I asked a boy in his twenties about his favorite mantinádes, he found the question slightly confusing and he asked me to specify which particular theme I meant. He then went on to explain that his favorite theme was *ya tis pérdikes*, about the partridges (a metaphor for unmarried girls; for more information on this conversation, see Chapter 6). Theme certainly corresponds to the topic of conversation that guides the dialogic poetic practice and imagination: further examples on performances and composition in the following chapters will shed more light on what a theme can be, and how it can be reflected under the requirement of thematic continuation in a performance.

Couplets as building blocks

Mantinádes "continued" (sinehómenes)

In Crete, besides the actual independent mantinádes, longer lyrical and narrative poems and songs, love songs, laments, and lullabies, for example, are almost exclusively cast in the form of a series of rhyming couplets. These are not usually called mantinádes, whose primary characteristic is the demand of conveying a full meaning within the two rhyming *dekapentasíllavo* lines. Often such longer compositions are called "songs" or mantinádes *sinehómenes*, "continued." While many people thus categorically separate an independent mantináda from a cluster of more than one couplet, there are others who do not see any problem in calling even larger clusters of couplets *mantinádes*.

The borderline between the mantinádes and mantinádes *sinehómenes* is not always clear, due to the determining role of the thematic connection between the successive mantinádes in a performance. Many poets are prolific, and even when they write their verses down later, they are not overly selective with regard to their production. As a consequence, their notebooks are filled with several poems evolving around a theme to which the composer originally reacted. Many informants say that some days, verses simply flood their mind, "*horís na to thélo*" (regardless of my own will; e.g. 010422). Romeos (1952–5: 282) noted a concern which today may sound rather amusing: how easily even the most experienced collectors of songs mistook these clusters of couplets on the same theme, persons, etc., for a longer song, and published it as one (c.f. Amaryanakis' [1988: 328] note on improvisation, p. 75).

Under certain conditions, mantinádes may very easily turn into *sinehómenes*, forming a discursive complex of poems on a certain theme. When the composer (and in traditional surroundings, this holds particularly for women) does not have access to social poetic dialogue, then the normally interpersonal chain of mantinádes in a *paréa* can be formed by one person. In the beginning of this book, we saw an example of this, when I referred to the *kafenío*-owner's elaboration on the theme of separation as a reaction to my excuse: one such chain took form in a performance by a single person.

The following verses illustrate how a special theme, in this case a mantináda heard in a television broadcast, inspires the composer to take the floor with a dialogic cluster of mantinádes (fieldnotes August 22, 2006). This incident took place in May 2006, when my informant Despina Papadaki had had to stay in the hospital for some weeks due to health problems. One evening she heard the following mantináda on the television:

> *Na zíso parakáleta / tou Hárou de yirévo*
> *Tin teleftéa mou-anapniá / den tou ti zitianévo*

> To live without request / I do not ask the Charos
> For my last breath / I will not beg him

Contesting the idea expressed, Despina had immediately composed her own response:

> *Eksanazítisa tou-egó / parátasi tou Hárou*
> *Ma ekínos mou apándise / 'timásou na se páro*

> I myself requested again / extension from the Charos
> But he answered me: / ready yourself for take off!

(And I answer him)

> *Den íne kríma ki-ádiko / horís kamiá etía*
> *Na m'aferésis ti zoï / ná 'his tin amartía*

> Is not that pity and unfair / that without any reason
> You will take my life / and take the sin above yourself

> *'Oso boró th' antistathó / de tha to váno káto*
> *Ya na tou díkso pos ki-egó / káno ta páno káto*

> As long as I can I'll resist / I will not give up
> To show him that as well I / can make the upside down

> *O ouranós na kateví / ki-i yí na pái-apáno*
> *Katálave to Háronta / pos hári de sou káno*

The sky to come down / and the earth to go up
Grasp this, my Charos / that I will not please you

'Ipa sou ke ksanápa sou / píyene se mia álli
Ksekóllise apó páno mou / páre mia pio megáli

I told and told you again / go to someone else
Release your hold on me / take an older woman

Lígo meró parátasi / zitó ma de mou díni
Tharís apó ti tsépi tou / vgáni leftá ke díni

A few days extension / I ask but he does not give me
You'd say from his pocket / he takes money and gives

Tharó pos thá 'rtho mia vradiá / ston ípno na se piáso
Ya na sou dóso ipnotikó / ísos na isiháso

I think I'll come one night / to catch you while asleep
To give you a sleeping-pill / maybe to rest for a while

The theme of the mantináda recited on television touched upon Despina's own situation, and she composed this "conversational" cluster of verses at once, writing the verses down on tissue paper. After she had left the hospital, Despina gave an account of these verses to a friend during a telephone call. This friend then asked for another mantináda. Despina made a short outline of the theme again, this time adding a new definition:

Ezítisa parátasi / tou Hárou déka hrónia
Ke toú 'pa den epántrepsa / akóma ta engónia

I requested extension / from the Charos for ten years
I told him I hadn't married off / yet my grandchildren

The friend responded laughingly: "Well, you didn't ask much; why didn't you ask for more years?" Whereupon Despina continued:

Mólis tha ftáso sta enniá / ke álla tha tou yirépso
Na ftáso ke sta dígona / mia balothiá na pékso

When I'll arrive at nine / I'll also request him for more
To arrive at great-grandchildren / to shoot one bullet in the air[10]

While an ideal mantináda compresses the message in one poetic picture, here the cluster elaborates the theme from different angles and arrives at

---

10 Until the beginning of the twenty-first century, gunfire was a traditional form of manifesting joy in festive occasions in Crete (still today this can be experienced especially during Easter Saturday night).

a conclusion only after debating the point through many proposals and narrative details. This cluster is a rhetorical dialogue that depends on narrative repetition and on a partial addition of information in building the point(s) of view; it does not compress the message in one image or give a final answer at once. In other words, the style is additive, as well as persuasive and rhetorical. Garcia et al. (2001: 178–183) indeed suggest that the term rhetorical best depicts the *bertsolaritsa*, which is poetry that normally contains eight or ten lines (4–5 couplets), as a genre. This example illustrates well the difference between the two types of improvised verses: the coherent imagery of the couplets (quatrains) and the argumentative rhetoric of the longer compositions.

Narrative songs

The compact form of the rhyming couplet serves to help in the composition and in memorizing longer entities, and it is therefore also used as a building block in the longer narrative songs that are often historical. In scholarly contexts, historical songs are referred to as *rímes* (Amaryanakis 1988; Beaton 1980; Kapsomenos 1979), but contemporary people seldom use this word or understand its meaning.[11] Instead, Cretans prefer to talk about songs, or a history in mantinádes. The verses cited above already provide an example of more narrative means and structural character, although here the objective is to show a rhetorical protest. Although the same metrical rhyming couplet form is used in longer songs as a building block, the identity of the couplet becomes quite different in style and structure. This is clearly a separate register, and most Cretans also regard it that way as well. In addition to purely linguistic or metrical features, the stylistic and performative parameters therefore always contribute to what can be defined as register, or genre.

The oldest known narrative song referred to as *ríma* is the *Daskaloyannis*, which tells the story of the 1770 Cretan rebellion in Sfakia in an epic of 1,034 lines, written down shortly after the event. The same characteristics and composition technique are also shared by some shorter and more recent compositions. (Beaton 1980: 155–158) Today, new compositions are written and published in leaflets or in local newspapers.

A special category of longer narrative songs is formed by the satirical stories narrating an event of getting rid of old donkeys, and the consequential exploitation of the meat and fur by the members of the family and friends involved. Since donkey meat is not used as food, the animal was useless when it aged, and to avoid needlessly taxing the family's meager livelihood, the donkey was put down. As carrion meat is a taboo, the whole donkey business provided a delicious subject for satire. Although the verses make fun of their target, these compositions were referred to me as *ikoyeniakés mantinádes*, family mantinádes, by one women interlocutor in Karanou,

---

11 This is evident in one quotation of our conversation with Kostoula in Chapter 6, page 173.

Hania (060515). I came across these donkey stories troughout Crete, although they were also unknown in many places (see also Herzfeld 1985a: 146–148; 1990).

Normally the donkey songs form a complete, long story, but most informants no longer remember the verses. The following few examples of these donkey verses are from a discussion involving Despina, Agapi, Despina's godchild (R), me and my husband (Y) in 2001 (010329):

R: About the mantinádes, god-mother, which you had created about one donkey that died?

D: Yes, and now recently I created another song about that, now lately I have created one of the donkey of Mitso, the one who died, that they wanted to roast it in the charcoal burning place.

R: Good Virgin Mary!

A: The mantinádes that you have created!

D: *(…) tou horioú i nearí / válane simadoúra*
      Ke pígan na skotósoune / tou Mítsou ti gaïdoúra

      The village's young men / made up a contract
      And they went to kill / the donkey of Mitsos

These first verses I remember, I don't know, I create a lot and I must remember a lot, by heart I don't remember everything. I remember that they got together, it says, at the other end of the village, and shouted that they will take it [the donkey] to the charcoal burning place, well…

A: To me, what did you create for me, then?

D: *I-Agapi, léi, zítise / na pári tin proviá tis*
      Na tin kámi páploma / tahiá sta yeratiá tis

      Agapi, says, asked / to take the donkey's fur
      To make it a quilt / soon for her old age

(Y) They said, they said during the old times…

/D: *(…) epróvale / apó to parathíri*
      Afísete mou dio kilá / yatí eho mousafíri

      (…) showed up / on the window
      Please, leave me two kilos / because I have a guest[12]

---

12 This couplet is a good example of the deeply formulaic character of such songs; the verses are presented identically by Herzfeld (1990), except for the replacement of the name.

The *rímes* are always introduced in the publications of Cretan folk poetry, although all researchers have found it difficult to fit these literary, titled poems and their poets into the category of real "folk" poems; but they also have not been accepted as written literature (e.g. Amaryanakis 1988; Beaton 1980: 160; Kapsomenos 1979: 16–17). The register approach suggested here, and advanced in the methodological concerns of John Miles Foley (2002; 2005), can be useful in analyzing these songs. The phenomenon of topical verse in rhyming couplets seems to concern all the linguistic groups that use rhyme in oral or written poetry. Field experience in Crete suggests that beside the question of competence, people have very different personal orientations towards the poetic expression. In her research on folk narrators, Anna-Leena Siikala (1984: 96–150) introduces the terms *narration tendency* and *tradition orientation* in order to delineate the differences between narrator types. Later, she turns to the term *habitus*, adopted from the writings of Bourdieu (1977) and further employed by Hanks (1996), to examine the variation in the rune-singing practices (Siikala 2000: 256–257). Similarly, if differences are perceived in the personal approaches towards the choice of register and style in the use of the expressive potential in the composition of poetry, it is understandable that some people in a community are intrigued by and can excel in quick communicational repartee, while others prefer making funny stories about the undertakings of their fellow humans, and further, that some are particularly interested in composing historical narratives.

The basic difference between the self-expression through concise mantinádes and through longer narrative compositions seems to be a question of the poet's personal character, orientation and competence. There is a continuum between the registers that use the same basic couplet form but differ especially in their aims, structural organization and poetic orientation. Here (between mantinádes and oral narrative songs) the continuum exists between the communicatively and poetically orientated verses and the more narratively orientated verses, with a multilevel inter-space of more or less bound clusters of mantinádes: songs or mantinádes *sinehómenes*. Competence in these genres emerges on a very different basis, and the handling of textual and contextual elements is completely different. The same conclusion was drawn by Charles Briggs (1988: 352–358) with regard to the difference between the short and longer conversational Mexicano genres. Both forms are "traditional" ways of self-expression in Crete, even if writing down the verses may have been a more common practice for the longer narrative songs until the past few decades. Longer compositions are also more likely to have been composed by writing poets who do not have a command of the oral expression of the register. During the past few decades, when the activity of composition has been expanding to the written and mass media arenas, the attraction of written oral poetry holds true largely for single couplets as well.

V The multidimensional performance

When Cretans are asked to define the main performance arenas for mantinádes, they name the following: 1) the *gléndi*, the collective feast with music and dance connected with life-cycle festivities, carnival time, and annual village festivals, and 2) informal singing accompanied by musical instruments in a *paréa*, which is a get-together of a group of friends or relatives. Both these forms have been important performance arenas in which verbal creativity has become one with music, in the *gléndi* likewise with dance, and socially significant discourse has taken place among the members of the community. In the traditional singing events up until the 1980s, mantinádes served as the essential language for all communication, from creating the atmosphere and the sense of solidarity, to the verse contests and detailed personal messages. Introduced in Chapter 3, Cretan musical and festive traditions are maintained continuously, although within a changed society.

Musical performance arenas and the musicality of poetic expression are essential parts of the verbal tradition. Even if the traditional forms of singing and entertainment rarely actualize in contemporary life, recognizing these arenas is still extremely significant, because the dialogic nature of the communication in the *gléndi* and *paréa* is implicitly present in the contemporary conceptualization of the tradition and poetry. Today, the mantinádes sung by professional musicians still introduce this communication with the tradition and the collective values expressed by it. It is important to notice, however, that even if mantinádes are an emblematic part of the musical life in Crete, much of the oral composition and many performative uses of the tradition breathe silently underneath and surface only in informal occasions between friends and families.

In the recent past, as well as today, the idea of performance in Crete is far from being exhausted by naming the singing performance contexts (or the written and mass media environments in contemporary society). In practice, it is much more common to be drawn into poems in speech for the purpose of citing, referring to, recollecting and telling stories, and for presenting and negotiating poetic inventiveness. Many villages still have people who can weave anything into a mantináda. Before, poems were often proverbially embedded in people's everyday speech situations, and they were recited to tease or to provoke a poetical dialogue, a verbal duel, and this occurred as much in casual confrontations as within the frames of a singing event. The emergence of performance will therefore be taken into consideration in this study, as Richard Bauman has advised (1977: 26):

> In the ethnography of performance as a cultural system, the investigator's attention will frequently be attracted first by those genres that are conventionally performed. These are the genres, like Chamula genres of pure speech or Bahamian old stories, for which there is little or no expectation on the part of the members of the community that they will be rendered in any other way. He should be attentive as well, however, for those genres for which the expectation or probability of performance is lower, for which performance is felt to be more optional, but which occasion no surprise if they are performed.

While Bauman refers to different parallel genres, this study focuses on how as representatives of a single register, the mantinádes emerge in very different kinds of performances.

This chapter offers an introduction to the basic discursive contexts and ways of performing mantinádes outside the frames of the singing events that have been presented in Chapter 3. After describing and analyzing these different performance arenas, I will proceed to draw some conclusions concerning the role of gender in a performance. I will thereafter discuss in detail the means of participation, improvisation and perceiving or creating a meaning in a performance by analyzing the special strategies of meaning used in poetry that have been introduced earlier in Chapter 2. I will conclude the chapter with a discussion on the performances in the current mass media contexts.

Recited performances

While sung performances are organized around the thematic development of the subject and thus within the collectively negotiated frames, recited performances are particularly personal utterances. These utterances can occur in different kinds of performance discourses, which I will introduce by sharing a story based on my own experiences of the performances of a composition in September 2005 (fieldnotes, September 22, 2005).

We had been passing time with 68-year-old Antonis Stefanakis in his workshop (see photos on page 87) in a village, sitting and talking about his life and about mantinádes. Leaving the workshop afterwards to go down to the village center to have supper and spend the evening with *paréa,* Antonis presented me with a mantináda that he had composed recently:

> *Sta héria sou-éhis tis harés / aftés pou-egó steroúme*
> *Ki-íha misí ke s'épsahna / ya na ti mirastoúme*
>
> In your hands you have the delights, the ones that I lack
> Once I had half, and I was looking for you, to share with you that

Antonis had initially been inspired to compose the poem after he had met a very beautiful girl. She had had "the delight" of exceptional beauty, but also a very pleasant personality. Antonis's poem tells about his admiration for this girl, endowed with all these good qualities which he lacks, and expresses his wish to be able to share with her what is good in his lot in life. The addressee of the poem, however, is a generic "you," so it could be addressed to anyone. The word *harés* (sing. *hará*) can also point to many other kinds of joys, skills, and delights (in plural, *harés* also means a wedding).

Antonis told me that after composing the poem, he recited it to his friend, a fellow poet and musician. He now expected the friend, were we to meet him, to refer to the poem somehow, because he had greatly appreciated it.

On the road, we first stopped by a small clothing shop for a fitting of a pair of jeans that Antonis had asked for from the woman owner previously. The jeans were fine, but the trouser legs had to be shortened. The owner offered to do this, just as she always had done. In response, as a "thank you," Antonis uttered the same mantináda to her; now by placing emphasis on the concrete idea of the delights (skills) she had *in her hands*.

Later, after we had had our supper in a very small tavern, sitting by one of the few tables outside, a man came from across the street and approached our table. He put two peeled cactus fruits on the table in front of us, reciting: *Ki-íha misí ke s' épsahna...* "*Once I had half, and I was looking for you...*" This was the friend who had valued the poetic picture and the traditional idea of sharing whatever little you have in Antonis's mantináda, as well as his invitation to come and join him.

Here, the new poem, after its composition, has been recited to a friend, a fellow poet. The poem is then later recited in a social, circumstantially motivated situation in a shop. The poem is being reused both by the poet, and by another performer, to refer to and to recollect earlier discussions and meanings. Antonis's friend uses a part of the poem to refer to the idea of sharing, both to express his approval of the poetic skill Antonis has displayed in capturing that idea in a mantináda, and within the social discourse, to issue an invitation. Antonis' reciting the poem to the shopkeeper is also a performance (a reference) to me. And now in this study, I tell a short contextualized story of past performances, which is likewise a typical local form of discourse.

This example demonstrates that performing a mantináda can adopt any of several *kinds* of performance discourses. Expressed succinctly, the performance discourse can serve the following functions:

(1) as a social communication: a poem uttered ex tempore to fit the current, face-to-face circumstantial context (to the shopkeeper);

(2) as a reference, a recollection by using a previously heard poem (*between those present* in the former recitations);

(3) as a short, contextualized story about a performance in the past (to *someone who has not been present* at the given situation); and

(4) as a performance for the distinct purpose of displaying poetic inventiveness (here between the active poets and to me: to show the quality of the poetic form and the contents of one's new poem; to share meaning and values).

Except for number three, telling a story, where contextual information is provided, all the other communicative forms are extremely short, referential and allusive. This means that a compact recitation contains a long story, and decoding it requires extensive knowledge of local and interpersonal factors.

Poems embedded in speech

The improvised proverbial and phrasal use of mantinádes in speech is certainly more closely tied to the traditional way of life in a village environment, and it is becoming rare in Crete. These verses are composed on the spot, or memorized, and the poem is uttered without preparations, on the spur of the moment. These verses may be used to greet, to joke, to create a certain kind of atmosphere, or to express one's feelings for or opinion or interpretation of something physically or referentially actual or present. A mantináda like this is often recited to direct the conversation or situation, just like proverbs or proverbial sayings are used in many cultures. Even if verbal contests have lost their role today as a serious negotiation of social status and boundaries, communicational situations contain many interpersonal and circumstantial elements which may be unforgettably negotiated through metaphorical or allusive expression.

In the beginning of this study, I introduced an example of a conversational situation where I was myself both the reason for the poetic expression, and the addressee of it. On that occasion, my interlocutor was using traditional mantinádes which, in the course of our interaction, alternatively took the form of provocation, accompaniment, possibly a hint, and an interpretation of the conclusion of the situation. Although the interlocutor put considerable persuasive power in his utterances, as an addressee, I was able to misread the seriousness and to stress instead the flirting playfulness of that dialogue. This was a remarkable firsthand experience, since it allowed me to comment on the part of the interpreter from inside the process.

Let us therefore compare this case to another personal example which took place a year later, in June 1999. When my Greek partner-to-be, Yannis Hadziharalambous, recited a mantináda to me during our first conversation, the situation was quite different. He was born in Athens and grew up there, but had just spent the eight years prior to our meeting mostly in Crete. Although not able to compose verses himself, Yannis was familiar with mantinádes from playing music with the local musicians. We had never met before, but having spent some evenings in the same *paréa*, Yannis as a musician and I as a listener, our eyes continually strayed towards each other, and then we were finally struck up a conversation. I told about my interest in mantinádes and that I was returning to Crete after the summer in order to carry out fieldwork research on the subject. He looked at me and said:

Na kámo thélo tarahí / sa do kakó Yenári
Naríkso hiónia ke nerá / állos na mi se pári!

I want to make disorder / like the wicked January
To throw snow and water / so that no one else will get you![1]

In tight village communities, this veiled and metaphorical way of talking in mantinádes was the only way to express the emotions between the two sexes. Even on this referential occasion, the atmosphere created by this romantic utterance completely changed the frame of reference for the following discourse. Choosing to use the playful imagery and the romantic aura evoked by the register, Yannis had opened his heart, but safely. I now willingly interpreted the challenge in the way he intended it, but had I not shared his feelings, I could have downplayed his words, without the situation becoming embarrassing. What is tangible in this example is how much the right timing can mean in switching the code to traditional poetic register, how much information can intuitively be packed into a short poem, and how immanent the simultaneous contextualization process is. In connection with the previous example, this experience also clearly displays the correlation between the freedom with which the addressee may interpret the metaphorical utterance and the freedom with which the performer may invest all his might in it. In this type of poetic discourse, using the register gives access to communication in a special performance arena, and the contextualization process either renders the results valid in "real life," or it does not. In the end, the rules are fair enough.

In the examples referred to above, the performers used poems intentionally to affect or to change the course of the ongoing situation. Examples of such intentional utterances are featured throughout this book. Besides occurring in conversational communication, the same also takes place, of course, in singing events, but within frames that are more ritual and prepared.

A mantináda can also occur in the course of a conversation much like a memory or a philosophical statement that is evoked by a personal interpretation or association. In the Village, my friends Agapi Moshovaki and Despina Papadaki continuously used mantinádes to illustrate various situations, or mantinádes were brought to their mind by lexical associations.

When we sat down to discuss for the first time in March 2001 (010329), Agapi casually mentioned, quite soon after we had begun: "and it says..." (*léei*; with this introduction she, like many others, often quoted a mantináda):

Miázi-i kardiá mou m' eklisiá / pou litouryá den éhi
Móno an bi kanís voskós / na mi vrahí-onte vréhi

My heart is like a church / that has no religious service ("proper use")
("It has use") Only if a shepherd goes in / not to get wet when it rains

---

[1] This mantináda is known from the repertoire of the lira-player Psarantonis, who in performance adds the phrase *pos m' évales sta páthi*, "since you made me feel passion", after the first half-line of the first verse (featuring also in the record: Psarantonis: *Na kámo thélo tarahí*).

A chapel in the countryside. Photo by the author, Milopotamos, September 2010.

She continued by saying: "As it is, it tells you…It has a lot of meaning!" Here, Agapi was referring to the typical, small Greek chapels that are located a short distance from the village and have been built even in very remote places in the countryside. These chapels were built to honor a particular saint, and often they hold a modest liturgy only on that saint's day; this is in striking contrast to the central churches that conduct regular liturgies weekly and which, except during these liturgies, are often frequented on a daily basis by locals and visitors, lighting candles in memory of their loved ones. By referring to the random entrance of a shepherd to keep rain in the building, using it for some other purpose than what it was built for, the poem enhances the metaphor of isolation and uselessness. Later on, we learned that this was indeed how this lively old woman herself felt her own life to be: her husband and some close relatives had died early, and although she had children and grandchildren, she regretted that her full life had passed too soon. Such an utterance gives voice to personal experience. While corresponding to a poetic picture of one's emotions and thoughts, this brings the satisfaction of self-expression, but it also brings a psychological release: others have felt the same.

Many of the poems by Despina, who had married in the Village, expressed a concern for moral principles and their adaptation in the village's social life and relationships in the village. On several occasions, she composed verses or took up a poem composed earlier to explain this philosophy to me: if you always treat others well, never talk about them bad behind their back, and always help those who need assistance, you have nothing to fear and can lead a respectable life in anyone's eyes.

Agapi Moshovaki and Despina Papadaki, September, 2010. Photo by the author.

Na páme s' énan árrosto / na ton episkeftoúme
Kouráyo na tou dósoume / ke na ton agapoúme

We should go to the sick / we should visit him
To give him courage / and to love him

San pas sto drómo ton kaló / tha vrís tin evloyía
Tha sou harízi o Theós / óli tin eftihía

When you walk on the good road / you will be blessed
The God will give you / all the happiness

When I took the above photograph of Agapi and Despina during my visit in the village in September 2010, Despina turned to me and commented (fieldnotes September 7, 2010):

Me ti fotografía sou / stéko ke kouvendiázo
Ma-íne hartí ke de milí / ke varianastenázo

With your photograph / I stand and discuss
But it is paper and doesn't speak / and I give a deep sigh

The poem most probably commented on the fact that although I was present that day, this presence would be short and soon followed by a long absence. I believe the performance of this poem got her to think about other people, familiar from the photographs hanging on her living-room wall, people whom she could no longer talk to, because she immediately began to recite poems about getting old. She first talked about her own advanced years, then turned to general reflections on the incapability of old age, subsequently made a moral observation about the lack of religious faith which only becomes relevant in times of trouble, and lastly, remembered an event from her youth of a mantináda being performed by a passing neighbor. This chain of associations was then disrupted when the name of a plant I am not familiar with required some explaining, and the discussion again turned to other themes on every-day subjects.

> *Esí 'se stin anatolí / k' éhis keró brostá sou*
> *Sti dísi ópou ím' egó / tha pó tou íliou stásou?*
>
> You are in the East / and you have time in front
> In the West where I am / shall I tell the sun to stop?
>
> *Tréhoun ta hrónia sa neró / pou tréhi sto potámi*
> *Ke sa yerási o-ánthropos / ínta borí na káni?*
>
> The years run like the water / which runs in the river
> And when the man becomes old / what can he do anymore?
>
> *Efígane ta hrónia mas / írthan ta yeratiá mas*
> *Ke tóra efonázoume / éla, Theé, kontá mas!*
>
> The years are gone / the old age came
> And now we are shouting / come, God, be with us!
>
> *Eyérasa ke psárina / ke práma blio den káno*
> *'Evgala ke stahtiá malliá / san ton aletouráno*
>
> I turned old and grey / and no more make a thing
> My hair turned ash-colored / like the *aletouráno**
>   (*name of a plant)

Several improvisers consciously render even ordinary messages in couplet form. In addition to this, an everyday utterance may begin non-poetically and while never consciously intended as a poem, it may turn into one. The words steer themselves towards the *dekapentasíllavo* meter and suggest a rhyming word.

As has been demonstrated earlier, mantinádes can be embedded into speech as references to past situations, in which both the reciter and the hearer(s) have been present. Such recitals are a mutual joy: simultaneously, they refer to the given past situation itself (and/or praise or comment on the individual communicative or compositional skill exhibited in that situation), and praise the unity of the interlocutors (or the community) by showing just how well-equipped the people sharing the same tradition can be in decoding these short, referential messages. The following example also refers to the significance of the poetic meter in terms of memory.

Half a year after my first longer stay in the Village in 2001, I returned again. Despina, now 71 years old, had composed poems about our friendship and about my forgetting the people in the Village (fieldnotes September 15, 2001). I had called her on the phone some weeks before I returned, and immediately after that, she had met with Agapi and extemporized the following poem:

> *Mia filenáda ékama / apó ti Filandía*
> *Véra tine fonázo 'gó / ke-aftí me léi thía*
>
> One (woman) friend I made / from Finland
> I call her Vera / and she calls me aunt

It is clear that the rhyme word "aunt" is arrived at through the pressure of finding a rhyme quickly, and the meaning has been enclosed into the poem along with this word. They told me that when she had come up with this poem, they had laughed their hearts out, and could not help laughing even now (or ever after). For them, the poem had already became a way to cite my presence. I did not immediately grasp the cultural background against which the poem appeared so amusing, so they explained: that Despina in the poem calls me by my name, and I call her "aunt," implies that Despina has to be *very* old indeed, with one foot in the grave already, because I am an adult myself (born 1962), a mother of an adult daughter, and not a child who would call any woman outside the family "aunt." This image keeps amusing us whenever we meet.

Then, some years later (fieldnotes July, 2006), we were sitting with Despina at a table during a feast, and in the course of our conversation, when someone referred to my home country, Despina tried to recollect which country I came from. I saw her striving to think back to this poem in her mind, and when she triumphed over finding the answer, I myself recited the poem to her. She could not believe that I had followed her thought so well, and after we had reminisced "our" moments of fun with the history of the poem, Despines entertained the others with this new story of my "psychologizing" her.

Stories of past performances

Some mantinádes remain in the local repertoire as fixed texts, poems, and some as stories. As the example above indicates, first the event and the inventiveness of the words can begin as an experience between only a few people, but it can be retold in new forms, and it can even take on a completely new shape and meaning. New associations, in turn, produce new events and new stories (see also Caraveli 1982: 132–135). Often those poems that once uttered in the stream of an ongoing discourse have irreversibly affected the course of that discourse, also need some contextualization in their retelling. For many Cretans, whose roots and memories lie in the old tightly-knit village life, these extemporized mantinádes form a very central point of reference. Therefore, even if mantinádes are today rarely extemporized, such past performances and events are recollected as stories. As I have noted earlier, this is the way that the event portrayed in a mantináda is narrated to those not present in the situation. These accounts are dramatized performances: for the outsider's benefit, the situation is now explained to the extent needed for grasping the point, and the mantináda enters as the punchline of the performance, often followed by comments and explanations. Several quotations included in this study reveal how a speaker may recite such verbal events in the middle of a conversation to illustrate his or her point.

The local people recollect many stories especially about those communicative situations where someone had the last word with a mantináda. They also like to tell stories about a sudden turn of events, which someone cleverly comments on by immediately producing a befitting mantináda. Moreover, people characterize and memorize other people through the mantinádes that are associated with them. These stories celebrate the individual's skill to improvise and reproduce the appraised values of his or her ready wit and dexterity in words, similarly to the referential citing of the mantinádes uttered in the past contexts when among the speech community.

> Kostas Kontoyannis, 1999 (991124):
>
> Once we were in the village, we were a *paréa* and we drank water from the spring: one bows down, drinks water, drinks the next; the moment when I bow – this happened in the reality – the spring stops! It was a spring, it was running water, and stops the spring, and I say:
>
> *Skífto sti vrísi ya neró / m' aftí me mia sterévgi*
> *Intá 'kama stzi míras mou / kakó ke me pedévgi?*
>
> I bow to the spring for water / but it runs dry at once
> What bad did I do to my fate / and she mocks me?
>
> We, that is, in Crete, we have the parable: "even if you go to the spring it will run dry", that is, you are unlucky and even if you go to a spring that runs, it will stop running. This happened to me."

Local folk musicians were important people in the villages because they most often were the center of the informal entertainment and *parées*. For example, an unmarried, self-taught *liráris* (lira-player) who had died about twenty years ago in the Village, was recollected by Agapi Moshovaki with the following story (010420). In the past, the Village had been notorious for its lack of water supplies, until the united village committee had water pipes constructed:

"A *paréa* who had also a lira, in the neighboring village, was making fun of our village. The other village's *liráris* said:

Kaló horió ín' ke (to Horió) / ma éhi éna psegádi
'Ospou na páne sto neró / tsouknóni to tsikáli

A good village is also the 'Village'/ but it has one shortcoming
Until they get to the water / the cooking-pot gets burnt

Then our village's *liráris* responds by saying:

To pos den éhome neró / den íne prosvolí mas
Kasída sto eláhisto / den éhi-i kefalí mas

That we don't have water / is not an insult for us
Dandruff, even a little / is not on our heads[2]

Our *liráris* then recites another mantináda, re-directing the blame and hinting that there are people in the other village who have dandruff, but Agapi does not remember the words of this mantináda.

The other *liráris*, from patrigroups named Katsamás, then replied:

To meraklídon ta hartiá / egó ta diorízo
Parákseno mou fénete / pos na mi se gnorízo

The cards of the merry-masters / are assigned by me
It looks odd to me / that I don't recognize you

And our *liráris* recited the following in response:

An thes na gnoristoúmene / na m' éhis to herió sou
Vres mou mia híra Katsamá / ná 'rhome sto horió sou!

If you want us to get familiar / and to have me in your hands
Find me a widow Katsamá[3] / and I will come to your village!

These stories and recollections reflect how people value situational improvisation and the capability of words to have a highly contextual meaning. At first, the event and the inventiveness of the words can be completely an insider experience, but the success in capturing the moment as an experience in a verbal repartee is truly cherished by Cretans, and therefore a story like this often becomes a permanent part of a person's repertoire.

---

2 My interlocutors explained that in those days, dandruff was thought to be a sign of poor hygiene, of not washing one's hair.
3 "Find me among your patrigroups a widow that I can marry." The Village's lira-player was a bachelor, and by improvising this utterance, he refers to the (in Crete) rather rare case of becoming a *sógambros*, a groom marrying into the village of his wife.

Just as people contextualize single poems as their own utterances and performances, people can adopt the stories of meaningful performances to reflect personal experiences. Once, when both I and my husband were present, we heard a mantináda bearing a striking resemblance to another, rather peculiar one we had heard before, concerning a man who had travelled around the world and then died of a bee sting the day he returned home; only this time, it was presented as an utterance of a mother, concerning the death of her child for the same reason. This experience cannot be verified because the first telling of the story had taken place in an unrecorded conversation, and neither of us could remember where. These kinds of recontextualizations could be expected even with these kinds of singular stories – especially in Crete, where both the stability and the re-formation of a text, as well as the acknowledgement of the situational meaning of a text, coexist so closely.

Presentation of poetic inventiveness

I introduced previously the presentation of a newly made poem as a performance. During my early fieldwork, I eagerly hunted for people's accounts of the socially significant recitations of poems that were improvised and contextualized. Although, as the previous presentation of the stories of past performances show, while people did appreciate such events, they gave them much less consideration than I had anticipated. Sometimes they even responded by taking a negative stance: in many districts of central Crete, as in the village Korfes near Iraklio, which is famous for its serious *parées* and quality mantinádes (see Papirakis 2004), people understood that I was referring to the habits associated with eastern Crete (Sitia particularly) of teasing, mocking or making fun with mantinádes, and made a point to clarify that that particular style was not much appreciated in their village. But could a poem be recited in a moment of daily life, outside the ritual singing events? They expressed that of course, if one had created or heard a good new poem, one could present it to others, for example, when going to the *kafenío*.

This makes evident how many Cretans, particularly performers and composers, conceptualize their talk about the mantinádes by turning to the aesthetic qualities and the story *incorporated into* the poem. They place importance on the individual poetic creativity and inventiveness, because for them, the end-product embodies a dialogic process. Furthermore, in addition to looking back to a certain performance, they look forward: they focus on the potentiality of the poems in future performances. Therefore the presentation and evaluation of the success in *capturing a theme* (for the definition, see Chapter 6) requires few words between those people who know each others' repertoire and performance history.

When I had assimilated this observation, which gave a more complex insight into the local evaluation of the poetic text, I also began to notice references made by the *mantinadolóyi* to the phenomenon of publicly "announcing" new poems. In September 2006, I explicitly asked Aristidis Heretis if he had felt an immediate need to announce a newly created poem.

He responded to my question by stating: "Think, when a baby is born, isn't it such a joy that you run around the village to tell it to everyone!? A poem born is like a baby born, you have to tell it to others!" (Fieldnotes September 9, 2006)

This "presentation of poetic inventiveness" is a discourse in which the individual ability to express oneself and to capture meaningful ideas, structures, and values of the surrounding reality and tradition in a poem is performed, received and evaluated without any necessary circumstantially contextualized frame. This discourse is a vital mode of being in the performance arena between the active composers and their immediate circles in Crete.

Performance as gendered and shared experience

Up until the time when the acoustic format of the *gléndi* was held, and the *parées* used to gather regularly, the ability to perform was a necessary skill at the feast and singing events. In what comes to the performance in *parées*, and in the singing in the *gléndi* in many areas of Crete, this applies especially for men. Musicians were all men and the singers in the *parées* were quite exclusively men. In fact, women were normally not allowed to learn to play musical instruments even if they wanted to: how could a woman play in male *parées*, stay up until the early morning hours, and possibly even travel from place to place? This was regarded as a direct path to a sinful life. (010422; 010430) Only the mandolin, which was popular in many areas and could be used for lyrical singing in one's home environment, was acceptable for women to play in some cases. In the mountain village of Anoya, people have told me that mandolin used to be played by many women, and that it is still played there. In 1997 in Rethimno, I interviewed an elderly woman, Tasia, who had come as a refugee with her family from Asia Minor in 1922 when she was two years old. She recounted that she had insisted so much on learning to play that she was allowed to do so in the end. She said that in addition to family occasions, she performed the mandolin and sung in the festive get-togethers of the local *kapí* ("center of occupation for the old people").[4] Tasia was, however, the only exception that I have heard about in Rethimno.

How women experienced and practiced poetic argumentation thus differed somewhat from how men did, particularly with regard to the male *parées*. In Chapter 3, it was noted that women did participate in the singing of mantinádes in the *gléndi*, particularly in the reciprocal challenges, and that in eastern Crete, women were important performers in the dance genres that consisted of improvised singing. Although women did not sing or play music in the *paréa*, they were excluded from these events only when they were exclusive male, *androparées*, which were more typical of some

---

4 These centers with their assembly halls are very active and they organize trips, for example, to various places of interest, *paniyíria*, monasteries and places of birth (for the refugees of Asia Minor).

A picnic trip to nature, typically organized on May Day. Thanasis Skordalos (1920–1998) on the lira, in the village of Spili. Photo private collection of Manolis Tzirakis.

villages and areas than of others. In other words, women were present in all major celebrations and in several other occasional celebrations, as can be seen in the photograph above and on pages 22, 94, 104. Of all the ritual events, *klídonas*, the midsummer feast, had its special rituals involving the mantinádes sung together by women and men. Anna Caraveli (1985) remarks that in Karpathos, women played a decisive role in the evaluation and re-performance of the poems sung in the *glêndi*: as attentive listeners, they evaluated the poetic and performative qualities of the poems sung and then decided what was valuable and worth remembering.

However, mantinádes were also sung in many other events, and some of these were especially the women's domain. For example, one exclusively female duty is the preparation of the bride and groom for a wedding, with mantinádes traditionally sung at each turn. Because lamenting in Crete uses the same metrical model of the rhyming couplet, many women who are often literally referred to as *piítries*, female poets, contributed to the poetic imagery and improvisation in this context.

Women were important performers and composers in the more intimate and conversational arenas, and several interlocutors have emphasized their poetic way of speech; in the old days, this everyday habit significantly supported their children's learning of the expressive principles of the register (see Chapter 6). Both sexes also cultivated the repartee in various communicational occasions of daily life. Local people do not report seeing any major gender-related difference in the talent to improvise or compose poems, but women are said to "know" more poems than men, and among the elderly, women are often acknowledged to have a much better command of words. This means that most people had a repertoire of mantinádes in their active memory; many interviewees claim that a person not knowing how "to say" a mantináda was an exception in the old days. New poems were actively collected in this repertoire. Especially the festive times served as important sources for new poems, because several mantinádes were performed then and the competitive tension contributing to the quality was intense. Furthermore, in addition to the poems people heard in their own village, sung either by the villagers themselves or by visiting musicians, they would also travel to other villages and there acquire new expressions, structures and repertoires to share with others in their own village. Despina and Agapi, as well as many other elder female interlocutors, have also said that young women would write the best poems down in their notebooks.

Participation, improvisation and meaning

During a performance, a poem can be composed on the spur of the moment, but even composers often recollect and use existing poems from their poetic reserve when they perform. All people actively connected to the tradition have a poetic reserve like this, a wealth of poems they have absorbed and memorized, which they reflect on creatively. With mantinádes – short, compact and incorporating a message in a linguistically independent image – memorization is often accurate. I will refer to this capability of storing and retrieving relevant poems from the memory "on the spur of the moment," as a *poem-memory*. It has been noted that a vast repertoire of poems is the basis for acquiring improvisational skills, but even people who cannot extemporize themselves are able to use the memorized poems fluently in a performance. In the following, I will analyze more closely the roles of ex tempore composition and the poem-memory as a means of engaging in a dialogue and in creating meaning in a performance.

In Chapter 2, I referred to Michael Herzfeld's article, *The Indigenous Theory of Meaning* (1981a), in which he establishes a semantic theory of the meaning of the mantinádes, basing it on an analysis of the commentary of his interlocutors in Rhodes. Drawing on my own experience of performances, local commentary and narratives of past performances, I have conceptualized four principal categories of meaning. Now that some examples of performances and commentary have been presented, these ideas can be analyzed closer. In Crete, the meaning of the mantinádes is explicitly or implicitly stated to lie in the following:

– the *performative, thematic continuity* between mantinádes: the poems adhere to the theme at hand;
– the *contextual relevance* of the poem performed. This relevance can be acknowledged in connection to the present situation or to a situation out of the immediate context;
– the creative *internal fitting* or textual manipulation of a mantináda, and
– the way a statement or an idea is incorporated into the imagery of the poem.

Thematic continuation

One of the most obvious statements made by my informants concerns the perception of meaning in the *continuity* between the mantinádes performed, that is, the *thematic connection* of the mantinádes recited in succession. This is the principle of meaningful communication with mantinádes and of disciplined communicational creativity. The notion of continuation, *sinéhia*, was emphasized to Herzfeld in Rhodes, to Caraveli (1982) in Karpathos, and to me in Crete, the thematic connection was underlined in all conversations in my fieldwork. Thematic connection means that the context of meaning is created in a performance and perceived in the intertextual context of the evolving dialogue. According to the basic rule, each singer in a singing event contributes to the current theme. During the course of the event, longer singing in turns in a *paréa* introduces new themes: continuation is demanded until the selected theme is naturally exhausted, as described by the singers. The conception consequently brings forth the significance of the performance as a dialogue. This suggests that such a performative verbal exchange has a value in and of itself.

Thematic continuation may be realized by varying methods. As a singer is required to reflect on a theme, the subject of speech, by a poem textually interconnected with it, a meaningful contribution can in most cases be made with a suitable poem selected from the singer's poem-memory. Since a singing event is always improvisatory by nature, I defined this act of "matching" as *contextual improvisation* (see p. 78).

In practice, thematic continuation is very often realized by repeating or reflecting on a *word* occurring in the previous poem or an idea embodied in the imagery already presented. This may be done in a congruent, questioning or contrasting way. The following example shows how common words can act as dynamic stimuli when they emerge in a poem, because they may lead one to the recognition of a certain theme even outside performative events. The example is an extract from one of the conversations I had with Despina and Agapi in the Village. This comment was recited by Agapi during our reading aloud of Despina's collection of her own compositions and of the poems she had heard, written down by hand (2001, 010430):

Despina: *Éfiyes díhos na mou pis / tou horismoú to yá sou*
Ma-i sképsi mou tha vrískete / pantotiná kontá sou

You left without saying to me / the good bye of **separation**
But (even so) my thought will / always be near you

Agapi: *O horismós íne varís / (léi) yatí afíni póno*
Ke propandós ótan skeftís / tis anamnísis móno

The **separation** is hard / because it leaves pain
And above all when you think of / only the memories

By selecting the word "separation," the poem continues to develop the same theme. Agapi's poem, however, implies a crucial displacement in the mood of the poetic self and in the level of argumentation: after the poem recited prior to this one, relevant to the situation only regarding our efforts to read the poems from the handwritten sheets, the poem cited by Agapi reflects a personal, philosophical conception of life. She could, nonetheless, have reflected on the theme only on the basis of a lexical association with no further deeper relevance, which is the case in the following example. Here, she seizes upon the expression of number included in one of the poems in a letter composed by Despina to a friend whom she had not seen for a long time (010430):

Despina: *'Ikosi hrónia eklísane / perásan ta triánda
pou s' ého mesa stin kardiá / k' ekí tha s' ého pánta*

Twenty years came full / **thirty** years have passed
That I have you in my heart / and there I'll have you always

Agapi: *Triánta mines s' agapó / yínonde pénte hrónia
Ke lemoniá na fíteva / tha étroga lemoniá*

Thirty months I love you / they'll become five years
Even if I had planted a lemon tree / I'd now eat lemons

The movement within the continuum of general–personal is recurrent. Although individuality and surprise are major pillars for successful communication throughout the register, solely the pull of the thematic continuity attracts both spontaneous associations and dialogic reactions.

Statements/ideas enclosed in the imagery

As was stated above, a thematic connection can be made by citing a poem that contains a relevant image, which Herzfeld called an *eternal truth*, referring to an experience shared by the singer and his audience. These images are "philosophy in the flesh"[5]: they express moral values, a general philosophy of life, or deliberations on themes such as love, friendship, sorrow, death or luck, which carry an intrinsic value and a potential of being adapted in the recurrent situations of human life. In understanding the value of such statements, shared cultural values play a major role: first, they justify such self-expression as a culturally valid way of speaking and matching emotions with the poems as a creative endeavor; second, they show that the register is not simply a mode and form of performance, but that it is also an archive of attitudes, norms, believes and hopes. These images can be used authoritatively or metaphorically as a vehicle to describe the situation or the personal emotional state, or to create an atmosphere. As composers have explained, most of these mantinádes are not composed on the spur of the

---

5 I refer to the title of the book: *Philosophy in the flesh. The embodied mind and its challenge to Western thought* by George Lakoff and Mark Johnson (1999; New York : Basic Books).

moment in a performance, but at other times (for additional information on this topic, see the following chapter).

In a singing event, a poem containing a certain image may be interjected only for performative reasons: to fulfill the need of thematic continuation. Or, it may be used to express an intentional statement or a point of view. Whether the meaning then is shared depends much on how the poem corresponds to the receiver's/hearer's own experience (age group, depth of the repertoire of poems, knowledge of the performance history), feelings, or the current life situation. For example, a young man in love will not find substantial meaning in an old man's philosophic verses about death and loss, and vice versa, as is made explicit in the following comments:

> Kostas Kontoyannis, 1999 (991124):
>
> A poem can be good for you, but not for me. If I have not felt the same, it does not touch me; it does not speak to me. But it can fit your experience; it can speak to you.

> Kostoula Papadoyanni, 2008 (080930):
>
> I can't say that this is good, it is strong, or how much it can touch people – or **which** people, because, other people like those of love, other those of separation...

The perception of meaningfulness in the imagery – and the evaluation of the poem – will thus commonly take place through a personal feeling of sharing of the experience or idea indicated by the imagery. Active poets and regular performers, however, will also evaluate the *potentiality* of the poem and its imagery, and they will therefore also perceive the meaning at an abstract level of creativity, even as being outside the realm of their own experiences. These concerns will become more concrete in the following chapter.

Contextual relevance

Meaning can be perceived in the external *contextual relevance*, which can be either present, or out of the immediate context. In this case, the meaning of a poem recited or sung is perceived with regard to how it refers to or comments on the current social situation, or how it alludes to any other situation or event which is familiar and relevant to the audience. The communicative utterances therefore build connections between the text and the context, possibly also between the implied earlier texts, situations or performances. These poems can be memorized or composed extempore: references can be bound in the text, or the citation of a poem can activate a shared memory.

References have the power to evoke very different kinds of referents that are in dialogue with the present moment. For instance, they can be explicit textual indications of or references to the current situation or to an earlier performance or poem. Another possibility is that references are metonymic in nature, deriving extra-textual meaning from the tradition. An example of this will be cited in Chapter 6: an argument of not wanting to play cards is based on the common saying that winning in card games means misfortune in love. As is certainly typical in all verbal traditions, the metonymy embedded in the code-switching is a common marker and creator of the atmosphere.

Internal fitting

In several cases, direct comments and contextually relevant references can be made very skillfully through contextual improvisation, but it is in the direct suggestions and in the explicit, context-sensitive manipulations of the existing texts – which Herzfeld refers to as the creative *internal fitting* of a mantináda – where actual textual improvisation plays a characteristic role.

Internal fitting is chiefly connected to the performative situation, just like making an external reference, but the meaning is now conveyed through the explicit manipulation of *textual* elements; particularly, this involves making morphological and lexical changes to the text presented immediately before, or to another text that is known to be part of the shared repertoire. As a result, meaning is produced through the intertextual play between the present mantináda and a past or preceding mantináda with an explicit and intentional manipulation of the textual components: in effect, this can be done either by using the components of the previous mantináda in a witty manner to create a contrast in the meaning, or by delicately modifying well-known verses and metaphors. In the internally created context, alterations in the form of a known or previously stated text can create a subtle play between the original and changed contexts. Often enough, these alterations are motivated by reproducing the effects of humor, irony or ridicule, as in the following example provided by Herzfeld (1985a: 142):

> A young Glendiot man had gone to the lowland village of Voriza, a place despised by Glendiots as merely agricultural and a good place to raid without fear of retaliation. The locals started to goad the Glendiot youth with suggestions that he should marry into their village. Irritated, he announced:
>
> Kallia 'kho na me thapsoune stsi asfendias ti riza
> Better-I-would-be to-be-buried at the asphodel's root
> Para na paro kopelia na' ne 'pou ta Voriza!
> Than to take a girl who is from Voriza!
>
> An old Voriza woman, standing nearby, heard the verse and replied:
>
> Kallia 'kho na me thapsoune se mia khiroskatoula
> Better-I-would-be to-be-buried in a puddle-of-pig-shit
> Para na paris kopelia na 'ne Vorizopoula
> Than that-you-should-take a girl who is a Voriza-girl

Adapted to the same formulaic structure, the famous romantic image of "asphodel's root" is turned into the vulgar "puddle-of-pig-shit;" and the way of stating the "girl-from-Voriza" is transformed lexically. The irony in the woman's immediate verbal dexterity is poignant (Herzfeld 1985a: 142–143).

These cases of internal fitting exploit as well as create formulaic patterns. Much of the humorous material I have heard tends to be constructed using modifiable patterns, or the poems play with recurrent metaphors like in the example above. The following examples were quoted by Yorgos Sifakis (041110) while describing to me how teasing and mocking used to be particularly common in Sitia:

>Ta portokália tou horioú / yemízoune vapóri
>O,ti skatá 'ne-o próedros / íne ke-i psifofóri

>The oranges of the village / fill up a motor boat
>The same shit with the president / are the ones who vote

>Stin páno bánda tsi koprés / fitrónoun i domátes
>O,ti skatá 'ne-o kafetzís / íne ke i pelátes

>Up above the dung / sprout up the tomatoes
>The same shit with the café-owner / are also the customers

This type of formulating communicative significance through the conscious manipulation of a text seems to occur rarely today. Evidently, this type is connected to the impulsive, humorous styles, to textual improvisation and to the face-to-face situations in closely-knit communities to a degree that is rarely represented in contemporary society. The communicational units that are improvised during the dance, in extemporized singing events and in situational commentary, have certainly taken full advantage of this factor and displayed it. Furthermore, one must keep in mind that communicative frames may differ widely in the different parts of Crete. These frames may also vary among the specific groups within each community, such as gender and age. Moreover, it is essential to consider these verbal arguments with respect to the aspect of the insider/outsider.

Written and media contexts

The most apparent poetic experiences of the mantinádes include the interaction and coexistence of oral and written texts, together with the orientation towards writing down poems. Today, in all age groups engaging in poetic language, the typical result is fully or mainly orally composed couplets, which then circulate in written form through mediated contexts. The television and radio broadcasts focusing on mantinádes and Cretan music as their primary subject are popular, and mantinádes are widely circulated as text messages sent by mobile phones among friends and relatives. These poems naturally operate in very different contextual arenas than those in the tightly-knit oral village societies. Today, composition can also be a hobby even for those people who were not immersed in the traditional poetic expression in their formative years, and for them, composition depends much more on writing. Oral arenas, however, existed in the recent past, and the traditional context of communicating with mantinádes is a current experience for many Cretans. Consequently, the value of a poem as a text is completed and enriched through the dialogic relationship with their tradition and their traditional ways of performing.

Written arenas

In Crete, the oral and literary have lived in an intertextual relation for a long time. This is evident from the mixed oral and literary origins of Cretan poetry, from the influence of the widely known *Erotókritos* romance and of a parallel narrative composition technique in rhyming couplets (*rímes*). Poetry is, perhaps, more susceptible to being written down than prose, due to the emphasis on the metrical form and the significance of the completed form for meaning, which are obligatory for poems. For example, in Crete, anecdotes are also featured as a particularly cherished and versatile genre, but although collections of anecdotes exist, people do not show a similar degree of motivation for their preservation.

Conversations with elderly women make explicit that mantinádes have been written down and collected in notebooks by young women for as long as writing has been possible. I first saw one of these notebooks in 1997 when my language teacher at the University of Rethimno brought me her mother's notebook to look at, when I had asked her about mantinádes. Later, both Agapi and Despina mentioned to me that their old notebooks had disappeared when they had been loaned to other girls. Some women have told me that in the old days, young men and women would write small notes in the form of a mantináda on a piece of paper, which could then be hidden in a secretly agreed place under a stone or delivered by a messenger. Engaged couples could keep in touch by exchanging love-letters: Despina, for example, had created her own mantinádes for her fiancé, and he had asked his cousin, Agapi, and other female relatives for help in order to write his own letters.

Today, both female and male composers write their verses down in notebooks. I have asked several informants why this written record of one's own and others' poems is regarded as being so important, and people are unanimous in their answers: to preserve them, not to lose them; to hand them down to their grandchildren. Such a "text-centered" attitude surprised me at first, but it appears rather that the question itself is ill-founded. Why indeed would the preservation of oral poetry be different from the written in a society where most people can read and write? This is probably the most crucial point in which any educated Westerner will have to be aware of how certain attitudes of artistic creativity and "pure" orality are inevitably contextualized in our minds. However, putting a mantináda into writing has never been regarded as a performance, but a way of storing – unlike in the communities and epic traditions where written versions of texts seem to have contributed to the idea of the existence of one "correct" version, with the result that the versatile oral performance has been eroded (Lord 1960: 124–138).

I have already referred at length to this logic of action and storing when discussing the collections and the local way of reading them in order to charge the poetic reserve. By Cretans who perform and compose, the printed poems are approached essentially as material which can be learned for situational improvisation and which give inspiration for composition. Contemporary composers print collections where poems are invariably divided into categories according to their theme. The theme, indeed, is the immediate *context* and the larger organizing principle for storing the poems, although, to an outsider, it looks as if it were completely context-less.

When television substituted the paréa

Today, face-to-face get-togethers for singing are organized only by the people most dedicated to Cretan music and mantinádes, but television and radio programs provide an easily approachable mass media parallel. For example, the most popular talk show in Crete is hosted by Yorgos Vitoros on the local "Créta" channel, and that show is broadcasted during the winter season from Tuesday to Saturday during the peak viewing hours, from 8:00 to 10:00 pm. During the summer, reruns are scheduled. The show's basic subjects are Cretan music, musicians, mantinádes, the *mantinadolóyi*, the latest anecdotes, as well as various current events, feasts and topics concerning Crete. Watching the show is one of the most popular regular pastimes in Crete today.

New mantinádes are the core subject of the show, and in every broadcast, a prewritten mantináda in presented as the theme of the following broadcast. When the show first started to provide these themes for the audience's contributions (at the time of my stay in the village), only the first *dekapentasíllavo* verse of a mantináda was presented, and people were asked to add a second verse. Towards the end of the broadcast, the original second verse would be revealed. Since this practice proved to be problematic in many ways, it was changed to reciting a full poem and the authorship was then announced. Currently in each episode, one poem (given in the previous broadcast) provides the theme, and the viewers are then asked to send in their own poems, which are composed around this theme, before or during the show as text messages, or they call in and recite their verses live. Vitoros, the talk-show host, reads these poems aloud, and sometimes he exchanges a few words with those who call (many are recurrent participants), but poems are not evaluated further.

Now, opinions about the "Vitoro" vary. The show has very good ratings and many Cretans view it only in an extremely positive light. The show's host, Vitóros, has played an important role in presenting and commemorating local musicians and *mantinadolóyi*, and he has worked with charitable cases as well. The show has also provided a performance arena for a number of talented poets to actively develop their skills, and I will refer to an individual case of this in the chapter on composition. There are those, however, who find the show's excessively popularizing style and the commercialization of the composition to be a problem. This is because all poems, whether good, mediocre or bad, are praised alike, which distorts the conception of a mantináda and leads people who do not have talent falsely to believe that they do. The supporters of the show feel that the themes presented stimulate people to compose and, in the course of time, these participants may become better composers, while the critics argue that a composition has to stem naturally from the composer's experience, and not be commercially forced. In my experience, most of those who are of the latter opinion are musicians and other people who were brought up in a traditional environment and consequently those who still have access to singing performance arenas, while those who eagerly participate in the show are people who would otherwise have no means of entering public arenas. This division, however, is not conclusive, because many experienced, improvising composers also participate on the show. Women in particular have taken an active role in all these contemporary arenas where traditional gender roles regarding the use of the public space do not exist.

For the sake of objectivity, I would like to say that the performative rules of singing events persist in these modern arenas in several ways. Just like in a singing event, a theme is introduced and the participants respond to it; the thematic organization of participation thus continues. However, references cannot work the same as they would in a face-to-face situation, and the evaluation of creativity is blurred. In this sense, a television show, where every message and phone call (as well as viewer ratings) is money, works entirely unlike the real performance arenas: both competent and less competent composers now participate in the same virtual *paréa* without immediate feedback. This means that everyone is brought on the very same level, and the village criticism, which would prevent people not capable of communicative repartee from appearing in public, does not intervene. Whether this is a loss or an advantage is up to the perceiver. On the other hand, the audience faces a situation very much like that in a real singing event, and it can evaluate, discuss and store the poems which are judged worthy of it. Another essential change is that the imagery becomes much more focused in a situation that downplays the immediate textual references that work in face-to-face communication.

Mobile phone messages

Today, mobile phones are not only used for sending compositions as text messages to television and radio broadcasts, newspaper columns and to an occasional competition; composers, friends and family members also use mobile phones extensively to exchange mantinádes in text messages. Indeed, mantinádes seem almost to be made for this medium, being perfect by size and by their nature as independent utterances. I was recently told that Cretan students have introduced the composition of couplets to university communities all over Greece: young people may, for example, improvise an invitation to go out in poetic form. Instead of the old means of writing, for example, on paper napkins, today people also use the mobile phone memory to archive their compositions and the significant poems they have heard. All these contemporary practices will be discussed in more detail in the following chapter.

Individual and shared: problems implied by the double-identity in modern arenas

While the poems are thus at the same time recognized as individually composed texts and as free material to adopt for situational contextualization, it is quite evident that their introduction into the modern arenas is not entirely problem-free. Particularly, the anonymity of composed poetry, a natural characteristic of oral tradition, becomes a problem when moving from the oral uses of poems and songs to their commercial uses in business, where the composer is not the one who benefits from them financially. The problem is that the nature of the tradition, where anyone can take and perform anybody else's poem, has been used as an excuse for copyright violations by many recording musicians, producers and publishers. The Cretan record industry and in general the Greek record industry have, until very recently, had nearly non-existing information on record sleeves about the performers, composers and other participants. During the early decades of recorded Cretan music, most name musicians continued what had been common practice in oral performances: the verses they performed were composed for them by someone else. Musicians would thus publish lyrics they had not composed under their own name on the record sleeve. Because everyone created mantinádes, it was not regarded as anything special and in line with the traditional oral performance, the owner of this performance was the musician. Mitsos Stavrakakis and Yorgos Karatzis were two of the first named mantináda-poets: in the 1980s, they started to demand that their names be mentioned in connection with their poems. Both can refer to many cases in which this was not done properly, however (991202).[6] Only very recently have the poets gained the rights to have their names published with their verses and to get paid, although as Yorgos Sifakis explained to me, *mantinadolóyi* still do not get copyright compensation, which all goes to the musician who has made the recording (041110).

Another problem, where economic harm plays a lesser role but which represents a strange type of pride, is that people may send mantinádes composed by others to radio and television programs under their own name. In fact, this is a recurrent practice. When other peoples' mantinádes are exchanged, for example, by mobile phone as text messages, they most often circulate without any mention of the original composer; someone picks up a poem he or she likes and presents it as his or her own. But, as Sifakis remarks, "That's how it is, this [the mixed character of the individual and the shared] is the nature of the Cretan tradition" (0411110).

---

6 During the past few decades, both have also made their own records.

VI Composition

This chapter will elaborate on several aspects of composition. Since composition is such a significant experience in the mantinádes tradition, and because poems are acknowledged as individual creations, I will let the composers speak for themselves and allow space for their quoted contributions. These quotations and examples are taken chiefly from conversations with two contemporary composers, with whom I had the opportunity to talk at length and in depth on these matters. I believe that they are more commonly representative because, as will become evident, these descriptions also reflect the conversations between the poets themselves. Drawing from a larger body of conversations, I will address the questions of how one internalizes the tradition and starts to compose; how the structure and meaning may be developed; and the kinds of motives people have presented for composition. The longer quotations provide examples of how composers describe the composition process, what it means to them, and how they talk about the poems among themselves.

Internalizing the tradition

Kostoula Papadoyanni, 2004 (040720):

I started (to compose) when I came to the village – I was eighteen years – to take care of my grandmother who was in her 80s then. My grandmother spent time with other old women – I had lots of live "hearings" (*akoúsmata*). During these years, being eighteen years old, a young woman is very sensitive to love and emotions. So, to me, that time was very positive and I was like a sponge that absorbs everything. The old women sang poems, stories as songs, old songs. As they did not know to read and write, they told them with their mouths, and from one mouth to the other, the tradition went on. That's also how I, in the beginning, I tried to hold in my mind some things. What was positive then is that I read the *Erotókritos*, since I had a lot of time. That was the most significant: that was the beginning.

Kostoula Papadoyanni, September 2009. Photo by the author.

In Crete, less than thirty years ago, most children heard mantinádes recited in their home environments and they heard them sung especially in the *glédi*, and boys also listened to them in the *parées*. Most adult male interviewees emphasize the significance of the *glédi* and *paréa* for listening to poems and for learning them. As has been discussed in Chapter 5, male and female experiences differed, since women did not participate in the singing *paréa* as a pastime; if a woman attended one, she would normally be there to listen. By contrast, the *glédi* was open to all members of society, and the pronounced attraction to the *glédi* as a source of repertoire is due to the framed focus on a verbal exchange and on the competitive atmosphere. For men, singing in musical *parées* was a casual way to practice and to become more competent. Despite the primary focus on the singing in the *glédi* and *paréa*, many adult composers and musicians noticed that usually there was a close female relative, a mother or grandmother, who was extremely verbally talented and poetic in her speech style, and that she was the one who fostered the child's interest and special love for the tradition. For a child who was being initiated into the world of poems and music, the home environment often served as an emotional anchor to the tradition. Nonetheless, to be able to build up a repertoire and to later gain in competence, these were more easily acquired in the specific environment of the *paréa* and *glédi*.

Repartee in communicative situations, although enthusiastically recalled by several adults, is rarely mentioned as contributing significantly in the learning process. One natural reason for this is the different semantic character of the poems recited ex tempore in situational speech communication and in the *gléndi*. The former are based on quick interpretations of the situations and social relations, whereas in a *gléndi*, the basic repertoire also contained a fair amount of more easily contextualized and absorbed material. When I asked the primary school children in the Village in 1999 (991013/1) if they had heard mantinádes from older people, they hesitated. Then one boy explained to me: *"they are difficult and I can't learn them."* Although the sources that the children currently use to learn poems are rather different from what they used to be (books and recorded material), I believe that this "difficulty" concerns especially the capturing of the situated, improvised meaning.

Children who practice composition must first practice the form, as the semantic contents develops later. An illustrative example of this is the following set of two conversations that took place during a day I interviewed the primary school children in the Village in September 1999. In the first example, I speak with an 11-years-old boy, Nikos (991013/1), and in the following, I speak with Manolis, a young self-taught musician in his twenties, in the presence of Nikos (991013/2).

In this village primary school, the favorite theme of all the boys had turned out to be the *"ya tis pérdikes"* (about the partridges). In Greek folk poetry, the most common game bird, the partridge, is a well-known symbol of a girl at a marriageable age and she is desired and "hunted," but like the partridge, she is difficult to get. All mantinádes on the partridges center on this metaphor. We had the following conversation which occurred first at school:

(Nikos)	– Let me tell you about "partridges"!
	Poté mou se mia pérdika / den épeksa dio bálles
	M' aftí íne diaforetikí / ke tha tis pékso ke-álles
	Towards a single partridge / I never shoot two bullets
	But this one is different / and I'll also shoot others
	Did you understand?
(V)	– *A partridge, basically, is ...*
(Nikos)	– A bird!
(V)	– Yes, but it is much used... (as a metaphor, I wanted to continue)
(Nikos)	– Yes, yes, they eat it, they eat it...!

The conversation immediately turned to hunting: Nikos now explained to me enthusiastically that he has a gun and that he could kill birds.

Some hours later, Nikos and I continued the conversation with Manolis, a self-taught local musician, at the latter's home across the street.

(V)	– *Which theme do you like most?*
(Manolis)	– The most beautiful theme is that of the partridges.
(V)	– *The children also told me many poems on that theme.*
(Manolis)	– The partridges, of course... every partridge has also one girl in what it says... it doesn't tell, it doesn't mean partridge, the bird, it is a girl... *léei*:

> *Pos na ksamóso pérdika / poú 'ne zevgaroméni*
> *Afóu katého-o horismós / pliyí 'ne pou de yéni*
>
> How can I approach a partridge / one who has a mate?
> Since I know that separation / is a wound that doesn't heal
>
> – They are strong mantinádes, it has strong meaning.

At this point, Níkos recited again the same mantináda that he had presented before:

> Towards a single partridge / I never shoot two bullets
> But this one is different / and I'll also shoot others

Manolis was clearly amused by the young boy's inability to understand the full metaphoric weight of the poem, so Manolis himself now plays with the double meaning:

> *Akloútha mou stis pérdikes / na máthis na ksamónis*
> *Yatí 'se akóma atzamís / ke práma de skotónis!*
>
> Follow me to the partridges / to learn to approach
> Since you're still a beginner / and able to kill nothing!

Growing up in a productive oral tradition means that one is given the tools to try to compose. Some contemporary composers state that they had practiced composition when they were young school children by making poems that "did not yet mean anything," whereas others, although declaring being keenly attracted by mantinádes, music and dance already at an early age, started composing much later. This whole process of taking an interest and learning to compose can happen suddenly even at an older age, but most often this occurs in one's early twenties; the most commonly cited reason to start to compose is emotional stress (see Kostoula's description above and also Mitsos Stavrakakis' description in Chapter 1). In the following, Kostoula Papadoyanni comments on some of the typical aspects of the composer's initial and subsequent steps (080930):

> I want to say to you that many things pass by – you can say something to me in prose words without it touching me, without my thinking about it. I can hear one mantináda, and it makes me happy! I can hear one mantináda and cry for two days.
>
> (V) *It is these images that move you...*
>
> /(K) The images, the images!
>
> (V) *The poetic form opens even with its form a door to another world*
>
> (K) And you enter that world, and when you enter, you speak, express yourself, you think with mantinádes...you dedicate...You see now that I spoke to you about the wishes, if I want to write something for any

feast, I write it with mantináda – because, because that shows exactly what I feel, to the other one, I make him understand that.

And that is something, like, like *infectious*, that is, when we two (female) friends talk something and start the mantinádes, then, the other girl will also enter this world and collects, eh, she as well collects mantinádes, and at some moment she will try to create, she as well tries to write, because we have this thing inside us, here in Crete we have this inside ourselves.

(V) *Do you have (female) friends who are engaged in?*

(K) Yes, I do! Certainly, I have friends who are engaged in, after a period of time, you understand at some moment: me, I can also create mantinádes! Later, of course, you are very selective, that is, you start to discard some, and you want the best ones – you want those that have the greatest image – you see?! Just like a painter starts to make a straight line, an oblique line, when he is a small child, and ends up making a perfect painting, that's the way with the mantináda as well!

A significant part of Kostoula's own process of practicing composition and developing her skills now takes place through her participating in the "Vitoro's" talk show which was described in Chapter 5. During the winter 2005, she started to tape-record the broadcasts at home, to study intensively those mantinádes that she liked, and to compose her own poems around the themes discussed. However, after a while, she also sent in her poems under a pseudonym. Because these poems were good, during one show Vitoros had asked their sender to phone and reveal who he was, which Kostoula did. That way Kostoula became a frequent participant with her poems. She has described to me how a competitive, dialogic relationship between some of the regular participants has been constructed and how this urges her to make all the more expressive poems, as well as how, in some cases, these dialogues have continued through mobile phone messages or in live situations between her and other participants (080930; 091030). In the continuation, Kostoula also became one of the composers whom Vitoros asks to create poems for specific themes beforehand, to display a theme for the following broadcast. Examples of these dialogues will follow.

Local definitions of composition

I have discussed throughout this work the fact that although textual improvisation is, and is recognized as a separate skill, it is not the only appreciated form or even a central form of composition or performance for the wide range of uses of register. The verbs used for creating[1] poems indicate this. The most common verb is: *vgázo* (take off/out) and today, *gráfo* (write); the verb *ftiáhno* (make) can be used, and the verbs *teriázo* (match/fit

---

1 With the exception of the verb "to write," which can be directly translated, in this work I have used the verbs to create, and to compose to gloss these local expressions.

together) and in eastern Crete, the verb *katevázo* (bring/pull/put/get/take down) have been cited to me as well. The most common verb, *vgázo*, just like the verbs *katevázo* and *teriázo*, point to the individual activity of using a personal fantasy creatively to capture something from the existing reality; to seize or to match a lexical unit of something that is available but not yet discovered. Although these terms can point to ex tempore composition, they do not make explicit when the composition takes place. Ex tempore composition is often characterized by supplementary definitions, like *epí tópou* (on the spot).

The use of the verb *gráfo* is inspired by the written performances and today it often denotes (apart from the actually written oral poems) the process of composition, which is completely or highly oral, although the poems are preferably written down and often performed in written arenas. The following examples illustrate this:

Despina Papadaki, 2001, (010329)

> V: *You (say you) write, but first you have them in your mind, and then you write?*
> D: The mind writes them like the tape-recorder!
> V: *Because I don't think anyone writes it like that, word-by-word...*
> D: No, first you think them and then you write.

Kostas Kontoyannis, 1999, (991124)

> V: *You write?*
> K: I may not write it immediately but the *mantináda* which I compose, I remember it, because I compose it myself.
> V: *You do not however sit down on a chair to write...?*
> K: No! Nobody can do that! To sit down and to say: now I write. Always, like I told you, first you have to be influenced by something, and that moment when you are influenced, you create the *mantináda*.

Kostoula Papadoyanni, 2004, (040727)

> A mantináda is not a set up thing, that means, you cannot say: write me this! Sometimes people say me: make a mantináda! I want this kind of mantináda, they tell me! And I say: tell me roughly the story, you know, just like, in order to play a role in the theater, the actors have to go into the skin of the role, like we say, eh? To come to the place of the person who made this thing, and not to remember that I am Kostoula, but to go into the skin of the other one to convey it better. I can't make a mantináda if you ask it – I will, but I first have to get into your emotional world, that is, to understand what you felt that moment and what you want to say. And since you can't say it, I will say it!
>
> (V) *This means that you will create a mantináda while alone, or can it come to you when...?*
>
> (K) Most often when I'm alone but when I am with company, as well, I don't have a problem, when I am in a company, I can. It's not necessary to sit down somewhere; I can do that also when I drive! This winter

when we were picking olives, my *koumbára* (the wedding sponsor) had her feast (name day), and I was picking olives but meanwhile I create the images – what to send to her, to congratulate her – although I was making another work, and when in the end, the wishes took form in my mind, I went to the car, I took a piece of paper and wrote down the wishes, and then, sent them as a message with the mobile phone.

(V) *And when do you write, only when it is ready? You don't sit down with an idea and write...?*

(K) No, in my mind I create it, in my mind. Just if it is a song, just if I want to write a long history, because I don't remember, when I start with the first couple of verses, that is, I can now write the first couplet, then however, then you bind it, with the *dekapentasíllavo*, I can forget the first one! And so, necessary, that is when I sit down and I say: I'll write a song about Vera whom I got to know...I'll sit down and start to write. So I will write it on a paper. I might make some small changes, but very few, since it comes, slowly, slowly to my mind, like an image, and I write, write, write and go on, that way.

As the above examples demonstrate, all these composers view the composition process primarily as a form of mental activity during which the poem is formulated in their minds.

Rhyming and structuring the verse order

End rhyme plays an emblematic role in the mantinádes. Several poets are unable to analyze what in fact happens when a poem is being created in their mind, but those who do, most often point to two alternatives: what the poet captures first is either the rhyme words, or one full verse (the first or the second).

Kostoula Papadoyanni, 2008 (080930)

(V) *Do mantinádes come to you completed, or, like that, that you first have, let's say, half a mantináda or an image?*

/(K) No, they do not come completed.

/(V) *Do you first have an idea...?*

/(K) Yes!

/(V) *...an end rhyme?*

/(K) An end rhyme, other times I get first the first verse, you know, the first two lines[2], sometimes I get the last two lines. Other times I get the end rhyme lines, the second and the fourth, so that I know that it will become a mantináda, that way.

---

2 I will keep in the translation the difference between the verse and the line corresponding to one full *dekapentasíllavo* verse (verse) and half verse, the octosyllable or heptasyllable hemistiches of the verse (line), because in this description, Kostoula uses the typical tetrapartite conceptualization of the poem in which the hemistiches of one full *dekapentasíllavo* are regarded as two lines.

(V) *Some have told me, Despina as well, that she always has to have the end rhyme first and then it becomes...*

/(K) Yes, that also happens, that happens most often, that is, you have to have the end rhyme – that takes place when you are asked to create a mantináda, that helps – In fact these two words, the last of the second verse, and the last of the fourth, that is the foundation of the mantináda. When you have that – how we build a house and we always have to have the pillars to lay the foundation, they are the pillars of the mantináda, these two words, so that you can have the end rhyme. And when you have the end rhyme, your mind is confined then to the rest of the syllables – then, you make the image. When you have these two words, then your soul cooperates with your mind and they create an image. You see.

(V) *Do you have an example in mind now?*

(K) There was, that mantináda I told you about the friends, that was a very characteristic mantináda, which I was asked to create for the friendship, about friends, and I created – look – not an image, but a feeling, that I, I want to have my friends when I go through difficult moments and not when I go through good moments. That was the basic meaning. That was the basic emotion, which I as Kostoula, wanted that from my friend. I said how I want my friend to be; I like him to be that way. Fine, how can we then say that the friend, I want him in bad moments and not those that are good, and I say:

> *Egó tous fílous tous metró / més' tis zoïs tis bóres*
> *Ke-óhi monáha stis harés / ke stou glendioú tis óres*
>
> I measure friends / during the storms of life
> And not only in joys / and during the hours of a feast

You see? That's it. Thus, there came the storms (*bóres*), then the hours (*óres*), you know, all that together with the feeling that this is the way I want my friends.

The need to find the rhyme words beforehand is particularly apparent in the cases of textual improvisation:

Yorgos Sifakis, 2004 (041110):

With the mantináda, basically I think of the theme, the theme and then, I think the two words, to make the end-rhyme – today at midday there was a *paréa* here (in his tavern *Mesostráti* in Rethimno) and there were two girls who had gotten their degrees, and they were drinking cups of *rakí*, they ate, there were their parents and other people. One girl was from (the island of) Hios (accusative form Hío) – from Hio, note – and they said she works in the Town Hall in Pireus. They drank *raki*, we sang mantinádes – she said to me: will you say a mantináda to me? I asked: where are you from? From Hio(s), she said, and someone else added: and she works in the Town Hall (*dimarhío*) in Piréus. So, I say:

Thá 'rtho mia méra na se vró / mésa sto Dimarhío
Na dó-an doulévis í masás / mastíha ap' ti Hío!

I will come one day to find you / in(side) the Town Hall
To see whether you are working or chewing / mastic[3] from Hios!

Well, I glued these elements...

V: *That is, you always have to have the two words in your mind, to make the end rhyme?*

Y: Not always, there's another beginning as well, to start with a theme, that is of course when – when the mantináda is spontaneous, you always have to have the two words in your mind, to say it at that moment, let's say, you have to, you can't wait to search, you have to say it at that moment, to glue it, eh – but when you create a mantináda in peace and quiet, there it is different, because you can concentrate on a theme. There, very basically, the theme plays a role.

The above descriptions demonstrate how, at the moment of the situational ex tempore composition, composers are very aware of the rhyme words, whereas at other times, other poetic elements come more to the fore in the organization of the working memory.

The other case presented by Kostoula above is that one full verse, quite complete, comes to mind first and this can be either the first or the second verse in the finished poem. Often, however, this idea-verse is a strong, declarative verse, which is typically what the second, conclusive verse is. After a suitable rhyme word is found, the first, leading verse is constructed to correspond with the second, as in the next example:

In September 2006, Kostoula told me an example of an unusually bothersome verse (fieldnotes September 5, 2006). She had listened to the sound of a big sea shell put to her ear, and that experience had turned into one, full *dekapentasíllavo* verse:

San to kohíli pou kratá / tis thálassas ton ího

Like the sea shell that holds /- of the sea - the sound

This is a beautiful, melodic verse, which Kostoula liked and did not want to change. She was, however, immediately facing a major problem: the word *íhos*, sound, only rhymes logically with the word *tíhos*, wall. Wall, on the other hand, is hardly a suitable rhyme word in verse, but Kostoula was determined not to change the word order of the original line. However, she told that she could not get rid of the verse, and in the end it took a turn by itself, the word *kohíli* (sea shell) placed itself now at the end of the verse, rhyming with the word *híli*, lips, which resulted in the following poem:

---

3 The island of Hios is well-known for its mastic, a resin obtained from the mastic tree (Pistacia lentiscus) and used in the production of chewing gum and sweats.

Krató to káthe s'agapó / pou lén' ta dio sou híli,
osán kratá tis thálassas / ton ího to kohíli

I hold every "I love you" / uttered by your lips,
Like the sea-shell holds / the sound of the sea
(= Like holds-of the sea- / the sound-the sea shell)

Inventing meaning through rhyme

The above cited example demonstrates how the process of establishing the rhyme can affect the substance of the message. I will mention yet another illustrative example provided by Despina Papadaki (010401):

Once, having finished a meal with her family in a recently opened new *kéndro*, Despina wanted to thank the landlord, Vitóros. She latched onto the rhyme words: *Vitóros – servitóros* (waiter) in her mind, and immediately produced the following mantináda (these key words end with an *o* both in the vocative and accusative forms):

Na zísis na to hérese / to kéndro sou, Vitóro
Ma mi skeftís kamiá forá / n'alláksis servitóro

May you live long and rejoice / your *kéndro*, Vitóro
But may it never occur to you / to change the waiter!

Despina elaborated on the second line:

> So that the verse would fit! But Vitóros was really pleased about the complement about the waiter and said: Did they take *so* good care of you...!? The verse would not fit otherwise, but the boy [waiter] was also very good, and so two works were made at once!"

These poems reveal how experimental the creativity can be in an ex tempore composition process. The meaning is invented in a very short feedback time; in this case, the poet has an idea of what she wishes to say (Despina wants to thank the landlord), and the substance of the message is delivered through an image that is inspired by the end-rhyme word that is figured out at that moment. In an example cited earlier (p. 146), an inspiration for poetic activity is only generally connected to the focus of the conversation (Despina tells her friend about my telephone call) and then this leads to a joke. Picking out the rhyme words leads to figuring out the point, which might follow a conscious, pre-existing goal, or be an entirely new one – brought into being by the rhyme words.

These oral poets have adapted the poetic register as a productive vehicle for creativity and they are not ashamed to disclose that their creations lack intentionality – quite the contrary. The associations created on the spur of the moment are especially serendipitous: they demonstrate the improvisatory capacity to find new interpretations and to turn any situation to one's advantage. Herzfeld (1981: 119) cites an informant who makes explicit even that: "sometimes you sing a song which has a meaning (*simasía*) which you yourself can't understand. Someone else, however…will get substances (*ousíes*) from within [the song]. I, however, don't [necessarily and at that moment] understand what substance it has within." As Herzfeld astutely observes, "this is an unequivocal statement about semantic *potentiality*."

Certainly such semantic potentiality and meaning discovered in many ex tempore compositions are mainly interpretable in the given surroundings and between the participants equipped with the situational and cultural knowledge required for picking out the meaning. Rhymes such as those found in the precedent example can hardly cross the borders of the situation or the *paréa* involved to a commonly shared, symbolic use. As we have noticed in chapter 5, such situationally striking poems are, however, eagerly re-recited between the participants – like the joke made by Despina about our age difference is between the three of us – or told as stories, in which case the details and explanations required for sufficient contextualization are provided for those not present in the first situation. The moment of the emergence and perception of a *meaning*, however plain or unintentional, is a remarkable experience of creativity, and it is this moment of creativity that is memorized and reported in the narrated event.

The ideal of coherence: building an image

The composition of a couplet differs from longer poems in its compact, completed, argument-like character. I had the pleasure of following and specifically addressing Kostoula Papadoyanni's conscious learning process through our conversations over many years. She had already composed longer poems in the *dekapentasíllavo* meter since her early childhood, for thirty years. This process originated from her wish to learn to compress the message into a self-dependent mantináda, and in 2008, it brought her to the level of creating images even completely ex tempore (080930). In October 2009, she acknowledged that this conscious process had taken a total of ten years (091030).

> (K) (080930) In the beginning, the first years, I merely wrote songs, I could not… Influenced by the *Erotókritos* – the *Erotókritos* is a history – I started to write in many, many *dekapentasíllavo-lines*. So that was a history, it was not a mantináda. Then, it is much more difficult to write mantinádes, because you must put all that inside (a pair of) *dekapentasíllavo* lines. And it's really difficult, very difficult! To create an image in this way!
>
> (V) *Also the vocabulary is different.*
>
> (K) You are restricted in the words, like you say, to the Cretan dialect, and there we use the apostrophe a lot, that is we cut the words, we can't write *stis óles*, we say: *sts'óles*, or, anyway you must cut some words, or, some moment when I like very much a certain theme and I want very much to make it into a mantináda, a full sentence can come to me and in

the end, I make all that one word. I cut it down, I compress it, I compress it, in order to manage to make one mantináda.

/(V) *It seems to me that there are mantinádes which are more narrative, let's say...in which you just add information, like when you make a ríma. But I think that a mantináda, when it is very good, is bound, that there's always something that binds the mantináda and makes it one, whole. You don't just add like: I wish you this, and that you will be fine*

/(K) No. A mantináda, Vera, has to be one complete theme.

/(V) *I mean that there are people who can create verses with end-rhyme, but the poem is narrative, if you understand what I mean... And I believe that it's another talent to create a mantináda which is like you say an image.*

/(K) And that's very difficult. And that's *very difficult*! Let me tell you why, because... when you create something in three four mantinádes, you create an image, it is like a puzzle, what you think, it is a puzzle which has four parts – when you read all the FOUR you will have the full image. This is much easier for the person who writes than for the one who has one mantináda in which to make ONE picture. ONE image. That is, to enclose EVERYTHING inside. (...) And this mantináda does not have one unnecessary word. That is, if you create four or five couplets, some words will be there just for you to create an end-rhyme, but they do not fill in the image. You have to read them all.

/(V) *You are adding information.*

/(K) Little by little, you add a little ... It is however very difficult to create one mantináda, to put one word, bam! That is, you have to observe all the words one by one. And to *which* position you place them, to which position, in order to the other person to see the image you want in front of her. Since one word can be placed at the end and the other person cannot grasp the point, and you say that well it didn't fit there, I meant the second word to be the fourth word – nobody will know that. A mantináda must be – and so we see VERY simple mantinádes which are very STRONG mantinádes! That is, it strikes you, bam! And you see immediately the image in front of you. There's no need for you to *seeearch*, to search to see, what the other wants to say.

In addition to this structural struggle to render a message in only the two fifteen-syllable lines, the process includes developing cognitive, metaphoric skills in order to be able to create an image.

Kostoula Papadoyanni, 2008 (080930)

We were talking about that someone could, once, for example, I saw the yard and I said: the yard is: it has a foot path, it has flowers, I see a tree, I see – that is, I saw the things that all people see. Or at least most people. When you are engaged in the mantináda, you see OTHER things, everything becomes alive around you. And everything can take the place of something else. That is, let's say, the stars, the moon can become human, they can make things, you can say that they can do things, that the moon can talk to you, that it is pale because it is worried, things that happen only to the humans – when one is worried one is pale. But how many times we write in a mantináda: pale moon. So, you start to see the world in a different way. Meanwhile, I learned to express myself, to my children, to my husband – all the significant moments in my life, I have clothed them with a mantináda. I have expressed them with a mantináda. That makes me content now. How a painter sees a view and says: I do not want to photograph it, I want to paint it myself to show how I see it with my own eyes. You see, it is about how you see it with *your own eyes*. And – that's why the mantináda is each one different, that is, there are 10,000 mantinádes about the moon, and they are all different! Since every person sees the particular thing in a different way. That's it.

Kostoula Papadoyanni states above that to create a mantináda is to create an image – an image as one sees it with one's own eyes. Contemporary composers invariably point to this: the poetic essence of mantinádes is to create an image. This means that one selected idea is presented, and also that the presentation of the idea is itself captive, telling and understandable: the poem immediately constructs a visual image for the listener. This means that the poetic ideal essentially requires both structural and semantic coherence. The following three poems are fitting examples of how Kostoula has depicted her emotions and arguments in semantically and structurally coherent, self-dependant images.

(080930) One day we were talking, we discussed with Manolis…and we said that we met, like everyone meets, and we continued together, now we have been twenty years together, and although our characteristics are not the same, nobody is the same with the other one, finally we made a very good couple, that is, we are contented with our married life, although we had some difficulties and we are different personalities. So we were talking about that – Well, said Manolis, I wonder how we are together since you are very sensitive, and I am an egoist, I have other matters in my mind, you know, all that. And then I said to him:

'Ilios esí, vrohí egó / ma ótan sinandithoúme
Me-ourániou tókso hrómata / ton ouranó kendoúme

You are sun, I am rain / but when we come together
In all colors of the rainbow / we'll embroider the sky

That is, there are two opposite things which together, however, make a really fantastic thing!

(080930) Like Manolis, once he told me: I suppress you, I have the children on your head, but it doesn't work otherwise because I have also other work to do – like he would justify, regret that: I can't do otherwise, maybe you feel bad about living with me. And I said then – he said you are deprived of some things and I wrote him that yes, sometimes I'd like to do some things but I'm deprived:

San to poulí mes' to klouví / esthánome kontá sou
Ma de zitó ti lefteriá / an íne makriá sou

Like a bird in a cage / I feel when I'm near you
But I do not ask for freedom / if that's far away from you

(V) *Very good!*

(K) Something must influence you for you to write.

In the following, Yorgos Sifakis supplies other examples and further specifies the qualities of the mantináda; he gives also a good example of how these images become subject to new ideas.

> Yorgos Sifakis, 2004 (041110): Yesterday, for example, I phoned to the *Creta* Channel, there was a broadcast dedicated to the Arkádi[4], and they recited many mantinádes, the poems were very good, in the [program of] Vitóro, and it came to me that moment and I said:
>
> > 'Ithela na yayérnane / kína ta hrónia opíso
> > Mésa st'Arkádi ya na bó / ki egó na martiríso
>
> > I would like that they return / those years back
> > That I could enter the Arkádi / as well to die a martyr
>
> That is, I created an image, let's say...this image which might have come out of my internal mental world.

(V): *Can you, each time you make a mantináda, understand immediately where this image comes from, or is it possible that even you yourself don't grasp where it comes from?*

(Y) I understand when there is an emotional loading, either positive or negative; there, it comes from inside you, really. There are other ones which are more superficial, like that I told you before (see pp. 169–170), about the Hio, that one is more superficial, let's say, of the moment, and in these cases the quickness of the thought plays role, and, the fitting of the words and the elements of the moment, which you can unite in a couplet. These are in principle couplets to me, not mantinádes. Mantinádes have a deeper meaning. But also the couplet in Crete, it is very popular.

(V): *Thus, you separate clearly...*

(Y): I separate, because...

(V) *Mantináda for you is the one which has poetic values?*

(Y): Poetic values, deep meaning, fantasy...and syntactic structure without mistakes. That is...today at midday I talked with one friend, who said to me – he's a very good *mantinadológos* – there's one mantináda which has been recorded, a good mantináda, of one woman from Iraklio (Despina Spatidáki) and it says:

---

4   The battle in the Monastery of Arkádi in 1866, which culminated in a decision to blow up the monastery and the people hiding there, is one of the central historical memories of the uprisings of the Orthodox Christian population during the Ottoman reign.

> *Píra mia pétra angaliá / kai ton kaimó mou ts' ípa*
> *Ke-íhe kardiá yati-ákousa / to béti mou ke htípa*
>
> I took a stone in my lap / and my worries told to it
> And it had a heart since I heard / as it struck my heart

And he said to me that this mantináda starts well but the second verse is not tied to the first very much. Because, it should say, for example, that something happened to the stone; there the: "had heart," someone can think that the person had heart disease (laughs). And I asked, well how would you say it? He said you could say it like this:

> *Píra mia pétra angaliá / ke ts' ípa ton kaimó mou*
> *Hília komátia yínike / ap' ton paráponó mou*
>
> I took a stone in my lap / and told it my worries
> Thousand pieces it became / from my grievances[5]

As this conversation shows, composers are influenced by the texts and actively debating about them. The words and imagery that are used produce new associations and suggest alternative frames of interpretation. Any text can be interpreted as an utterance which signals the thematic opening of a discussion.

Motivations for composing

> Kostas Kontoyannis 1999 (991124):
>
> The Cretan mantináda is a fifteen-syllable verse, with end-rhyme, it expresses the feelings of the person, and everyone who has created a mantináda, the one who sings a mantináda which he has created, has made it from conditions which he has lived, that is, his life was influenced by something and he created the mantináda. You do not create a mantináda randomly: they are pieces of your life.

The above description provided by Kostas Kontoyannis states that the poems that one creates, and sings, are parts of one's life. Using this quotation, I wish to direct attention to the plurality of meaning in the mantinádes; since this type of oral poetry, couplets and quatrains, is most often presented from the perspective of performance. Furthermore, as performances, they are particularly characterized as comments that are extemporized to reflect on the social relations and carryings-on of the poet's fellow human beings. This identity as a humorous, satirical and critical commentary is one significant aspect of communicational oral poetry, but it is not the only one. For this reason, I will now turn to take a closer look at the kind of motives given for composition.

---

5 To compare this poem to Yorgos's later adaptation of the latter verse in a singing event, see p. 114.

Verbal interaction

Intersubjective communication is certainly the primary reason for performing poems. By communication, I refer here to the engagement in verbal interaction between two or more persons, either in the sense that someone has a need or a wish to pass a message on to somebody else or in the sense of "small-talk," communication as social interaction for its own sake. As was described by Mitsos Stavrakakis earlier (see the quotation on page 23), in the previously close-knit village communities, messages between the two sexes were conveyed through poetry, because that was the only means available. Many other kinds of messages – humor, irony, hints, teaching, etc. – were channeled through proverbial comments in speech or in singing-events, either one way, or reciprocally.

> Kostoula Papadoyanni, 2004 (040727):
>
> Many times I discussed with my father by using mantinádes. I was very sensitive and if someone was angry with me, I started to cry. I could not say it. So I wrote it! I always wrote with mantinádes. My father, for his part, gave me good advice. One day we were sitting at the table and I told him about one disappointment; something happened and I quarreled with my girl friend, and I was worried. He was writing some papers, I don't know what. So, I thought that he was not listening to me, and I was worried that he doesn't listen to me. But on the pad he had written:
>
> > *'Oso ki an klés mi fantastís / pos tha se lipithoúne*
> > *Tóra to éhoun se hará / ptómata na patoúne*
>
> > As much as you cry, don't imagine / that people will pity you
> > Nowadays they have it for fun / to tread on the corpses
>
> That is, people like to see others to sink low and to laugh. This is an advice that has stayed with me. My father died five years ago, but that is advice from my father, which has stayed with me and is a valuable thing to me.

Very similarly, Kostoula now speaks to her children with mantinádes, as described in the following example (080930):

> Let's say now with my children. Whatever happens to them, I will – We are not talking about it anymore, I will say one mantináda to them, since I know that it also touches them much more! That is, it touches them, either I give them self-assurance, or I make them a wish, eh, they will never forget it, while would I say it in prose they *could* forget it (laugh) – They will never forget it, yes, yes, and little by little they also begin to (compose)...
>
> When, let me tell you an example, when my Nikos (her son) went to the exam to get his driver's license – he passed the written test, he passed the driving, he got the license. The boy was in Hania, I was in Rethimno, so he phoned me and told me: Mama, I got the license on the first attempt!

Eh, bravo! I said to Nikos – he said: Mama, don't you have anything to say to me? (laugh) Yes, yes, now my children also require something to understand exactly what I feel! If I say to them that well, fine, bravo, I'm happy – you know that doesn't make them content anymore. You see? That doesn't make them content anymore. And so I sit down and I write, but the feeling was so strong that well here's my son – but I didn't think that only. I thought that, ok, this boy, now that he is, let's say, in few years he can steer ships since he goes to the officer academy… your mind LEAVES entirely, to the other paths. (…) You know, since I had the fear now that he is driving... I could have said: Niko, I'm happy that you drive, but I'm also afraid because so many accidents take place – all that, I put:

Oti timóni-i héra su / is ti zoï su piáni
Afine tópo ke-o Hristós / ti héra tu na váni

Ke-an tóra 'máksi odigís / mésa se líga hrónia
Ta dio su héria na kratún / ton kavión timónia

Me to Hristó st'aristerá, / tin Panayá deksá su
Ke me tis mánas tin evhí, / yé mu kalostratiá su!

Whatever steering wheels, your hand / in your life will hold
Let there be room for Christ / to put his hand as well

And if now you drive a car / in a few year's time
Your two hands will hold / the steering wheel of ships

With Christ at your left side / and Mary at your right
And with your mother's wish / may you have good roads, my son!

That is, have good roads, I could have said, and I expressed it like this!

In this cluster of three poems, Kostoula's good wishes take shape and are interwoven into the communication of her larger ideology of life. The argument now covers three mantinádes, rather than just one, which appears to be typical of expressing felicitations and wishes.

The communication of situational remarks is the privileged setting for textual improvisation. Local recollections recount that in the smallest villages, there was always at least one person who was a known *rimadóros*, a rhyme-maker, and who would "say it to you at once" or "say it on the spot," namely, clothe your personal characteristics or involvement in a given situation in a poem immediately. The following is one of the stories narrated by Agapi in the Village (fieldnotes August 19, 2006) while describing this spontaneous rhyme-making habit of the local *mantinadológos* at the time of her youth:

Once he had taken us, three young women, to help to gather the crops. We were chatting while working, but whereas the two of us were working hard, one girl was lazy, and often stopped working when she was talking. He followed the situation for some time, and finally said to this girl:

'Oles sas íste ómorfes / ma-esí 'se san ti vióla
Ke-ótan milas mi káthese / ma na therísis kióla!

Every one of you is beautiful / but you are the viola
And when you talk don't sit / but gather the crops as well!

The ability to compose witty poems ex tempore has always been admired. On the other hand, when encountered, these poets would also give cause for anxiety, since the witty words were often sarcastic. Since few were able to respond in kind, the extemporized poems could easily render their subject open to ridicule. In the high mountain shepherd communities, where verbal duels were apt to be very pointed, Michael Herzfeld (1985a: 142–146) offers examples of the power balance between the ages and sexes in these duels, and of how far one can go. Today the skill of extemporization is rare; except for a few cases, such as Kostoula, it is no surprise that one is likely to encounter only elderly people being ex tempore composers and in such village surroundings where *parées*, verbal rivalry and the need for an ability to read social situations all have played an active role.

Communication is not always warfare; it also does not necessarily involve the need to pass on an *intentional* message. Similarly, as many informants have described, the interchange in the musical parées, contemporary composers chiefly recount only good-humored, cooperative verbal activities. Here is one example: In July 2004, in a *paniyíri* in the neighboring village, my landlord introduced me to Papa Nikolis, a priest, hagiographer and *mantinadológos*. Papa Nikolis was born in this village and is now living in Rethimno. After my landlord had told him that I was conducting research on mantinádes, Papa Nikolis immediately related to me the following exchange of words between the tavern-owner Yorgos Sifakis (Simisakoyoryis), a fellow priest Papadoyannis, and himself (fieldnotes July 20, 2004):

And we, our *paréa*, the other day, had this conversation:

Simisakoyoryis:	*Se tsánta ítan to psomí / stin pórta kremasméni* *fénete mou to klépsane / pentéksi pinasméni*
	The bread was in a bag / hanging on the door It seems that it was stolen from me / by five to six hungry men
Papadoyannis:	*Eklépsane sou to psomí / ma 'sí epíres állo* *prin na yení to próvlima / apó mikró megálo*
	They stole your bread / but you provided another one Before the problem became / from small to a big one
Papa Nikolís:	*Eklépsane sou to psomí / ma léo den pirázi* *áma tha klépsoun to faï / tha íne to marázi*
	They stole your bread / but I say it does not matter If they'll steal the food / that will be a disaster

This exchange of mantinádes between a *paréa,* a group of friends, indicates a relaxed focus on the verbal creativity in an everyday occasion.

Composition for emotional self-expression

During one's twenties, the erotic emotional stress tends to be very strong, and in several conversations, the mantináda has been described to me as an *emergency exit,* or a *release, "lítrosi"* (fieldnotes July 7, 2004). To be able to feel that one's sentiments can be channeled through images, through one's own words, is of great help, even if the result is similar to a thousand other poems describing the joys and pains of love, or the beauty and loveliness of the loved-one. The declarations of love are, of course, transmitted both by personally composed poems as well as traditional poems and images: everyone has feelings, but not everyone can compose. Although, as Mitsos Stavrakakis and Kostoula Papadoyanni have put it, one of the most opportune times to try to is when one is experiencing one's first love.

The composition of (lyric) poetry in general is strongly connected to the need for self-expression and for the deliberation of emotions. When one is filled with emotions and overwhelmed by them, it is natural to wish to express them, and to find comfort in poetry. While interpersonal communication is always a social domain and communicative composition is open to outside evaluation, regardless of how seriously or leisurely it is taken, this is the area where *personal creativity* takes place as well: the end result is significant in its own right.

Regarding the aspect of privacy of emotional self-expression, Crete as a community, however, differs from many others. Even in everyday speech, men in particular boldly declare that Cretans are a people with strong emotions. Sentimental self-expression in poetic form is open to every member of the community, which seems to be in contrast to that related by Caton and Abu-Lughod of the Arabs and Bedouins, respectively: manly men do not touch upon such themes, and sentimental poetry is composed and transmitted only by those who hold a weak position in the community, such as women and young men (see Chapter 1).

> Kostoula Papadoyanni, 2008 (080930):
>
> *(V) Once we were talking about if there is, if women express themselves in a different way from men. And we had exchanged a few words on that, but what is your opinion now, do your mantinádes differ from those of the men? Is there any difference in the expression, in the style...?*
>
> (K) Eh, no... No, and many times, let me tell you, I have understood that, since here in Crete the men are proud, and they have also a bit of self-regard (*egoismós*), you know, often they become very good mantinadolóyi with words that they would not accept, they would not say them in prose words.
>
> */(V) That's certainly so.*

/(K) Because, in order not to lower their self-regard – they want to create through the idea that I am a tough man, however the mantinadolóyi are more sensitive than thousands of women. There's one man here in the next village, who is, I don't know – when you hear one of his mantinádes, you must, you will say: is this possible! However, if you see him, if you see him with the beard, like he has a beard with, with, always black clothes, I don't know what, black shirt, you will say, Virgin Mary, what a wild human being! You do not believe that he hides such an emotional world inside himself, by nothing, what should I say to you now. He might understand the love much better than ...I believe that they do this, because they don't want, they think it is degrading...

/(V) *To the men, it is more significant to express themselves like that.*

///(K) Yes and I believe that since a mantináda is a way of self-expression which is not misunderstood, you know – that you are not a tough man because you create mantinádes. But if one creates a good one, they will say him, you are two times a man, that's why they express themselves so beautifully – that is, it is their emergency exit, there, and you can see men very tough, or let's say who at least show that they are tough, however they create pearls. Marvelous things.

As suggested by Kostoula above, most probably the sentimental aspect of the mantinádes is cultivated by Cretan men particularly because it can balance the otherwise rather severe qualifications for their self-regard. Furthermore, there are two further possible reasons for this romantic aspect. First, the most probable origins of the mantinádes in Crete are the medieval love songs and serenades, *kantádes*, introduced on the island by the Venetians, and young men widely practiced the habit of communicating their emotions by making *kantádes* until the 1970s. Second, in connection with the previous point, the sentimentality in mantinádes stems from the model of the written verse narrative *Erotókritos*. In their explanations quoted earlier, Mitsos Stavrakakis and Kostoula Papadoyanni refer to the singing of *Erotókritos*' verses in everyday life during the active learning period as an important *ákousma*. Equivalent to a national epic for Cretans, the *Erotókritos* follows the romantic narrative model of the Middle Ages, binding strong emotions and defeats and victory in love to heroic deeds in very masculine battles. This model enhances the association of the masculine gallantry and the verbal capability with (emotional) poetry.

Following the different characteristics of these two models, emotional male poems can be very sensitive and touching, but they can also be very dramatic. Explicit expression of tenderness is present in many poems, and I would especially note its presence in poems created by older men for their wives (explicit expression of tenderness is rare in the everyday communication between Cretan couples due to the rather separating gender model that is typical of Crete that separates them). One example is the following poem quoted by Yorgos Sifakis (041110):

Many men are also very emotional when it comes to death. One man said to his wife:

Thélo louloúdia plastiká / stou táfou mou to vázo
Ya na min kouvalís neró / ke se políkourázo

I want plastic flowers / in the vase on my grave
So I don't make you carry water / and tire you out

The most popular records give a good idea of the continuum between these ends: from sensitivity to emotional drama. Poetry may serve as a roundabout way in two senses: it is an emergency exit helping to express emotions that one could not express in any other form, or for those that one would otherwise have no words. Yet the possibility to shut down one's emotions in a detachable form can make it possible to avoid exposing one's vulnerability in "real life."

Emotional poetic self-expression in Crete is thus an established act. A full array of sentiments – love, erotic feelings, disappointment, suffering a bad fate, etc., – is openly declared in poems with no fear that these recurrent themes or similarities to other poems would reduce the originality or weight of the personal expression. In composition, emotional self-expression is a dominant motivation and the majority of all poems created are emotional. Since personally meaningful emotional poems are socially approved, there are few obstacles in publishing them in print or in broadcasts on the television and radio. On the contrary, it is this very aspect that has made the poems so popular in the modern arenas.

Capturing a theme

Much like the turn-taking and personal argumentation in a singing performance, the images constructed in composition are connected to a larger conversational or existential background, a *theme*. This is defined by Sifakis as follows:

> Yorgos Sifakis, 2004 (041110):
>
> The theme is very essential; to me, the theme is very essential in a mantináda, that you have an original theme, *original*, that is. One of these days I had created one mantináda, and I say:
>
> *Salévo stin akroyaliá / ke karteró na vgáli*
> *To mínima ts'agápis sou / to kíma sto bukáli*
>
> I'm walking on the seashore / and await [the wave] to pull out
> A message of your love / the wave [to pull out] in a bottle
>
> The bottles that there used to be in the old times, you remember, which some seamen...
>
> (V): *and you wait for years...*

(Y): A, Bravo!
Well, that is a capturing of one theme – a capturing of a theme. Like that one I referred to before, about the stone, that's Despina Spatidaki's, she's also a very good *mantinadológos*, that one which says I took a stone in my lap...on that theme, of the stone, many mantinádes can be created. But she created the first theme. On that, others have answered, other mantinádes have been created... About the theme now, since many mantinádes are created, thousands, it is clear that there will be similarities between them, it's not possible that there are not similarities... the fact is that people from Anoya are original, they do not have many similarities. Then there are many, you know, who join: *Kríti* (Crete) – *Psiloríti* (name of a central mountain range),[6] the classic ones, they are very classic, and, eh, very worn, these.

(V): So you believe that you can continuously find new solutions?

(G): Yes, that's essential for a *mantinadológos*, to find themes and to have ideas that differ from the other's ideas. To create something new. Just like in poetry, in songs... A mantináda for me is very much like a cartoon. It is the capturing of an idea. Like the cartoon: an event takes place now and the cartoonist depicts it with the pen on the paper, with figures, and writes also two words. Well, that is very much like the *mantináda*. Not all the *mantinádes,* but part of them, those which come out due to a certain event. Since there are also *mantinádes*, as I said earlier, which come out of our internal world without reason.

Although Yorgos Sifakis addresses the applicability of the idea of capturing a theme only in connection with situational, improvised poems, it is my view that this idea can easily be applied to describe the general artistic urge of capturing an idea in a short and compact poetic image. Whether a theme is introduced in a conversation, in a singing event, or in a talk-show, or whether it occupies the mind for personal reasons, the poet seeks to take hold of it and to condense the core of it into a poetic picture. Capturing the theme is relevant in ex tempore composition where, for example, situations, circumstances, or personal characteristics are woven into verses. It is also relevant in creating lyric poetic pictures that communicate emotions or in depicting the proverbial, normative principles or a philosophy of life. Here the thematic objective, in addition to reacting to and catching a fleeting moment, as to create something *eternal*, and in this way help anyone else to find the right words at a similar moment.

These quotations reveal how the goal of imagining a theme and capturing it in a poetic image is a dynamic artistic urge for many experienced composers. The example of the evaluative conversations between composers further indicates how this artistic ideal is also a dialogic ideal: poems, and poets, contribute to a certain dialogue on a certain theme. Not only do performers produce this contribution in their performance, but composers also do it in their imagery.

---

6   See the photo on the cover page.

Although capturing a theme in a single poem is a fundamental ideal in verse-making, it is necessary to remember how the reverse is true, as well: as a conversational, dialogic center of versatility, variation and rhetoric elaboration, a theme is a typical stimulus for creating several mantinádes, a cluster of poems on an arousing theme. This has already been discussed in connection with register in Chapter 4. In reciprocal performances, one poem is selected as an argument for each turn; however, when the turn-taking goes on, the theme is also elaborated on at length. The following description provides one more example of how this performative dialogism also has its parallel in composition.

Kostoula Papadoyanni, 2004 (040727)

Here is the mantináda I told you about, about the snow, when I came out and it was snowing, that one, as I told that one day it was snowing here, and I came down to the road, and above of one log there was a little bit of snow and I wrote – I held the car keys and I wrote "I love you" into the snow, I carved it, and when my husband said to me what are you writing there, I answered him:

Ipa tu íliou símero / ts' aktínes tu na hósi
Yati-égrapsa to s' ágapó / sto hióni ke tha liósi

I told the sun today / to hide away her rays
Since I wrote "I love you" / on snow and it will melt

Yes, maybe, if he didn't ask me, I had not created that mantináda – but he asked: what are you doing there? He said, fine, I'll go on, and I said to him:

Hionízi, vréhi ke fisá / ke ríhni ke halázi
Ma ti fotiá ts' agapis mas / práma den tin pirázi

It snows, rains and winds / hailstones batter down
But the fire of our love / nothing will bother that

(V) And did your husband understand it? Was he still there?

(K) Yes, of course, of course – because he has learned up to now that when I enter this process and open this door, he has learned to follow me, silently, of course, but he follows me because he knows that at that moment I am creating and he doesn't want to stop the creation, because he likes it.

(V) I have understood that he values it highly.

/(K) Yes, yes, he esteems it much since it is a way of self-expression! That's it! (...) He may not be able to communicate the same way, however he respects me. He understands! The same day I wrote:

Hionízi ke stin pórta mu / dio métra hióni sténi
Ma ti fotiá ts' agapis su / ého ke me zesténi

It's snowing and on my door / two meters of snow arise
But the fire of your love / I have and it keeps me warm

Then he told me: go inside because it's cold and light the fireplace and write there the remaining mantinádes (laugh); you will catch cold in the end! So I go in but since I was still influenced – you see, it snows here seldom – and because it was snowing, it is a wonderful image to see the snow falling softly, softly, indeed. I lit the fireplace and said:

*To tzáki anávo ke o hioniás / ókso tis stúpes stróni
K' éla min pésune i anthí / ts' agápis mas sto hióni*

I light the fireplace and the snow / outside heaps up the flakes
Come in, so that the flowers / of our love won't fall on the snow

When the snow weighs on the trees the flowers fall...Then... Manolis came in and said to me: are you still composing mantinádes? And I said: yes, I'll tell you:

*Poté mikró mu s'agapó / mi gráfis ís to hióni
Yatí htipá ts'ahtínes tu / o ílios ke to lióni*

Ever my little one "I love you" / don't write in the snow
Since (the sun) beats its rays / the sun will make it melt

An unusual phenomenon, snowing, followed by an act of carving the text "I love you" in the snow and by the speech act – these all give a poetic impulse first realized in a summary of all these elements. The elements, however, are woven into a *frame* which establishes a delicate analogy between the appeal to the sun not to shine and cause the (text in the) snow to melt and the human need to protect love from harming elements. In the continuation, the primary lexical and semantic elements "snow" and "love" are combined within the frame of the contrasting nature of these two: snow and winter as cold, and love as warming. The last poem, still elaborating on the same lexical elements, returns to the original impulse and idea, now in a form of an instruction.

The creativity of making the point: reframing

A special talent is needed to create the point during the process of composition. Although this can often mean framing a piece of reality with images and arguments that are powerfully descriptive, narrative, normative or lyric, the emblematic characteristic of a mantináda seems to be that through the image, the poem opens up a new perspective on the situation. In brief, it presents something that has not yet been thought of. I have noted earlier that I became intimately aware of the existence of this special cognitive creativity only when my own attempts at making couplets revealed a complete lack of these skills. While it is quite easy to find rhyme words and make up one line, difficulties arise when one tries to build a pair of matching phrases. And even should this succeed, the result would be only additive in nature – hardly something to create a coherent or surprising image. Kostoula's verbalizations of the composition process below show that acquiring the spontaneity and competence in handling the register is a creative process that is time-consuming, conscious and also self-rewarding (080930).

(V) I don't know, maybe all kinds of forms of creativity have always to do with that you can see alternatives...

(K) Yes.

(V) ...maybe the first thing that you have to have inside yourself is that you can see alternatives?

(K) But that to happen, it takes a lot of work! And it takes, that your soul is like that, that you are a person – that you have live images (*akoúsmata*). That is, according to the place where you live. Because that means that you know the people well. You know the local customs, what people feel, what they feel in their sorrow, what they feel when happy – eh, you open other paths.

(V) And then – instead of thinking that bravo, you took your license, you see...

//(K) VERA, that will never end! That will never end! And the more, the deeper you get in to this matter, that is, the more new paths open up, the more you want to walk on them. You don't want to leave any of them. And some moment when you arrive at a point and you say, now, from here onwards, I *can't*. Eh, you get worried and you try, and you say: no, I CAN! I *can, I have to think of it another way.* Do you know how many times I have created a mantináda and I say no, no, it is not this, it is not JUST this, it seems very little to me, this – and I say no, no, I didn't say what I feel.

(V) So consciously, you put, you force yourself to go forward?

(K) That's it, consciously! Because do you know what? Now I, as a person – a person who creates mantinádes – the more one creates, the more demanding one becomes with oneself, that is, the more one wants to create better ones, to say mantinádes in which each word expresses oneself, if *that* is possible! That is, one pays attention even to the last word. Since one says... one wants to make it perfect! The perfect however never comes. Because... (...) All the more you make it better, the more – you see that, ah, I have also other possibilities, ah, that one is more beautiful!

You go ahead and you progress and you go upwards, and you get into difficulties...let's say once in the program they said, they put one mantináda on the screen, mm, and I said – I was maybe tired, I don't know what, it was winter, I started a fire in the fireplace here, I was tired and I said baa, this mantináda is very strong – you always have the demand to create something stronger than that one which is put in the broadcast because it pulls you – and I said: tonight, I'm not working on, let it be, I don't create. Since to create, I have to create something good, I'm tired, thus I can't. But, UNTIL the broadcast is finished, I have created a mantináda! (Laughs) Yes. Since I saw the theme so good that I could not, I wanted to take part, I wanted, I want, that is something...like a *disease*, I don't know what! You get addicted, my friend, addicted! (Laughs)

Ah, let me tell you an example. He (Yorgos Vitoros) called me and said where are you? I said I'm in the Village. – And what are you doing? – I am cooking. Where are you? – I'm in one place and playing cards with some friends of mine. Do you, he asked, play cards? Do you like it? And I tell him, "no." And he asks me why? And I say to him that I will tell him some other time. So when we then finished the call, I write, with mantináda, and tell him:

Poté mou zária ke hartiá / sta héria mou den piáno
Na min kerdíso ke mou poún / pos stin agápi háno

Never do I dice or cards / pick up in my hands
Not to win and people say / that I will lose in love

Here there's something that people say that the one who wins in cards, loses in love. You see! Yes, and I said how will I justify the situation, that I don't play cards (laughs). But, I didn't want to say to him, simply, I don't like it. I could not say that. I wanted to say to him something which would surprise him, which he would like. That what we said before... which we said before...that...*the mantináda is a game...*

An analysis of the above poem shows that the image conveying Kostoula's argument (that it is not profitable to play cards or games) is rhetorically constructed of two components. The first, described here by the first verse, is the existing reality including the general question of playing cards and Kostoula's specific wish to express the opinion that she does not like to play cards. The second component, expressed in the second verse, is an *analogy* brought about by her fantasy, in this case in the form of a common saying, from which she draws to *justify* her argument of *not being able* to play cards. By building on this analogy, the poem opens a new perspective on the matter.

The composer picks up something existing in the moment and combines it with an idea forming in his or her mind, making these ingredients into an image. This image leads the hearer to see something which was not present in the situation in that form before the poem revealed it – an interpretation, a connection, a possibility, a joke; there are many possibilities for the linking element and the style of the point are many. For the point to be effective, it has to be found in something familiar, easily and quickly grasped by the listener and not *new* in that sense. Nevertheless, the image yields a new association, a *new frame*. This turn of the mind, or the art of processing a part of the present reality in combination with personal imagination and turning them into an image that looks at reality in a new light or from a different perspective, thus particularly concerns changing the conceptual frame.

Let us call this creative skill *reframing* – a term widely used for the practical philosophical and psychological skills in looking at things from a new perspective.[7] Although poetry in general places special emphasis on the inventiveness of the arguments and imagery, and reshapes the world effectively through metaphors and analogies, such dialogic poetry takes full advantage of the narrowness of a human's everyday perception and the selective, categorizing organization of human thinking and cognition. The very selectiveness with which the mind frames perception gives the tools to build arguments on interpretations, making *alternative* slices of the world visible. Let us now turn to analyze this idea by reviewing more examples.

It has been stated earlier that mantinádes are often constructed very much like the punch lines in jokes, utilizing the relation between the first line, which gives a certain setting, and the second line, which in a mantináda qualifies and interprets the image given in the first line. The following poem of Kostoula, cited earlier, builds an image by using a clearly rhetorical structure:

San to poulí mes' to klouví / esthánome kontá sou
Ma de zitó ti lefteriá / an íne makriá sou

Like a bird in a cage / I feel when I'm near you
But I do not ask for freedom / if that's far away from you

The first line presents a simplified statement through the metaphoric image of a bird in a cage, which is seen by the hearer automatically as a negative state (deprivation of liberty), only to show in the second verse that the opposite alternative, again a simplification, is an option that is even less desirable. The second line is especially clever, since the "bird in a cage" metaphor is widely used and normally alludes to the need or appreciation of freedom. Having heard the story of the poem's origin and knowing Kostoula, I can interpret the image resulting from this rhetoric as a balanced, even tender acceptance of the circumstances. Other interpretations would also be possible: obtaining closure in the poem-argument is certainly a circumstantial goal in the composition which, however, does not restrict other interpretations that are fitting to other circumstances.

The next example shows how an answer to a poem selects and reframes an element of the first poem's observation. Kostoula had previously described how an exchange of poems by text messages between herself and another, according to Kostoula much more experienced *mantinadológos*,

---

7 For reframing in psychotherapeutic conversation, see Mattila 2001; 2006. With the frame theory as an integrative metaperspective, Mattila introduces the following perspectives to reframing: categories, analogies, metaphors, "seeing as," dialectics and interpretation (Mattila 2001: 13). As he widely analyzes in his dissertation (2001), all these elements which are used by humans to conceptualize the world and experiences, to reduce the incoming information and to help to predict situations and behavior, also make the perception always partial. This is why therapists can so effectively help people only by convincing them of alternative models and ways of interpreting and perceiving the same reality.

Yoryis Berkis from Anoya, had started and continued from six o'clock in the afternoon until two in the morning (080930):

> And the morning, I tell you, early morning, he sent me:
>
> *Kita pu s' oniréftika / ke den katého yánda*
> *Fenete m'epiréasan / ta htesina simvánda*
>
> Look, I was dreaming of you / but I don't know why
> It seems that I've been impressed / by yesterday's events
>
> And I sent to him:
>
> *Mu les pos m'oniréftikes / ma de mu les sináma*
> *Inta kontó se ksípnise / to yélio í to kláma?*
>
> You say you dreamed of me / but tell me also this
> What made you wake up / laughter or crying?

The first utterance could be interpreted as a positive statement. Kostoula, however, seizes upon the pondering (I don't know why; it seems) of the dream's reason, interpreting this as hesitation, and formulates this into a counter question of the exact quality of the dream (and thus of their poetic exchange from the day before): positive (laughter) or negative (crying)?

In the next example, we can see how an argumentation, a typical example of *antikristés* mantinádes as a dramatic performance between a woman and a man, is carried on by traditional poetic metaphors. In 2009 (091030), Kostoula had recounted to me another exchange of poems between herself and Yoryis Berkis, which had taken place the previous winter by text messages after an evening spent singing in Anoya with her husband – the first time she herself had been *singing* mantinádes. She had initiated this exchange with her wish to thank Berkis for the previous evening, and the improvised exchange of poems had later continued to other themes.

> In any case, at one moment the mantináda came to the flowers, the theme of the flowers, and he sends me this:
>
> *Na pápsis sto balkóni sou / louloúdia na potízis*
> *Ke na provérnis pou ke poú / esí na to stolízis*
>
> You should stop in your balcony / to water the flowers
> And come in front at times / to decorate it yourself
>
> He said me... And I said him:
>
> *Ná 'ksera ap' to balkóni mou / pos íthela perásis*
> *Ya na yenó vasilikó / st' aftí sou na kremásis*
>
> Should I know that by my balcony / you are passing by
> I would become a basil plant / for you to hang on your ear

Klonári sou vasiliké / poté de sou lavóno
M' arései akoutsotroúlisto / na s' apokamaróso

A branch of yours, basil plant / I will never take
I like with all your tops / to admire you

– without that some tops are missing, you know. And I say him:

Ama de thes ta klonária mou / éla na sou haríso
Ti mirodiá áp' ta fílla mou / ya na s' efharistíso

If you don't want my branches / come so that I can present you
With the scent form my leaves / to give you pleasure

– see now how it began and where it goes! And he said me:

'Opou ki an íse viola mou / me vríni i mirodiá sou
Akóma ke hiliómetra / apó ti yitoniá sou!

Wherever you are my viola / your scent will find me
Even many kilometers / away from your neighborhood

– A whole conversation thus took place again, we discussed with
Berkis that way.

In the final example, Kostoula shares with me one of her answers to the poems sent to her by the broadcast host Vitoros (080930). This poem shows how the reframing of an argument can take place at the level of the imagery:

Ah, wait a moment, some days ago Mr Yorgos sent me – because he sends me even now during the summer, I tell him, send me when you receive a good one, to stimulate me to create! So that I won't stop, I tell him, because I can't stop. And he sends me:

Egó 'me pu me ta theriá / íthela na kimoúme
K'edá 'me stin agápi su / deménos ke fovoúme

It was me who with the beasts / wanted to go to sleep
(that is, I was not afraid)
And here I am to your love / bound and that frightens me

He sent me this.[8] I wrote him:

Móno ts' agápis to therió / me lávose sto béti
K' edá 'hi kámi tin kardiá / spiliári ya na théti

---

8 Unfortunately, it was no longer possible to trace the identity of the author of this poem.

>Only the beast of love / has wounded me in the chest
>And here it has made the heart / a cave to lie in to sleep

>After that he calls me only after a few days and he tells me: leave me alone since I can't bear... (laughs). Yes, because he loves so much the mantináda and cannot compose himself, whoever sends him a strong one, the man goes mad, he goes mad... And I tell him, Dear Yorgos, that's all right!

Building on the metaphoric associations of the "beast," and the words "sleep," "love" and the formula "and here," but immediately contesting, as far as I know her, the idea that being in love (bound to love) would be *the* thing to be afraid of, Kostoula reframes these ingredients by new metaphoric associations into an image with quite different, multilayered meanings.

Commanding a poetic world as a productive language

In Crete, one can encounter composers and performers who have several levels of readiness and experience. The ability to create poems is regarded as a *hárisma*, an innate gift in the person, but further, two types of composers are recognized: those who in general can compose, and those who are spontaneous and capable of extemporizing new poems on the spot. Ex tempore composition is therefore regarded as a special talent, although, as noted above, the composers' opinions about the value of the ex tempore verses differ (they are not necessarily regarded as being any better). Extemporized compositions can draw the meaning both from the circumstantial realm and from the composition process itself: the process of rhyming closely coexists with the invention of meaning. Most composers also get their poems "out, down" in oral processes, but mainly during a longer time span and during private moments. Composition in general is regarded as a mental activity where ideas and arguments take shape aesthetically, linguistically in a poem, and although it is possible for a performer to attain fluency in spontaneity through practice, some particular cognitive skills are clearly needed for extemporized composition. Most Cretan composer-interviewees emphasize the fact that their internal moods dictate when they enter the performance arena, not only because of the pressure to perform or due to some other contextual stimulus from outside. However, as the examples above indicate, these certainly helped in arousing poetic imagination and particularly contributed to the art of reframing.

 One of the questions I posed in the beginning about composition was whether the poems change when entering a different communicative society, and if so, in what ways they change. Above I have presented different perspectives on composition that are based on the composers' own views and words. While discussing the modern written oral poetry and mass media arenas, I have pointed out that these arenas attract many kinds of composers and that they cannot be seen to generate only a specific type of poetry. In these arenas, composers with very different skills participate and demonstrate both recognized and experienced creativity. Certainly the focus on the textual, poetic side in building an image has become a more central goal than interactively communicating interpersonal, situational events and tensions. However, as is evinced by the in-depth exploration of the commentary and compositions of one individual, Kostoula Papadoyanni, even a contemporary composer can master a wide variety of skills. The inquiry will thus have to deal with those factors which allow one to command a metrically defined register as a productive language.

Some useful guidelines toward answering my question concerning composition are available in a study by the Finnish linguist Pentti Leino (1975). In his study, Leino analyzes the differences in the *kalevala-meter* line as used both in traditional poems performed in song and by contemporary folk and learned composers.[9] Among the composers of the topical verse, a decisive difference emerges between those who have heard folk poetry and learned the *kalevala-meter* in their formative milieu as children, and those who have learned the meter as adults. Leino refers to the contemporary theory of children's language acquisition, as well as to an oral poet's process of learning the oral epic language, as reported by Lord (1960) among the living Serbo-Croatian folk song culture. Thus, as a child first learns idiomatic expressions, the aspiring poet first learns songs that already exist and he can then repeat them. In the second stage, both learn the productive rules but still use them hesitatingly and often incorrectly. The rules overrun the exceptions, which were learned in the first stage of idiomatic repetition. In the third and final stage, both rules and exceptions are adapted to a system which can now be used flawlessly and with stylistic nuance. (Leino 1975: 44–46)

With reference to this three-stage path of learning a language, Leino (1975: 47) notes that features of the second stage often characterize the way the composers of topical verse use the *kalevala-meter*. However, the use of the alliteration is hyper-correct – which suggests that neither the theory of Lord, nor the theory of children's learning actually fit the Finnish folk composers. Instead, these composers have learned the poetic language in much the same way as adults learn a foreign language, with the typical lack of control in their use of the structures of the foreign language. The corpus of kalevala-metric topical verse was collected at the end of the creative era of folk poetry, and Leino concludes that most of these learned and folk composers acquired the poetic language as adults; they were not *bilingual*, as were the best traditional poets who had learned the poetic language

---

9 Leino compares the poems and metrical lines of (1) the epic folk poetry as sung by the traditional folk singer Arhippa Perttunen, (2) the composers of topical verse who were still connected to this traditional singing of kalevala-metric poetry, and (3) learned, non-native writers (a fourth category is taken from a linguistically distinct group in Viena). Differences arise between these groups on the following points: the proportions of the use of the basic metrical line and the enlivening deviances from it; the use of alliteration and parallelism; and the congruence of the metrical and the syntactical structure. Although the metrical model is well adapted by the composers of topical verse, their poems deviate largely from traditional folk poetry in the amount of parallelism (much less) and especially in the *syntactic structure*: instead of simple structures and the nearly exclusive use of main clauses, a dominance of subordinate clauses (Leino 1975: 39–41).

together with (or indeed as) their native language. Instead, they had learned a foreign language *through* their native language: "*kalevala-meter* was for them a foreign language, of which they had learned only the elements, not the more complicated structures and stylistic nuances" (Leino 1975: 48; translation by the present author).

Although it is possible to advance poetic competence through written and recorded materials, which is very common in Crete and elsewhere[10] today, the oral traditions are *traditions* especially in the way that one becomes familiar with them through the acoustic experience as a child. Cretan and Greek people refer to this with the indigenous notion of having *akoúsmata* ("live hearings"; live images, live experiences); this is a point made several times in Kostoula's descriptions and which also appears frequently in the conversations on their improvisational musical traditions.

All the active Cretan composers and performers with whom I conversed in the framework of this study had internalized the poetic register of mantinádes by immersion during their youth. Festive occasions, *parées*, *kantádes*, old women's songs, poetic confrontations, parents' and grandparents' speech, had all rounded their acquisition of a pliable, improvisatory model of poetic expression. However, even those children who were born in the early 1960s and who grew up in the years when new, alternative models of entertainment quickly conquered a place in Greek life, actively had to *choose* to make the expression intimately their own, rather than to find themselves constantly faced with it. The parées with *kritiká*, singing mantinádes and playing Cretan music, were now an option rather than a central way of celebration and self-expression. Nevertheless, this generation, as well as the following ones up to today, often combined the different ways of spending time. During the last few years, a counter-movement has been evident, as many young people have turned to Cretan music and mantinádes even after a period of denial of these roots.

Much like the acquisition of a native language, however, the adaptation of the register as a productive language involves learning a much wider system than something that can be acquired merely in occasional events. Several Cretans, although still aware of the cultural basis, and able to acknowledge competent performers and to occasionally participate in performances, therefore have only a partial, simplified model available for production. For this reason, the question of how profitable this basis is of the engagement and attainment of fluency for anyone with the relevant talent and energy to practice, is closely related to the question of whether the register is acquired as a productive medium or, as in an average modern society, as an author-centered, esoteric and distanced production.

Moreover, even if the adoption of a poetic register as a native language signifies the access to its linguistic flexibility and expressional, idiomatic potentiality, the *akoúsmata*, live acoustic experiences, have to be combined with an active adaptation of the means of action. As the study of the Frame Theory in the cognitive science shows, experts do not simply have more

---

10 See esp. Yacub 2007 and the *betsolaritsa*-performers' accounts in Garcia et al. 2001.

frames available than novices, but they also "possess more links between frames, better organized frames, better cross-referencing between frames," which makes them more flexible and efficient in their area of expertise (Mattila 2001: 38, drawing on Dreyfus 1992 and Howard 1987). How does one then learn to master alternative frames, build links among them and reframe the reality into poems successfully? Linguistic, poetic and imaginative skills are certainly needed in using the wealth of rhetoric, analogical, metaphoric and interpretive structures and frames. Cretans invariably see the talent to compose as an innate skill, but in her comments on composition, Kostoula Papadoyanni recurrently also referred to conscious activities: one has to know the local customs, how other people feel, what moves them; one has to practice and look for other possibilities, since new paths open up only if one walks on them; one has to exercise criticism and to learn to tell good ideas from bad ones. These requirements appear to be very similar to those that arose in Csikzentmihalyi's study on creativity (1996) that emphasizes the following factors: an intimate knowledge of the domain and existing solutions, devotion and hard work, sincere criticism, as well as enjoyment of the work for its own sake.

VII A theory of dialogic oral poetry

Dialogic oral poetry

According to my interpretation of the performances and composition as outlined in the previous chapters, the mantinádes are a tradition in which the dialogic, communicative goals are primary; these dialogic goals are, however, essentially partnered with the structurally inventive and, in several cases, explicitly artistic expression of the poetic register. Since I find that dialogism is the most pervasive single feature of the tradition, my conclusion is to refer to the mantinádes as *dialogic oral poetry*, or as a *dialogic register*.

I have used the attributes *short, productive, improvised, communicative* and *conversational* to depict this tradition, but during the process of analysis, the notions of *dialogue* and *dialogic* repeatedly surfaced as ways of capturing the essence of the tradition. The basis for the use of this concept is practical: people create poems and use them to engage in discourse and to exchange ideas with others. This exchange of ideas as dialogue can be very concrete and readily apparent. During recreational and festive singing, just as in many recited performances, the poems are exchanged back and forth by the participants. The creation of poems and the exchange of ideas through poems are also markedly dialogic implicitly and internally. These implicit ways of creating a dialogue, which do not point only to concrete verbal exchange in communication, require a more precise term of their own. In the case of this register, I underline both the structurally inventive element inherent in the register (a language for making poems) and the package-like, independent nature of the single poem (poems as the units of a language). I thus point simultaneously towards the internal dialogism of the language and the external dialogism of using the poem units as utterances.

By referring to the mantinádes as a specifically dialogic register, I do not intend to imply that the other verbal registers or traditions would not be dialogic. Instead, I have aimed to demonstrate that dialogism is indeed a fundamental force that the individual users of a shared poetic register consciously strive to attain. However, just as narrativity can characterize certain genres to such a degree that we can speak of narrative or epic genres, I use the term dialogic here to point to the special, essential character of this type of oral poetry. While Briggs' use of the definition of conversational genres is appropriate to describe recited utterances, mantinádes are also sung poetry. In addition, as shown in Chapter 6, the rhyming couplet form is also used as a building block for the longer compositions in which narrativity is much more prominent. By recognizing the short, compact and versatile form, by acknowledging the use of the poetic unit as an utterance in both sung and recited dialogues, and by noting that the primary *raison d'être* for mantinádes is as a vehicle for engaging in a dialogue, I therefore suggest classifying the register of mantinádes as a dialogic register among the various genres and registers of oral poetry. These genres can be recognized as scholarly genres or analytic types (epic, lyric, lament, genealogy, folktale, etc.), or they can be indigenously identified (e.g. Bauman 1984 [1977]; Ben-Amos 1976; Timonen 2004). John Miles Foley proposes the biological metaphor *ecology*[1] or *ecosystem* to depict the coexistence of the different kinds of forms of oral poetry in a society (Foley 2002: 188–218; 2005: 75–78)[2]. The present analysis on the Cretan tradition of mantinádes demonstrates that even if a dialogic register would not exist as an all-encompassing language of oral expression – as it does in central and eastern Crete – the use of this type of register in the indigenous ecology of genres can exclusively serve some needs and significantly complement others – as mantinádes do in western Crete.

In this conclusive chapter, in addition to analyzing how dialogism is established in the tradition of mantinádes, I will draw conclusions from the aspects implied by it: the wide access to the poetic register in performance and composition; the conceptions of creativity; the double identity of the poems as text and process; and the plurality of the aesthetics of performance and composition.

Individuals and tradition

Folklore genres vary tremendously within and between cultures as to how open they are for performance. As a register, mantinádes are simultaneously "open" and "closed" for performing and composition: these actions can take place at very different levels of competence. Until the 1980s, singing poems during collective celebrations was an experience which touched everyone either as a singer or as a listener. The extreme focus on performativity in some local speech communities has shaped the role of the repartee in public performances into a target of sharp criticism. In any public performance, one's ready wit and quick repartee form the appreciated norms of communication. At the opposite end of the spectrum, in addition to the contemporary expansion of the composition as an activity fueled by the mass media

---

1 The use of this notion differs from the concept of tradition-ecology, which as an "*approach accounts for the natural variation of traditions in social life*", as described by Honko (2000: 17–18; see also Kamppinen 1989: 37–46).
2 For the coexistence and interaction of genres in a community, see also the notion *ethnocultural substrate*, Harvilahti 2003, here in Chapter 2.

arenas, the accounts given by several elders attest to the fact that people have always created oral poems as self-expression, similarly to how people write poetry for their own pleasure in any contemporary culture. The double focus on the process and the text allows a freedom of choice, for example, in how much significance is placed on the elements in each case, and in the openness of the register for composition and performance in close circles, thus capable of being enjoyed at very different levels of competence. These factors, among others, made me conclude that although it is crucial to study and understand the components of competence, this concern does not exhaust the common experience of meaning in this register. For besides the communicative, socially defined and competence-centered uses of the register, the lyric and philosophical modes of expression and the compositional and aesthetic dimensions make this type of oral poetry work as a personal tool for creativity and self-expression. One of the conclusions is that in addition to the mantinádes being a vehicle for social sharing and communication in performance, they are also a means of personally sharing the values, ideas and attitudes crystallized in the tradition; they are an important language of dealing and coping with one's experiences and emotional life. In other words, the traditional is heavily intertwined with the individual, and the communicative dialogue is intertwined with each person's internal dialogue.

During my fieldwork in Crete, people have made it clear to me that a living tradition necessarily consists of two poles: there is the vehicle, which is the tradition, and there are the individuals who use this vehicle. The tradition of mantinádes is markedly a special language, a register. The register, apart from it being especially suited to allow composition and improvisation, carries diachronic elements, well-tested in the given society over the course of time; the register has diachronic elements in giving the people emotional, conceptual and communicative parallels for expressing themselves. This means that the register allows people to approach their current needs to make and convey meaning in a larger frame of reference, and to express these needs in an artistic, economic and understandable way. This economy and artistry, just as the ready wit and dialogically challenging communication, are appreciated by Cretans. The use of the register is based on these values and makes the process of dialogue evident even in the composition or recitation of single poems. The register thus represents the community's core ideal of communication: spontaneity.

Today, to an increasing degree, poems occur in contexts other than interpersonal communication and without immediate situational context, engaging their context in mental processes. I have therefore noted that in this tradition, we must recognize not only its performative value, but also its value as a productive register. Production, in addition to being a creative process, brings forth products: in Crete, new poems are valued as texts, as poetry, for their own sake – as well as they are valued as items carrying a potential for creating meaning in future processes. Hence, apart from the communicative, improvisatory process, the textual, poetic aspect plays a significant role in the evaluation of meaning. This parallel identity of the tradition as poems, as texts in their own right, and as an improvisatory process, has been of primary interest in this work. This reflects another dual identity: poems are considered to be individual compositions which, however, in the course of time, become a part of the shared tradition.

A person who composes new mantinádes can locally be called a *mantinadológos* (a specialist of mantináda). When performing, a *mantinadológos* may improvise verses on the spur of the moment, *epi tópou*, or may perform verses composed earlier. Any performer can sing or recite traditional verses, verses "heard," or those made by someone the performer knows. People are conscious of the fact that poems are made by a certain individual and they emphasize the individuality of the expression. People often express their admiration for the individual talent impersonally by referring to a poem: "The one who made this poem really felt this thing." When, however, people perform poems in singing events or in other communicative situations, they do not name any particular composer in connection to the poem, even if they are aware of who the composer is. Among regular *parées*, each person's characteristic repertoire is known, and the members of a close circle can easily recognize or guess who has created a certain poem. Nevertheless, a good poem is quickly circulated and separated from the acknowledgement of its origin. In brief, the individual talent that is reflected in a poem or in a performance is acknowledged in terms of its potential to speak to other individuals.

Four aspects of creativity

Mantinádes, as a rhyme language or as a register-based tradition, can stylistically vary widely in the continuum of prosaic–poetic and textual–contextual. Mantinádes can also range from structural play to finalized self-expression, and from first attempts to masterful compositions. I find that the uniting factor in the local perception of the meaning of mantinádes, for actors and perceivers alike, is best described by the notion of creativity – when this notion is understood to include both recognition and experience. This is why, while searching for the factors that produce recognized mastery and competence, I have also focused on the individual experience of creativity in the various personally significant uses of the register. By this I mean that the poems, performance and composition have the capacity to provide experiences of creativity and meaningfulness from the individual perspective of each person, according to their background, intentions and competence. The role of the structure is enhanced in the short couplet form, and making rhymes attracts everyone from the masters of communication to those composing their first verses. All participants, regardless of their levels, experience creativity in this poetic activity. The locals are extremely concerned with linking the poems to their personal experience, so the meaning and creativity of the text is essentially in the eye of the perceiver.

A dialogic poetic tradition such as the mantinádes gives multiple options for creativity. The locals perceive creativity in the creative process of composition and performance as well as in the resulting end product, the poem. Furthermore, the poetic domain differs even from many other domains of verbal art in that people experience creativity both collectively as well as from a very personal perspective. From my observations, I have concluded that four major forms of creativity can be distinguished.

The first type of creativity involved is *performative or improvisatory creativity*. Here, the focus is on the communicative process in which poems are matched with the theme of the exchange of poems in a singing event or with one's personal self-expression in speech. The poems may be composed ex tempore, or they may be poems that already exist. Creativity is felt in the possibility, and recognized in the ability, to make use of the poetic idiom and existing poems, and to apply these to new situations. This is the basic level of action in oral societies, and it gives the experience of creativity to most people practicing the dialogic tradition of verbal art. The competitive aspect of the performance also stimulates individuals with particular imagination and sociolinguistic talent to create ever better poems.

The second type of creativity is *productive creativity*. Because good mantinádes are locally appreciated as poetic end-products, the ability to provide new and commonly recognized poems must be noticed. This is true for poems that are regarded as excellent poetry; these poems contain a message that touches many people, and they are added to the shared oral repertoire. Productive creativity may or may not go together with the sociolinguistic talent to act in a situation, in a performance; nevertheless, these poems are mainly formulated in the mind of highly experienced and devoted people who have special innate skills, which have already been fully developed.

The ideas of *domain* and *field* as introduced by Csikszentmihalyi (1996; see Chapter 2) continue to be pertinent for both performative and productive creativity. In these two cases, creativity goes together with competence – that is to say, it is expressed and recognized in public arenas and as subject to shared criteria. Most often feedback is part of the parcel; feedback can either be immediate or conveyed through the poem being adopted in poetic reservoir of other individuals, that is, incorporated in the tradition. Most individuals capable of performing creatively or of composing great poems have internalized the tradition at an early age and gone through a long period of practicing. Furthermore, competition and exposure to evaluation are crucial, since oral arenas need a quick response and a good sense of what is good and what is bad.

The final two forms of creativity are *experienced* rather than recognized, because in these cases the creativity is evaluated with personal criteria and based on individual experience. One of these is what Csikszentmihalyi refers to as *personal creativity*. As to the mantinádes, personal creativity indicates the compositions that people create for their own pleasure, which make them discover something personally new (in the register or of their own capacity to act) and which fulfill their personal expectations. In other words, the register is easily available and open to anyone willing to try their hand in composing, and although many of the poems remain private and might not endure the criticism of the more experienced composers, the private composers themselves experience creativity in the process and enjoy the results.

All the above-mentioned cases refer to concrete *action* in performance or composition, but there is also an important creative process present in mental activity. This is the *creativity of perception* and it relates to individuals who experience creativity by processing poems in personal mental dialogues. If we agree that creativity is present in the processes that help us see things from new, alternative perspectives and that this process is crucial for a good performance and for creating new products, it follows that the same logic can be applied to the poems, as well: discovering a meaning in a poem, and applying this meaning to one's personal experience, is likewise a creative act.

It is my observation that all these perspectives are essential for understanding the improvisatory, associative and dialogic characteristics of the poetic performance arena. Composition is a creative challenge to many. The nature of a metrical, register-based tradition is a pyramid-like organism, where accessibility, extensive poetic practice and personal experience with the register all help people to recognize their own skills, and become competent in recognizing and enjoying true mastery. It is quite evident that participation in the singing events (which, in the past, recurred often) provided a field where many couplets were composed as well as performed purposely to fulfill the demands of participation. The same phenomenon is evident today in media talk shows: composing and participating with one's own compositions is encouraged widely, and there is no discrimination concerning competence. The poems composed in and for the traditional and modern participative performance arenas certainly differ: along with the movement from interpersonal, face-to-face communication to the decentered presentation of poems to a distant audience, compositions strive to create imagery rather than to produce contextually oriented and relevant expression. In both arenas, however, participation is a way to reach out from one's personal experience towards shared topics and messages.

Creativity is present in all these aesthetic and cognitive processes in which people create poems or match already existing ones to their needs. On the one hand, individuals produce the images and models which not only renew and refresh the tradition, but bring it into being in the first place. On the other hand, becoming aware of the creativity which poems engender in the various performative and mental dialogues causes people to recognize the significance of their traditions and this motivates them to uphold the tradition with their individual acts and choices.

The self-dependent poem and the economy of tradition

Registers in metrical form have the special characteristics of a strict mould. This mould consists of fixed meter and/or rhythm, rhyme and/or other poetical elements and means. Thus, while requiring the composer to confine his or her words to the limited possibilities of these conventional elements, this mould allows an explicit structural creativity. The natural word stress of the Greek language has to conform to the poetic pattern, which may make this especially obvious. In addition to offering the possibility of fulfilling the communicative and narrative needs for self-expression, this structural element provided by the metrical form is in itself a remarkable source for the composer to find satisfaction in creativity. Especially in the cases based on such a shared, productive idiom, focusing on the tradition as a language or as a register helps to allow a dynamic perception of traditional forms, with room for both shared meanings and referents as well as for individual creativity and aspirations.

Ideally, a mantináda is one coherent, self-dependent image, which is enjoyable and also understandable. According to the local definition, a mantináda is independent and it is poetry. The indigenous concept of mantináda as an image (*ikóna*) suggests something that is rendered immanent by poetic means.

> Kostoula Papadoyanni 2008 (080930):
>
> (Referring to the *Erotókritos*)…I liked the images of it. But you may say that well, in prose one also creates images. But maybe you need more time – like we talked last time – to show what you feel. To show what you see in your head, the image. Whereas with the *dekapentasíllavo* you show that immediately, you show the image. An artist can paint an image, someone can narrate an image – I believe that a *mantináda* closes that all inside, I mean, with a mantináda I feel it, I express it. I show what I feel inside myself, my emotions take form: love, hate, revenge, something…complaints (laugh) – complaints, yes! Everything, everything comes out more sweetly, comes out in the right form, in its own form. That is, I make someone understand [what I feel, what I want to say] with a mantináda.

Kostoula's reference to understanding explains why the independence of the poem is a different concern for insiders and outsiders: the net of textual and contextual referents embedded in the poems is wide, and the dialogic space the receiver/hearer/reader has to cover is remarkable. The interdependence of the concepts *parole* and *langue*, in their sociolinguistic sense, can therefore be aptly applied to the present context. This interdependence justifies the local perception of the poems as individual, independent *paroles*, but also recognizes the intimate relationship of the poems to the *langue*, the register which, for the locals, is so self-evident that it does not have to be mentioned. The recognition of this intimate relation is all the more important for outsiders, because in most cases, background knowledge is needed to unlock and appropriate the image, to *see* it, and especially to grasp the argument itself. A poem thus must be a semantically, structurally and circumstantially fully representative of the register, a meaningful and personal participant in the chain of poetic dialogue. A poem may not, however, be complete or autonomous in a vacuum – and why would it, when with so much less, one can say so much more? The charm of the dialogic register is essentially a result of extended communicative economy.

An essential counterpart of the possibility of a poem striving for such extended referentiality in creating an image is the role of an experienced audience as interpreters. Drawing from the work of Wolfgang Iser and Hans-

Robert Jauss, John Miles Foley (1991: 38–48; 1995: 42–47) adjusts their Receptionalist approach of the literary theory to explain the co-creation of the experience in traditional oral performance. In a literary work, the implied reader participates in the formation of the work by filling in the "gaps of indeterminacy," the necessary blank spaces in the text, which activate the reader and only in this way the process may allow a full experience of art. The implied reader receives the guidelines for filling in those gaps from personal literary and general experience and knowledge, as well as from the signals in the text. (Iser 1974, in Foley 1995: 43) Similarly, the contextualization of a performance proceeds in a simultaneous interpretation of the immanent textual and contextual cues and of a larger traditional textual, historical, aesthetic and moral knowledge. With regard to mantinádes, my analysis suggests that this referentiality is based on a heightened awareness and a conscious exploitation of the dialogic orientation of the language (Bakhtin 1981; 1986). The tradition, therefore, is not a *langue*, but essentially the acts of activating this langue through personal, contextualized and dialogic utterances – *paroles*.

The plural aesthetics of performance and composition

For a conclusion of the interaction between text and context, I will return to the beginning: the poems inserted by the *kafenío*-owner into our conversation presented a perfect introduction to the variety of means in a performance. These poems manifested several characteristics and means that are native to recited performances, and many features typical of singing events. Both poems, the first and the last, fit the basic dialogic idea of reacting to a situation and commenting on it or on another person's words. The first poem includes a clear textual deictic: "you are…," describing and evaluating the other person and her behavior.

> *Is' ómorfi, íse sklirí / íse ke pismatára*
> *Ke pos pligónis mia kardiá / de dínis mia dekára*
>
> You are beautiful, you are hard / you are stubborn too
> And that you hurt one heart / you don't give a penny

The last poem contains a coherent, well-balanced and metaphoric poetic picture. It draws on the intended message by employing the imagery to point to the parallelism between the situation and the poem.

> *Pollá ta déndra pou anthoún / ma líga pou karpízoun*
> *Pol' ín' ekíni p' agapoún / ma líyi pou kerdízoun*
>
> Many are the trees that bloom / but few the ones that bear fruit
> Many are the ones who love / but few the ones who gain

The four poems recited in the middle of our conversation as one cluster reveal that this man used to sing mantinádes in a *paréa*: my reasoning for having to leave was based on the idea of a long, confidential relationship between a couple, and the state of separation was immediately perceived by him as a familiar *theme*.

Horísame prosoriná / mi hásis tin elpída
Ma tin kardiá mou kivernás / sa naftikí piksída

We separated temporarily / don't lose your hope
Since you govern my heart / like the compass the seaman

Horísame, de sou zitó / elpída na mou dósis
Móno ta tósa mistiká / poté na min prodósis

We separated, I don't ask you / to give me any hope
Just that all those secrets / you never betray others

De tha mas ksehorísoune / i stratiyi ts' Evrópis
Yatí agapithíkame / ís ton anthó tis niótis

We cannot be separated / by Europe's generals
Because we fell in love / in the bloom of youth

'Ithela ná' me sínnefo / na me fisá t' ayéri
Na me fisíksi mia vradiá / kontá sou na me féri

I wish I were a cloud / to be blown by the wind
To be blown one night / and brought by your side

As a local, indigenous concept, the theme is the organizing principle guiding the singing in a singing event; it means that the mantinádes sung by each participant always have to build on the theme at hand. The performative rule of the exchange of poems is thereby *thematic continuation*. The *kafenío*-owner's poems elaborate on the theme of separation between two people having a long, confidential relationship. He performs a set of poems alone on this occasion, which was fuelled by his surprise over the fact that although a foreigner, I had perceived his code-changing from ordinary speech to mantinádes. This elaboration also demonstrates how the thematic continuation is essentially realized by *thematic associations* – the textual pull of the theme thereby links even a contextually disconnected participant (the second poem) in a chain of poems.

This performance consists of traditional, fixed poems, which are selected from a personal poetic reserve to meet the needs of the situation. Another possibility for a performance is to compose a mantináda *epi tópou*, "on the spot." Several, but not all or possibly even most, of the performances contain ex tempore composition. Ethnographic studies on mantinádes and similar traditions, however, concentrate primarily on extempore composition, which stimulates the researcher and the local observers alike in a special way. The fundamental identity of the tradition, both in the method of composition-in-performance (a term referred to and explained in detail by Albert Lord with reference to narrative oral poetry (1960)) and among the contest poetry genres (specifically called *improvised oral poetry*) in the Basque and Hispanic traditions (esp. Garcia et al. 2001), is the oral composition taking place at the very moment of performance. These traditions also clearly distinguish between the identities of the composer-performer and the audience.

My conversations with contemporary composers revealed a different focus in their own approach to composition. Even those whom I knew to be capable of extemporizing, stressed the primary role of poems as self-expression, as "parts of one's life." These contemporary composers emphasized that although an extemporized poem has its value in manifesting one's quickness of thought and one's skill in capturing a situation in a couplet, *meaningful* new poems are more likely to spring to mind when one is contemplating a personal feeling or experience. Several composers also told me that the moment a poem first comes into being holds more significance for them than the moment when they perform a previously created or an extemporized poem. One could draw the hasty conclusion that this difference in significance is due to the contemporary habit of writing down the poems and the changed ways of transmitting and performing them. However, several detailed accounts referring to decades back soon revealed that in addition to the communicative goals, these artistic and expressive urges have always been a significant part of the tradition in Crete.

Cretan mantinádes thus turned out to have a mixed identity within one register: while they are individually composed poems, they are also a reserve of poems in fixed form ready to be used to meet the needs of a situation. Ex tempore composition is but one form of composition and composers are but one category of performers. This means that the aesthetics of a performance and the aims of composition are also plural. Most fixed poems maintained by the tradition, for example, those recited to me by the *kafenío*-owner, contain a coherent image and universally applicable elements, which is often the result of a composition process carried out by the composer in peace and quiet. The Cretan tradition consequently stretches the concept of oral composition to encompass two kinds of activities: ex tempore composition in performance and composition as a less instantaneous, more coherence-oriented mental activity, which can occur outside of a performance. This is also made evident in the local definition of composition.

The most common verb used for creating poems is *vgázo* (take off/out). This verb is also used for taking photographs, *vgázo fotografíes*. Taking photographs is a good parallel to express how common the composition of mantinádes is in Crete, as well as how different the aesthetics, technique, talent and aims of the process can be. Everyone knows that an amateur photographer's snapshots rarely are exemplary aesthetically, although they may be among the amateur's dearest personal memories; the long preparation and staging of the setting can improve composition quality, but it can also result in lifeless images; true talent captures more and requires engagement and experience, and it rests on the combination of technical skills and an eye both to *find* and *frame* objects.

Interchangeably with the *vgázo*, composers today widely use the verb *gráfo* (write). Although the term *vgázo* can point to ex tempore composition, neither of these terms makes explicit when the composition happens. While composition in general is regarded an innate talent that cannot be learned, ex tempore composition is regarded as yet a special talent in a composer, and is often characterized by supplementary definitions, such as *epí tópou*, (on the spot). The verb *gráfo* is inspired by the written performances. This verb is used today very often to denote the process of composition, even when this is yet completely or highly oral, although the poems are preferably written down and usually performed in written arenas. In other words, a distinction between the oral and the actual written composition in the genre is not made explicit in any of the definitions used.

Today the skill of ex tempore composing in a situation is quite rare in Crete. This skill is certainly appreciated, but as the poems that continue to be referred to let us imagine, and as the accounts given by the composers straightforwardly tell, in most communities, ex tempore composing was never the sole standard for successful performance or composition. Instead, it is generally understood that situational poems created in performance have their own aesthetics, as do poems created at moments when personal impulses take form from one's thought, experience or feelings. This means that while new poems are composed in performance, they are also much more frequently composed during other moments as well. Nonetheless, although these aesthetics differ, they both share the challenge of choosing and framing the objects.

From oral to modern performance arenas

The singing of poems in festive and recreational events has provided a major traditional frame for performing mantinádes. Although these events are no longer featured as the primary contexts for the actual emergence of poems, as they constitute the very recent past and yet occasionally the actual events, they still provide a relevant mental *locale* for the tradition.

As performance, however, I have also included all casual, referential forms lacking the explicit characteristics of performance as a framed, situated event. This makes the important point that people in a living oral community can communicate meanings to each other with very little framing. I found the notion *performance arena* as introduced by John Miles Foley (1995: 8, 47–49) particularly suitable for my analysis, since it emphasizes, in connection to the use of the register, the state of performance as a mental readiness to perceive and decode meanings with an immediate awareness of the stylistic and referential codes. It is easier to understand the creativity of the metrically "limited," economical registers if one includes the informal, unframed performances, as well as the being in the performance arena in one's thoughts. The economy of communication and the identity of the texts, both as ends and as stepping stones, enhance the dialogic potential of the register.

For presentation, I grouped these oral arenas into the following five frames: first, the sung performances (1) in a *gléndi* (feast), (2) in a *paréa* (a get-together), and second, the recited performances 3) embedded into speech (proverbial, referential, meditative, etc), 4) of telling a story of a past performance, and 5) of presentation of poetic inventiveness. Each of these groups provides information on the frames for the discourse – of how much the addressee/audience is expected to have earlier knowledge concerning the rules of communication and of the local or individual repertoires and performances. In each case, the performer takes over the responsibility of speaking in socially appropriate ways, as Bauman defines the mode of performance[3], although in Crete this may be realized merely by the act of reciting a poem and showing, correspondingly, that *this poem speaks to me*. This factor alone also paves the way for the poems to enter the contemporary mass media.

To conceptualize how this poetry also works entirely outside the performative, face-to-face situations in the modern written and mass media arenas, one needs to understand the way traditional singing evolves through semantic continuation. As repeatedly pointed to, *théma*, the theme, is the central force in the performing of the poems in a singing event: the singing is essentially organized around a chosen theme to which each singer contributes. Therefore the dialogue in a singing event may be a net of reciprocal comments and responses, or it can as well (and often does) reflect the individual associations each participant has in mind at that moment and related to the theme in focus. The thematic connection is indeed largely a question of personal associations: each participant sings essentially the songs he or she likes, recollects or creates due to these personal associations. In other words, the theme and thematic continuation as major local conceptions define the rules and boundaries of the expression, all the while allowing and calling for imagination and creativity. Here the meaning is attributed as much to accomplishing a disciplined activity as it is to portraying a personal experimentation within the contextual elaboration and imagery of the specific theme.

Performative, contextual and textual dialogue

The analyses of the performance situations and composition processes have demonstrated that the different parallel or alternative ways of making and perceiving meaning are always dialogic. According to my interpretation, dialogue and dialogism are modes of verbal interaction and thinking that are based on special engagement in these actions. In Chapter 1, based on the work of Gadamer (1975) and Bakhtin (1981; 1986), I analyzed the concept of dialogue as an engagement in an interpretive process and specifically as a way to engage in a study. In Chapter 2, I referred to Briggs' analysis (1988) of the textual and contextual features in the performance of a variety of conversational genres and to his consequential conclusions of internal

---

[3] "Fundamentally, performance as a mode of spoken verbal communication consists in the assumption of responsibility to an audience for a display of communicative competence. This competence rests on the knowledge and ability to speak in socially appropriate ways." (Bauman 1984 [1977]: 11)

and external dialogic methods. While Briggs' analysis applies to a set of genres ranging from the conversationally defined genres to the genres with a narrative core, here I have attempted to shown how the performances and composition in one register are dialogic in different ways. This is based on my analysis of how people invest meaning in various elements on the different occasions of performance and composition. Various aspects of dialogism can thus be discerned in the kinds of relations, and in which elements the single poems are chiefly situated and perceived to be.

In performance, it is proposed that this engagement may signify three kinds of dialogic relations. The first type concerns the concrete exchange of poems and poetry as a mode of challenging the other to participate in a dialogue. During a singing event or recited exchange, the interaction takes place under the guiding principle of thematic continuity. I have described this type of dialogism as performative. The implication is that participants find singing together to be meaningful in itself as a collaborative arena of expressing themselves and of exchanging and developing their ideas. Although strictly speaking, the sung dialogue is not necessarily formed of reciprocal answers to what the former sang, but of thematic associations in which each person's contribution can vary in the different parameters, the turn-taking always adds something to the handling of the chosen theme and shapes the participants' ideas further. In short, the performative dialogism of a ruled, concentrated performance gives deep satisfaction to the participants.

Among the frame of such singing event, or when poems enter spoken utterances, a performer can create dialogic relationships between a poem and something that exists in, is performed, or recalled during the event. In addition to participating in a performative dialogue, a person can insert a more carefully contextualized or more personal utterance. This engagement concerns the perception or creation of specific ties between the present and past, between the text and context. For this reason, I refer to dialogism as being referential (or contextual) when a single poem sung/cited explicitly turns to reflect the situation or the shared past either through its textual referents, or as a whole. This reflecting on a situation can be accomplished by setting the present situation in an analogy with another event or shared knowledge. Sociolinguistic, communicative competence enables a person to point to a selected meaning, to draw analogies and to recall earlier meanings that are present either through the recitation/singing of the memorized poems or through extempore composition.

Images also create a dialogue with other images and give impulses to create new ones at the textual level. Hence dialogism can also take place at the textual level. Furthermore, the textual, thematic connections occur in performative dialogues both on the semantic level and on the lexical, surface level. Intertextuality is encoded in the requirement of a thematic continuation in performance and the textual dialogism often goes hand-in-hand with the performative as well as the contextual dialogism. However, due to the vitality of the poetic register, the dialogic impulses embedded in the imagery are also active outside the performance. At the textual level, the poems also participate in forming the meaningful units of tradition.

New images are created through associations, which join together the tradition and the individual through this special engagement. As for images, they are also understood to enclose a personal process: they are internally contextualized. Consequently, people can engage in a polyphonic dialogue through these images. This is especially evident in the composition of poems in privacy and in the emotional dialogues where thoughts and feelings are partnered with existing poems. To conclude, images speak to people because they create a mental state of mind that can be shared and discussed in a collective and individual manner concurrently – one can perform oneself as an individual while pointing to the shared experience and to the understanding guided by the tradition.

In addition to the syntactic and morphological flexibility of the poetic register and the variation in themes and imagery available for improvisation and composition, the expression in the register is characterized by cultivating the cognitive skills needed to look for new solutions, for which I applied the term reframing. Like literature and the visual arts, oral traditions have always been used for introducing new perspectives to current human matters, and this element is fundamental for short, communicational genres such as proverbs, aphorisms and jokes. Indeed compact, coherent mantinádes take full advantage of this cognitive resource in their textual and contextual improvisation and in composition as a mental activity.

By focusing on the thematic associations in sung performances and on the associations created by the imagery in composition by recognizing them as essentially dialogic ways to navigate among the poetic expression, these have all helped to open new perspectives in the research of oral poetry. Scholars have tried in several ways to solve the utilitarian versus artistic debate that characterized the Parry-Lord scholarship. One of the most prominent of these is Foley's endeavor to show how structures convey meaning; how, for example, do traditional formulas carry extra-textual referents which, like the necessary gaps in a literary text, require that the addressee/hearer enriches the poetic experience and the significance of what is said by entering into the entire universe of the traditional expression. A related concern touches on the semantic discrepancies in the associative chaining of poetic motives and the question of whether or not they are formed intentionally. Has the singer always expressed an intentional semantic message that we need to try to interpret (but often cannot because the poem texts are performed at time in the distant past), or has the pull of the poetic material already sung invited associations at the surface level without a special intentional purpose?

The composition and performance of the Cretan mantinádes suggest that these associations are a significant part of the internal dialogism of the imagery within the register, which has its own laws beyond the intentionality of normal speech acts. Nevertheless, the poems also are often featured as intentional, individual utterances, and the problem of interpretation as to how intentional or not an utterance is evidently arises in many cases. Even so, awareness of the performative and referential dialogism should not, however, hinder one's recognition of the textual dialogism and its improvisatory potential in poetic creativity. The foundation for the competent performance and composition of mantinádes is learning to use the cognitive skill of reframing effectively in real situations. Just like the skill of finding a fitting solution in each case requires an extended residence in the performance arena to gain experience in *possible cases* and to arrive at *alternative solutions*, poetic creativity acquires its power of striking accuracy from being inherently experimental, permissive and associative.

Bibliography and primary sources

Primary sources

All recordings made by the author. Original material (1999/cassettes, 2001–2008/ minidiscs, 2009/digital recording) archived by the author. The code numbers refer to the date of the interview. (Other participants, Yannis Hadziharalambus = Y.H.)

Code	/ Date /	Interviewees	/Place	/Other participants
991013/1	13.10.1999 /	Primary School children	/Village (Milopotamos)	
991013/2	13.10.1999 /	Nikos (11), Manolis (22)	/ Village	
991123	23.11.1999 /	Aristidis Heretis	/ Anoya	/+ Y. H.
991124	24.11.1999 /	Kostas Kontoyannis	/ Rethimno	
991202	02.12.1999 /	Mitsos Stavrakakis	/ Iraklio	
010328	28.03.2001 /	Despina Papadaki, Agapi Moshovaki	/Village	/+Y.H, +R
010401	01.04.2001 /	Despina Papadaki, Agapi Moshovaki	/ Village	/+Y.H,
010420	20.04.2001 /	Despina Papadaki, Agapi Moshovaki	/ Village	/+Y.H
010422	22.04.2001 /	Katerina Kornarou	/ Milopotamos	/ +Y.H
010429	29.04.2001 /	Mihalis Troulis	/ Village	
010430	30.04.2001 /	Despina Papadaki, Agapi Moshovaki	/ Village	
010430/2	30.04.2001 /	Katerina Kornarou	/ Milopotamos	
040715	15.07.2004 /	Despina Papadaki, Agapi Moshovaki	/ Village	/ +Y.H.
040727	27.07.2004 /	Kostoula Papadoyanni	/ Village	
040925	25.09.2004 /	Despina Papadaki, Agapi Moshovaki	/Village	/+women
041108	04.11.2008 /	Despina Papadaki, Agapi Moshovaki	/ Village	/+Y.H
041110	10.11.2004 /	Yorgos Sifakis	/ Rethimno/	+ Y.H.
050511	11.05.2005 /	Kostas Mangoufákis	/ Ano Vianos	
051102	02.11.2005 /	Vangelis Vardakis	/ Ierapetra	/ +Y.H.
050906	06.09.2005 /	Antonis Stefanakis	/ Zaros	
060504	04.05.2006 /	Maksimos & Irini Tsiburakis	/ Hania	/+Stelios Tsiburakis
060511	11.05.2006 /	Antonis Stefanakis	/ Zaros	
060515	15.05.2006 /	Mihalis & Irini	/ Hania	/ +Y.H.
060516	16.05.2006 /	Lefteris Kalomiris & paréa	/ Anoya	/ +Y.H.
060712	12.07.2006 /	Stelios Tsiburakis	/ Helsinki	
060823	23.08.2006 /	Mitsos Stavrakakis	/ Iraklio	
080930	30.09.2008 /	Kostoula Papadoyanni	/ Village	
091030	30.10.2009 /	Kostoula Papadoyanni	/ Village	

Bibliography

Abu-Lughod, Lila 1986: *Veiled Sentiments: Honour and Poetry in a Bedouin Society.* Berkeley: Berkeley University of California.
Ahola, Joonas (forthcoming). The Saga Outlaw. Ph.D. dissertation at the University of Helsinki, Folklore studies.
Alexiou, Margaret 1974: *The Ritual Lament in Greek Tradition.* Cambridge: Cambridge University Press.
Alexiou, Margaret and Holton, David 1976: The origins and development of "politicos stichos": a select critical bibliography. *Mantotofóros* 9: 22–34.
Alexiou, Margaret and Lambropoulos, Vassilis (eds.) 1985: *The Text and its Margins. Post-Structuralist Approaches to Twentieth-Century Greek Literature.* New York: Pella Publishing Company.
Alexiou, Stilianos 1969: *Kritiki Antholoyia.* Iraklio: Eteria Kritikon Meleton.
Amaryanakis, Yorgos 1988: Kritiki Vizantini kai paradosiaki mousiki. In: *Kriti: istoria kai politismos.* Second edition. Kriti: Sindesmos topikon enoseon dimon & kivotiton Kritis.
Anoyanakis, Fivos 1972: Neoellinika hordofona. To Laouto. *Laografia* 28: 175–239.
Anttonen, Pertti J. 1994: Ethnopoetic Analysis and Finnish Oral Verse. In: Anna-Leena Siikala and Sinikka Vakimo (eds.): *Songs Beyond the Kalevala: Transformations of Oral Poetry*: 113–137. Helsinki: Finnish Literary Society.
——— 2009: Arjen runous ja etnopoeettinen metodi. In: Seppo Knuuttila and Ulla Piela (eds.): *Korkeempi kaiku. Sanan magiaa ja puheen poetiikkaa*: 86–96. Helsinki: Suomalaisen Kirjallisuuden seura.
Armistead, Samuel and Zuleika, Joseba (eds.) 2005: *Voicing the Moment. Improvised Oral Poetry and the Basque Tradition.* Reno: Center for Basque Studies, University of Nevada.
Asplund, Anneli 2006: Runolaulusta rekilauluun. In: Päivi Kerala-Innala, Anneli Asplund, Petri Hoppu, Heikki Laitinen, Timo Leisiö, Hannu Saha, Simo Westerholm, *Suomen musiikin historia (8). Kansanmusiikki*: 108–165. Helsinki: WSOY.
Bailey, Clinton 2002 [1991]: *Bedouin Poetry from Sinai and the Negev.* London: Saqi books.
Bakhtin, M. M. 1981: *The Dialogic Imagination. Four Essays by M. M. Bakhtin.* Ed. by Michael Holquist. Austin: University of Texas Press.
——— 1986: *Speech Genres and other Late Essays.* Austin: University of Texas Press. Translation by V. McGee.
Barber, Karin 2007: Improvisation and the Art of Making Things Stick. In: Elizabeth Hallam and Tim Ingold (eds.): *Creativity and Cultural Improvisation*: 25–41. Oxford: Berg.
Bartók, Béla 1976: *Turkish Folk Music from Asia Minor* (ed. by Benjamin Suchoff). Princeton: Princeton University Press.
Baud-Bovy, Samuel 1936: *La chanson populaire grecque du Dodecanèse. Les textes.* Thèse à l'Université de Genève. Genève: Imprimerie A. Kundig.
Baud-Bovy 2006: *Mousiki katagrafi stin Kríti 1953–1954.* Tomos a&b. Ed. by Lambros Liavas. Athina: Kentro Mikrasiatikon Spoudon – Mousiko Laografiko Arhio Melpos Merlie.
Bauman, Richard 1984 [1977]: *Verbal Art as Performance.* Prospect Heights, Illinois: Waveland Press, inc.
2004: *A World of Others' Words. Cross-Cultural Perspectives on Intertextuality.* Oxford: Blackwell publishing.
Bauman, Richard and Briggs, Charles L. 1990: Poetics and Performance as Critical Perspectives on Language and Social Life. *Annual Review of Anthropology*, Vol.19 (1990): 59–88.
Bauman, Richard and Sherzer, Joel (eds.) 1989: *Explorations in the Ethnography of Speaking* (second edition). Cambridge: Cambridge University Press.

Beaton, Roderick 1980: *Folk poetry of Modern Greece*. Cambridge: Cambridge University Press.

────── 1989: *The Medieval Greek Romance*. Cambridge: Cambridge University Press.

Ben-Amos, Dan 1976: Analytical Categories and Ethnic Genres. In: Dan Ben-Amos (ed.): *Folklore Genres*: 215–242. Austin: University of Texas Press.

Berliner, Paul 1994: *Thinking in Jazz: the Infinite Art of Improvisation*. Chicago: The University of Chicago Press.

Boden, Margaret A. 2004 [1990]: *The Creative Mind. Myths and Mechanisms*. Second edition. London: Routledge.

Boulay du, Juliet 1974: *Portrait of a Greek Mountain Village*. Oxford: Clarendon Press.

Bourdieu, Pierre 1977: *Outline of a Theory of Practice*. Trans. by R. Nice. Cambridge: Cambridge University Press.

Bowra, Sir Maurice 1961: *Mediaeval Love-Song*. London: The Athlone Press (University of London).

Brenneis, Donald 1978: Fighting words. *New Scientist*, vol. 78 (No 1101): 280–282.

Briggs, Charles L. 1986: *Learning How to Ask: a Sociolinguistic Appraisal of the Role of the Interview in Social Science Research*. Cambridge: Cambridge University Press.

────── 1988: *Competence in Performance. The Creativity of Tradition in Mexicano Verbal Art*. Philadelphia: University of Pennsylvania Press.

Bronner, Simon J. (ed.) 1992: *Creativity and Tradition in Folklore. New Directions*. Logan: Utah State University Press.

Brown, Mary Ellen 1992: The Forgotten Makars: The Scottish Local Poet Tradition. In: Simon Bronner (ed.): *Creativity and Tradition in Folklore. New Directions*: 239–254. Logan: Utah State University Press.

Campbell, J. K. 1964: *Honour, Family, and Patronage: A Study of Institutions and Moral Values in a Greek Mountain Community*. Oxford: Clarendon Press.

Caraveli Chaves, Anna 1978: Love and Lamentation in Greek Oral Poetry. Ph.D. Dissertation at the State University of New York at Binghamton.

Caraveli, Anna 1980: Bridge Between Worlds: The Women's Ritual Lament as Communicative Event. *Journal of American Folklore*, vol. 93: 129–157.

────── 1982: The Song Beyond the Song: Aesthetics and Social Interaction in Greek Folksong. *Journal of American Folklore*, vol. 95: 129–159.

────── 1985: The Symbolic Village. Community Born in Performance. *Journal of American Folklore*, vol. 98: 259–286.

Caton, Steven C. 1985: The Poetic Construction of Self. *Anthropological Quarterly* 58: 4: 141–151.

────── 1990: *"Peaks of Yemen I Summon". Poetry as Cultural Practice in a North Yemeni Tribe*. Berkeley and Los Angeles: University of California Press.

Cerwonka, Allaine and Malkki, Liisa H. 2007: *Improvising Theory. Process and Temporality in Ethnographic Fieldwork*. Chicago: The University of Chicago Press.

Cook-Gumperz, Jenny and Gumperz, John J. 1976: Papers on language and context. Working Paper No. 46, Language Behavior Research Laboratory, Berkeley: University of California.

Crapanzano, Vincent 1992: *Hermes' Dilemma and Hamlet's Desire. On the Epistemology of Interpretation*. Cambridge: Harvard University Press.

Crease, Robert 1997: Responsive order: The Phenomenology of Dramatic and Scientific Performance. In: Keith R. Sawyer (ed.): *Creativity in Performance*: 213–226. Greenwich: Ablex Publishing Corporation.

Csikszentmihalyi, Mihaly 1997: *Creativity. Flow and the Psychology of Discovery and Invention*. New York: Harper Perennial.

Csikszentmihalyi, Mihaly and Rich, Grant 1997: Musical Improvisation: A Systems Approach. In: Keith R. Sawyer (ed.): *Creativity in Performance*: 43–66. Greenwich: Ablex Publishing Corporation.

Dalianoudi, Renata 2004: *To Violi & i Kithara os paradisiaki ziyia stin anatoliki Kriti. Kourdismata – repertorio – tehnikes*. Iraklio: Pagkritios sillogos kallitehnon kritikis mousikis.

Danforth, Loring M. 1982: *The Death Rituals of Modern Greece*. Princeton: Princeton University Press.
Dawe, Kevin 1996: The engendered líra: music, poetry and manhood in Crete. *British Journal of Ethnomusicology*, vol. 5 (1996): 93–112.
─── 1999: Minotaurs or musonauts? 'World Music' and Cretan music. *Popular Music* (Cambridge University Press). Volume 18/2: 209–225.
Diktakis, Athanasios P. 1999: *I Haniotes Laïki Mousiki pou den iparhoun pia*. Kastelli (self-published book).
Detorakis, Theoharis 1990: *Istoria tis Kritis*. B ekdosi. Iraklio (self-published book).
Droudakis, Alexandros 1982: *10.000 mantinades tsi Kritis*. Hania (self-published book).
Dubisch, Jill (ed.) 1986: *Gender and Power in Rural Greece*. Princeton: Princeton University Press.
DuBois, Thomas A. 1995: *Finnish Folk Poetry and the Kalevala*. New York: Garland Publishing, Inc.
Dundes, Alan and Leach, Jerry W. and Özkök, Bora 1970: The Strategy of Turkish Boys' Verbal Dueling Rhymes. *Journal of American Folklore*, vol. 83: 325–349.
Filippidis, S.N. 1987-89: Metashimatistikaa oria ton Kipriakon distihon (tsiattismaton). *Laografia* 35 (1987-89): 164–168.
Fine, Elizabeth C. 1984: *The Folklore Text. From Performance to Print*. Bloomington: Indiana University Press.
Foley, John Miles 1985: *Oral-Formulaic Theory and Research: an Introduction and Annotated Bibliography*. New York: Garland.
─── 1988: *The Theory of Oral Composition. History and Methodology*. Bloomington: Indiana University Press.
─── 1991: *Immanent Art: from Structure to Meaning in Traditional Epic*. Bloomington: Indiana University Press.
─── 1995a: *The Singer of Tales in Performance*. Bloomington: Indiana University Press.
─── 1995b: Folk literature. In: D.C. Greetham (ed.): *Scholarly Editing. A Guide to Research:* 600–626. New York: The Modern Language Association of America.
─── 2002: *How to Read an Oral Poem*. Urbana: University of Illinois Press.
─── 2005: Comparative Oral Traditions. In: Samuel Armistead and Joseba Zuleika (eds.): *Voicing the Moment. Improvised Oral Poetry and the Basque Tradition*: 65–81. Reno: Center for Basque Studies, University of Nevada.
Friedl, Ernestine 1962: *Vasilika: A Village in Modern Greece*. New York: Holt, Rinehart & Winston.
Gadamer, Hans-Georg, 2004 [1975]: *Truth and Method*. Second, revised edition. London: Continuum.
─── 2005: *Hermeneutiikka. Ymmärtäminen tieteissä ja filosofiassa*. Edited and translated by Ismo Nikander. Tampere: Vastapaino.
Garcia, Joxerra and Sarasua, Jon and Egana, Andoni 2001: *The art of bertsolaritsa. Improvised Basque verse singing*. Donostia: Bertsozale Elkartea.
Gilmore, David (ed.) 1987: *Honor and Shame and the Unity of the Mediterranean*. Washington: American Anthropological Association.
Granqvist, Kimmo 1997: Notes on Eastern Cretan Phonology. A Corpus-based Study. Ph.D dissertation at the University of Stockholm. Stockholm: Almqvist & Wiksell international.
Greene, Molly 2000: *A Shared World. Christians and Muslims in the Early Modern Mediterranean*. Princeton: Princeton University Press.
Guggenheimer, Eva H. 1972: *Rhyme effects and Rhyming Figures. A Comparative Study of Sound Repetitions in the Classics with Emphasis on Latin Poetry*. The Hague: Mouton.
Hallam, Elizabeth and Tim Ingold (eds.) 2007: *Creativity and Cultural Improvisation*. ASA Monographs 44. Oxford: Berg.

Halliday, M. A. K. 1978: *Language as social semiotic. The social interpretation of language and meaning*. London: Edward Arnold Ltd.
Hamilton, Andy 2007: *Aesthetics and Music*. London: Continuum.
Hanks, William 1996: *Language and Communicative Practices*. Boulder: Westview Press.
Harvilahti, Lauri (ed.) 1985: *Lehmuksen tytär tammen poika. Latvialaisia dainoja Krišjanis Baronsin kokoelmasta*. Helsinki: Suomalaisen Kirjallisuuden Seura.
—— 1992: *Kertovan runon keinot. Inkeriläisen runoepiikan tuottamisesta*. Helsinki: Suomalaisen Kirjallisuuden Seura.
—— 2001: Substrates and Registers. Trends in Ethnocultural Research. In: Wolf-Knuts, Ulrika and Kaivola-Bregenhøj, Annikki (eds.): *Pathways. Approaches to the Study and Teaching of Folklore*. Turku: Nordic Network of Folklore.
—— 2003: *The Holy Mountain. Studies on Upper Altai Oral Poetry*. In collaboration with Zoja Sergeevna Kazagaceva. Helsinki: Suomalainen Tiedeakatemia.
—— 2004: Vakiojaksot ja muuntelu kalevalaisessa epiikassa. In: Anna-Leena Siikala, Lauri Harvilahti and Senni Timonen (eds.): *Kalevala ja laulettu runo*. Helsinki: Suomalaisen Kirjallisuuden seura.
Heinonen, Kati 2008: Inkeriläisen runolaulun monta estetiikkaa. In: Seppo Knuuttila and Ulla Piela (eds.): *Kansanestetiikka*. Kalevalaseuran vuosikirja 87: 249–270. Helsinki: SKS.
Heretis, Aristidis 1996: *Ti mantináda na sou po...*. Iraklio: Panepistimiakes ekdosis Kritis.
Herndon, Marcia and McLeod, Norma 1980: The Interrelationship of Style and Occasion in the Maltese *Spirtu Pront*. In Norma McLeod and Marcia Herndon (eds.): *The Ethnography of Musical Performance*: 147–166. Norwood: Norwood Editions.
Herzfeld, Michael 1974: Cretan Distichs: 'The Quartered Shield' in Cross-Cultural Perspective. *Semiotica* 12: 203–218.
—— 1981a: An Indigenous Theory of Meaning and its Elicitation in Performative Context. *Semiotica* 34–1/2: 113–141.
—— 1981b: Performative Categories and Symbols of Passage in Rural Greece. *Journal of American Folklore*, vol. 94: 44–57.
—— 1982: *Ours Once More. Folklore, Ideology, and the Making of Modern Greece*. Austin: University of Texas Press.
—— 1983: Semantic Slippage and Moral Fall: The Rhetoric of Chastity in Rural Greek Society. *Journal of Modern Greek Studies* 1: 161–172.
—— 1985a: *The Poetics of Manhood. Contest and Identity in a Cretan Mountain Village*. Princeton: Princeton University Press.
—— 1985b: Interpretation from Within: Metatext for a Cretan Quarrel. In Margaret Alexiou and Vassilis Lambropoulos (eds.): *The Text and its Margins. Post-Structuralist Approaches to Twentieth-Century Greek Literature*. New York: Pella Publishing Company.
—— 1986: Within and Without: The Category of 'Female' in the Ethnography of Modern Greece. In Dubisch, J (ed.): *Gender and Power in Rural Greece*: 215–233. Princeton: Princeton University Press.
—— 1987a: *Anthropology through the Looking-Glass: Critical Ethnography in the Margins of Modern Europe*. Cambridge: Cambridge University Press.
—— 1987b: "As in Your Own House": Hospitality, Ethnography, and the Stereotype of Mediterranean Society. In: David Gilmore (ed.): *Honor and Shame and the Unity of the Mediterranean*. Washington: American Anthropological Association.
—— 1990: Literacy as Symbolic Strategy in Greece: Methodological Considerations of Topic and Place. *Byzantine and Modern Greek Studies* 14 (1990): 151–172.
—— 1991a: *A place in History: Social and Monumental Time in a Cretan Town*. Princeton: Princeton University Press.
—— 1991b: Silence, Submission, and Subversion: Toward a Poetics of Womanhood. In Loizos, P and Papataxiarchis, E (eds.): *Contested Identities: Gender and Kinship in Modern Greece*: 79–97. Princeton: Princeton University Press.

―――― 1992: *The Social Production of Indifference: Exploring the Symbolic Roots of Western Bureaucracy.* Oxford: Berg.

―――― 2004: *The Body Impolitic. Artisans and Artifice in the Global Hierarchy of Value.* Chicago: The University of Chicago Press.

―――― 2005: Cultural Intimacy. Social poetics in the Nation-State. New York: Routledge.

Holton, David (ed.) 1991: *Literature and society in Renaissance Crete.* Cambridge: Cambridge University Press.

Honko, Lauri 1998: *Textualising the Siri Epic.* Helsinki: Suomalainen tiedeakatemia.

―――― 2000: Thick Corpus and Organic Variation: an Introduction. In: Lauri Honko (ed.) 2000: *Thick Corpus, Organic Variation and Textuality in Oral Tradition*: 3–28. Helsinki: Finnish Literature Society.

Hymes, Dell 1974: *Foundations in Sociolinguistics: an Ethnographic Approach.* London: Tavistock publications.

―――― 1981: *"In vain I tried to tell you". Essays in Native American Ethnopoetics.* Philadelphia: University of Pennsylvania Press.

―――― 1989: Ways of Speaking. In: Richard Bauman and Joel Sherzer (eds.): *Explorations in the Ethnography of Speaking* (second edition). Cambridge: Cambridge University Press.

Ingold, Tim 2007: Introduction. In: Elizabeth Hallam and Tim Ingold (eds.): *Creativity and Cultural Improvisation*: 45–54. Oxford: Berg.

Ingold, Tim and Hallam, Elizabeth 2007: Creativity and Cultural Improvisation: An Introduction. In: Elizabeth Hallam and Tim Ingold (eds.): *Creativity and Cultural Improvisation*: 1–24. Oxford: Berg.

Jakobson, Roman and Bogatyrev, Petr 1980 [1929]: Folklore as a Special Form of Creation. *Folklore Forum*, volume 13, number 1, pp. 3–21.

Just, Roger 2000: *A Greek Island Cosmos. Kinship & Community on Meganisi.* Santa Fe: James Currey. Oxford / School of American Reseach Press.

Kallio, Kati (forthcoming): Länsi-Inkerin lauletttu runo. Ph.D. dissertation at the University of Helsinki, Folklore studies.

Kaloyanides, Michael 1975: The music of Cretan dances. A study of the Musical Structures of Cretan Dance Forms as Performed in the Irakleion Province of Crete. Ph.D. dissertation at the Wesleyan University, Middletown, Connecticut.

Kapsomenos, Eratosthenis 1979: *To singhrono kritiko istoriko tragoudi. I domi kai i ideologia tou.* Athina: Ekdoseis Themelio.

Kafkalas, Mihalis 1992: *Mnimonio kritikis dialektou me parallili anafora se sighrones mantinades.* Athina: Vivlioekdotiki Anastasaki.

―――― 1995: *Ta epirrimata tis kritikis dialektou.* Athina: Vivlioekdotiki Anastasaki.

―――― 1996: Kritiki Mantinada. Orismos, glossa, metriki, omiokataliksia. In: *Ereisma. Periodiki ekdosi logou kai tehnis.* Tevhos 5-6, Ioulios 1996: 9–26.

―――― 1998: *Odigos Kritikis Mantinádas. Apo ti theoria stin praksi.* Athina: Vivlioekdotiki AE.

Kavouras, Pavlos 1991: 'Glenti' and 'Xenitia': The Poetics of Exile in Rural Greece (Olympos, Karpathos). Ph.D. dissertation at the New School for Social Research, New York. UMI Dissertation Services.

Kiriakidis, Stilpon P. 1978: *To dimotiko tragoudi. Sinagogi meleton.* Ed. by Alki Kiriakidou-Nestoros. Athina: Neoellinika meletimata.

Kezich, Giovanni 1982: Extemporaneous Oral Poetry in Central Italy. *Folklore*, Vol. 93: 193–205.

Kligman, Gail 1988: *The Wedding of the Dead. Ritual, poetics, and Popular Culture in Transylvania.* Berkeley: University of California Press.

Kontosopoulos, Nikolaos G. 1988: *Glossikos Atlas tis Kritis.* Iraklio: Panepistimiakes ekdosis Kritis.

Koukoules, Maria (ed.) 1983: *Loose-tongued Greeks: a miscellany of neo-Hellenic erotic.* Paris: Digamma.

Ksanthinakis, Antonis 2001 [2000]: *Lexiko erminevtiko & etimilogiko tou ditikokritikou glossikou idiomatos.* Iraklio: Panepistimiakes ekdosis Kritis.

Kuusi, Matti 1963: Sananparsiston rakenneanalyysin terminologiaa. *Virittäjä* 1963: 339–347.

――― 1985: *Perisuomalaista ja kansainvälistä*. Helsinki: Suomalaisen Kirjallisuuden Seura.

Laitinen, Heikki 2003: *Matkoja musiikkiin 1800-luvun Suomessa*. Tampere: Tampereen yliopistopaino.

――― 2006: Runolaulu. In: Päivi Kerala-Innala, Anneli Asplund, Petri Hoppu, Heikki Laitinen, Timo Leisiö, Hannu Saha, Simo Westerholm, *Suomen musiikin historia (8). Kansanmusiikki*: 14–77. Helsinki: WSOY.

Lauhakangas, Outi 2004: *Puheesta ihminen tunnetaan. Sananlaskujen funktiot sosiaalisessa vuorovaikutuksessa*. Helsinki: Suomalaisen Kirjallisuuden Seura.

Leino, Pentti 1975: Äidinkieli ja vieras kieli: rahvaanrunouden metriikkaa. In: *Wäinämöisen Weljenpojat. Tutkielmia talonpoikaisrunoudesta*. Kalevalaseuran vuosikirja 55.1975: 26–48. Joensuu: Pohjois-Karjalan Kirjapaino Oy.

Lioudaki, Maria 1936 (n.d.): *Kritikes mantinádes*. Athina: Gnoseis.

Loizos, Peter and Papataxiarchis, Evthymius 1991: Gender and Kinship in Marriage and Alternative Contexts. In: Peter Loizos and Evthymius Papataxiarchis (eds.): *Contested Identities: Gender and Kinship in Modern Greece*. Princeton: Princeton University Press.

Lord, Albert B. 2001 [1960]: *The Singer of Tales*. Second edition. Edited by Stephen Mitchell and Gregory Nagy. Cambridge: Harvard University Press.

――― 1975: Perspectives on recent work on Oral Literature. In: Joseph J. Duggan (ed.): *Oral Literature. Seven Essays*. Edinburgh: Scottish Academic Press.

――― 1989: Theories of Oral Literature and the Latvian Dainas. In Vikis-Freibergs, Vaira (ed.): *Linguistics and Poetics of Latvian Folk Songs*, 35-48. Kingston and Montreal: McGill-Queen's University Press.

Lortat-Jacob, Bernard (ed.) 1987: *L'improvisation dans les musiques de tradition orale*. Paris: Selaf.

Lönnrot, Elias 1919 [1849]. *Kanteletar elikkä Suomen Kansan vanhoja lauluja ja virsiä*. Seitsemäs painos. Suomalaisen Kirjallisuuden Seura, Helsinki.

Magrini, Tullia 2000: Manhood and Music in Western Crete: Contemplating Death. *Ethnomusicology. Journal of the Society for Ethnomusicology*, vol. 44, No3: 429–459.

Mannheim, Bruce and Tedlock, Dennis 1995: Introduction. In: Dennis Tedlock and Bruce Mannheim (eds.): *The Dialogic Emergence of Culture*. Urbana: University of Illinois Press.

Mattila, Antti 2001: *"Seeing Things in a New Light". Reframing in Therapeutic Conversation*. Helsinki: Rehabilitation Foundation. Electronic dissertation: http://ethesis.helsinki.fi/julkaisut/laa/kliin/vk/mattila/. Helsinki: University of Helsinki.

――― 2006: *Näkökulman vaihtamisen taito*. Helsinki: Werner Söderström Osakeyhtiö.

Mikkola, Kati 2009. *Tulevaisuutta vastaan. Uutuuksien vastustus, kansantiedon keruu ja kansakunnan rakentaminen*. Helsinki: Suomalaisen Kirjallisuuden Seura.

Miner, Earl 1993: Poetic Competitions. In: Alexander Preminger and T.V.F. Brogan (eds.): *New Princeton Encyclopedia of Poetry and Poetics*: 925–927. Princeton: Princeton University Press.

Mintz, Jerome R. 1997: *Carnival Song and Society. Gossip, Sexuality and Creativity in Andalusia*. Oxford: BERG.

Moutzouris, Kostas D. (ed.) 2002: *Pepragmena Sinedriou "i kritiki mantinada". Kounoupidiana Akrotiriou 4–5 Avgoustou 2001*. Akrotiri: Dimos Akrotiriou Hanion.

Nettl, Bruno with Russell, Melinda (eds.) 1998: *In the Course of Performance. Studies in the World of Musical Improvisation*. Chicago: The University of Chicago Press.

Nikolakakis, Dimitris 2007: *Haniotiki mousiki paradosi. Organa ke kallitehnes*. Hania: Nomarhiki Aftodiikisi Hanion.

——— 2008: *Kritiki Horeftiki Paradosi. Haniotes horeftes.* Hania: Nomarhiki Aftodiikisi Hanion.
Opland, Jeff 1983: *Xhosa oral poetry. Aspects of a black South African tradition.* Cambridge: Cambridge University Press.
Oras, Janika, 2008: Viie 20. sajandi naise regilaulumaailm. Arhiivitekstid, kogemused ja mälestused. Eesti Rahvaluule Arhiivi toimetused 27. Tartu: Eesti Kirjandusmuuseumi Teaduskirjastus.
Pagliai, Valentina 2009: The Art of Dueling with Words: Toward a New Understanding of Verbal Duels across the World. *Oral Tradition,* 24/1 (2009): 61–88.
Palonen, Tuomas 2008: Vapaata mielenjuoksua. Suomenkielisen freestyle-rapin ilmenemismuodot estetiikka ja kompositio. Pro gradu -työ. Helsingin yliopiston folkloristiikan laitos.
Panayotakis, Nikolaos M. 1989: *O piitis tou Erotokritou ke alla Venetokritika meletimata.* Iraklio: Dimos Iraklion.
——— 1990: *I pedia ke i mousiki kata ti Venetokratia.* Kriti: Sindesmos topikon enoseon dimon & kinotiton Kritis.
Papadakis, Konstantinos B. 1989: *"Kritiki" Lira enas mithos. I alithia ya tin gnisia Kritiki paradosi.* Hania (self-published book).
Papadakis, Manolis Milt. 1992: *Maria Lioudaki. I Ierea tis pedias.* Athina: Morfotiki steyi Ierapetras.
Papadakis, Manolis 2002: *I istoria tis kritikis mousikis ston ikosto eona.* Thessaloniki: Ekdosis Ziti.
Papirakis, Manolis M. 2004: *I mantináda stis Korfes.* Rethimno: Politistikos sillogos Korfon.
Parry, Milman 1928a: L'Epithète traditionelle dans Homère: Essai sur un problème de style homérique. Paris: Société Editrice "Les Belles Lettres".
——— 1928b: Les Formules et la métrique d'Homère. Paris: Société Editrice "Les Belles Lettres".
Pavlakis, Yannis 1994: *Kritiki dimotiki piisi. I mantinades.* Athina: Vivlioekdotiki A.E.
Pennanen, Risto Pekka 2004: The Nationalization of Ottoman Popular Music in Greece. *Ethnomusicology,* Vol. 48, No. 1 (Winter, 2004): 1–25.
Peristiany, J. G. (ed.) 1965: *Honour and Shame: The Values of Mediterranean Society.* London: Weidenfeld & Nicolson.
Peristiany, J. G. and Pitt-Rivers, Julian (eds.) 1992: *Honor and Grace in Anthropology.* Cambridge: Cambridge University Press.
Pernot, Hubert 1931: *Chansons Populaires Greques des XV et XVI siècles.* Paris: Société d' edition "Les Belles Lettres".
Petrakis, Savvas 2009: *Asterousia. Mousikes Fotografies.* Dimos Asterousion.
Petropoulos 1954: *La comparaisen dans la chanson populaire grecque.* Athènes.
Politis, Alexis 1984: *I anakalipsi ton Ellinikon dimotikon tragoudion. Proipothesis, prospathies ke i dimiouryia tis protis silloyis.* Athina: Themelio.
Psaros, Nikos 1996: Stihourgiki, glossa ke i grafí tis mantinadas. In: *Ereisma. Periodiki ekdosi logou ke tehnis.* Tevhos 5–6, Ioulios 1996: 46–49.
Romeos, Konstantinos 1952–55: Tragoudia distiha tou Pontou. *Arheiou Pontou* 17–18 (1952–55): 279–284.
Sawyer, Keith 1997: Introduction. In Keith R. Sawyer (ed.): *Creativity in Performance*: 1–6. Greenwich: Ablex Publishing Corporation.
Scott, Clive 1988: *The Riches of Rhyme. Studies in French Verse.* Oxford: Clarendon Press.
Siapkara-Pitsillidou Themis 1990: Thimisi Samuel Baud-Bovy kai i meleti "Distiha tis Pontou". *Laografía* 1987–89 (1990): 146–161.
Sifakis, G. M. 1988: *Ya mia piitiki tou Ellinikou Dimotikou Tragoudiou.* Iraklio: Panepistimiakes Ekdosis Kritis.
Siikala, Anna-Leena 1984: *Tarina ja tulkinta. Tutkimus kansankertojista.* Helsinki: Suomalaisen Kirjallisuuden Seura.
——— 2000: Body, Performance, and Agency in Kalevala Rune-Singing. *Oral Tradition,* 15/2 (2000): 255–278. http://journal.oraltradition.org/issues/15ii/siikala

Siikala, Anna-Leena and Siikala, Jukka 2005: *Return to Culture. Oral Tradition and Society in the Southern Cook Islands*. Helsinki: Suomalainen Tiedeakatemia.

Siikala, Anna-Leena and Vakimo, Sinikka (eds.) 1994: *Songs beyond the Kalevala. Transformations of Oral Poetry*. Helsinki: Suomalaisen Kirjallisuuden Seura.

Silverstein, Michael and Urban, Greg (eds.) 1996: *Natural Histories of Discourse*. Chicago: The University of Chicago Press.

Sokolov, Y. M. 1950: *Russian folklore*. American Councel of Learned Societies.

Sowayan, Saad Abdullah 1985: *Nabati Poetry. The Oral Poetry of Arabia*. Berkeley: University of California Press.

Spiller, Michael R. G. 1992: *The Development of the Sonnet. An Introduction*. London: Routledge.

Stavrakakis, Mitsos 1984: '*Ilie mou kosmoyirefti. Mantinades*. Athina: Dorikos.

―――― 1999: *...sti dini ton anemo. Mantinades – piimata*. Iraklio: Ekdosis Anemomilos.

Sugarman, Jane C. 1988: Making Muabet: The Social Basis of Singing Among Prespa Albanian Men. *Selected reports in Ethnomusicology. Volume VII. Issues in the Conceptualization of Music*: 1–42. Los Angeles: University of California.

―――― 1997: *Engendering Song. Singing and Subjectivity at Prespa Albanian Weddings*. Chicago: The University of Chicago Press.

Sykäri, Venla 2003: Mantinádes in Crete. A Tradition of rhyming couplets as a poetic language. Unpublished master's thesis. University of Helsinki, Folklore studies.

―――― 2009a: Dialogues in Rhyme. The Performative Contexts of Cretan Mantinádes. *Oral Tradition* 24/1 (2009): 89–123. http://journal.oraltradition.org/issues/24i/sykari

―――― 2009b: Riimiruno puheenvuorona. In: Seppo Knuuttila and Ulla Piela (eds.): *Korkeempi kaiku. Sanan magiaa ja puheen poetiikkaa*: 110–126. Helsinki: Suomalaisen Kirjallisuuden Seura.

―――― 2010: Improvisointi ja runon tuottamisen tulkinnat. In: Seppo Knuuttila, Ulla Piela and Lotte Tarkka: *Kalevalamittaisen runon tulkintoja*: 276–286. Helsinki: Suomalaisen Kirjallisuuden Seura.

Tapaninen, Anna-Maria 1996: *Kansan kodit ja kaupungin kadut. Etnografinen tutkimus eteläitalialaisesta kaupungista*. Helsinki: Suomen Antropologinen Seura.

Tarkka, Lotte 2005: *Rajarahvaan laulu. Tutkimus Vuokkiniemen kalevalamittaisesta runokulttuurista 1821–1921*. Helsinki: Suomalaisen Kirjallisuuden Seura.

―――― forthcoming: *Songs of the Border People – Genre, Intertextuality and Tradition in Kalevala-Meter Poetry*.

Timonen, Senni 2000: Thick Corpus and a Singer's Poetics. In Lauri Honko (ed.): *Thick Corpus, Organic Variation and Textuality in Oral Tradition*: 627–660. Helsinki: Finnish Literature Society.

―――― 2004: *Minä, tila, tunne. Näkökulmia kalevalamittaiseen kansanlyriikkaan*. Helsinki: Suomalaisen Kirjallisuuden Seura.

Troulis, Mihalis 1998: Rethimno. Istoria – periiyisi – sighroni zoi. Rethimno: Mitos.

Tsouhlarakis, Ioannis Them. 2000: *I horí tis Krítis. Mithos istoria parádosi*. Athina: Kentro Spoudon Kritikou Politismou.

Tsouhlarakis, Ioannis Them. 2004: *Ta laika mousika organa stin Kriti*. Athina: Enosi Kriton Metamorfosis.

Vasenkari, Maria 1996: Mitä se sanoo? Mistä se kertoo? Dialoginen näkökulma kenttätutkimusaineiston tuottamiseen. In Tuija Hovi and Lotte Tarkka (eds.): *Etiäinen 3. Uskontotiede – Folkloristiikka. Kirjoituksia opinnäytteistä*: 84–109. Turku: Turun yliopisto.

Vasenkari, Maria and Pekkala, Armi 2000: Dialogic Methodology. In Lauri Honko (ed.): *Thick Corpus, Organic Variation and Textuality in Oral Tradition*: 243–254. Helsinki: Finnish Literature Society.

Vikis-Freibergs, Vaira (ed.) 1989: *Linguistics and Poetics of Latvian Folk Songs*. Kingston and Montreal: McGill-Queen's University Press.

Virtanen, Leea 1968: *Kalevalainen laulutapa Karjalassa*. Helsinki: Suomalaisen Kirjallisuuden Seura.
—— 1973: Kannakselainen laulukoulu. In: Hannes Sihvo (ed.): *Karjala. Idän ja lännen silta.* Kalevalaseuran vuosikirja 53: 146–158. Porvoo: WSOY.
Williams, Chris 2003: The Cretan Muslims and the Music of Crete. In Dimitris Tziovas (ed.): *Greece and the Balkans: Identities, Perceptions and Cultural Encounters since the Enlightenment.* Ashgate.
Yaqub, Nadia G. 2007: *Pens, Swords, and the Springs of Art. The Oral Poetry Dueling of Palestinian Weddings in Galilee.* Leiden: Brill.
Zedda, Paulu 2009: The Southern Sardinian Tradition of the Mutetu Longu: A Functional Analysis. *Oral Tradition* 24/1 (2009): 3–40.
Zemke, John 2005: Improvisation, Inspiration and Basque Verbal Contest: Identity in Performance. In: Samuel Armistead and Joseba Zuleika (eds.) 2005: *Voicing the Moment. Improvised Oral Poetry and the Basque Tradition*: 83–93. Reno: Center for Basque Studies, University of Nevada.

Index

Abu-Lughod, Lila 31, 34, 180
Alexiou, Margaret 118
Amaryanakis, Yorgos 75
antikristés 99, 128, 189–190
Asplund, Anneli 32

Bailey, Clinton 31
Bakhtin, M. M. 44–45, 65, 202
Barber, Karin 57
Bartók, Béla 31
Baud-Bovy, Samuel 28–29, 35, 71, 75–76, 121–126
Bauman, Richard 56, 139, 206
Beaton, Roderick 118, 120, 121
bertsolaritsa 75, 124, 135
Boden, Margaret 67, 69
Bogatyrev, Petr 10, 71, 80
Briggs, Charles 28, 33, 43–44, 61–62, 64, 66, 137, 196, 206–207

Caraveli, Anna 29–30, 61, 151
Caton, Steven 11, 31, 44, 98, 180
contest poetry 26, 33, 204
Crapanzano, Vincent 45
Csikszentmihalyi, Mihaly 68–69, 194, 199

daina 28, 33, 77
dekapantasíllavo 21, 25, 117–118, 121–122, 145, 159, 170, 172

Erotókritos, 119–120, 127, 158, 162, 172, 181

Foley, John Miles 55–56, 58–61, 71, 80, 137, 196, 202, 205

Gadamer, Hans-Georg 43
gléndi (pl. *gléndia*) 93, 138 et passim
Granqvist, Kimmo 86

Hallam, Elizabeth 68
Halliday, M. A. K. 58–59
Hamilton, Andy 73–74
Harvilahti, Lauri 57–59
Herzfeld, Michael 9, 28–29, 36, 39, 43, 47, 50–51, 61, 63–64, 66, 75, 82–83, 98, 125, 136, 152, 156–157, 172, 179
Holton, David 118
Honko, Lauri 50, 55, 57, 69, 131
Hymes, Dell 55, 58, 66

improvised oral poetry 26, 204
Ingold, Tim 68

Jakobson, Roman 10, 71, 80

Kafkalas, Mihalis 37, 125
kalevala-meter 9, 25–26, 32, 57–58, 72, 76, 192–193
Kallio, Kati (né Heinonen) 33
kantáda (a serenade), 115–116
Karas, Simon 35, 91
Kavouras, Pavlos 29–30
kéndro (pl. *kéndra*), 100–101
Kiriakidis, Stilpon K. 90, 119, 121
Kligman, Gail 31
kondiliés 21, 88, 105–106
Kuusi, Matti 72

Laitinen, Heikki 70
langue/parole 10, 71, 80, 201–202
Leino, Pentti 60, 192–193
Lioudaki, Maria 36, 97, 130–131
Loorits, Oskar 70, 76
Lord, Albert 37–38, 54, 58, 71–73, 77–78, 159, 192
Lönnrot, Elias 70

mantinádes sinehómenes 26, 132–135, 137

mantinadológos (pl. *mantinadolóyi*),
 a mantinada-composer
Mattila, Antti 188, 193–194
mezodopolio (pl. *mezodopolia*) 105

Ong, Walter 54
Opland, Jeff 73

paréa (pl. *parées*), 39–40, 104–105, 138
 et passim
Parry, Milman 37–38, 58, 126
Petropoulos, 126
Politis, Alexis 31
Porthen, Henrik Gabriel 70

quatrain 25–27, 31–33, 122

rekilaulu 32
rímes (sing. *ríma*), 93, 135–137, 158

rizítika 92–93

Sawyer, Keith 68
Siikala, Anna-Leena 56, 137
Sowayan, Saad Abdullah 31
Sugarman, Jane C. 30

Tarkka, Lotte 9, 58, 60
Tedlock, Dennis 55
Timonen, Senni 9, 58, 70
topical verse 26, 60
Tsantiropoulos, Aris 83
tshastushka 32

Williams, Chris 30
Virtanen, Leea 32–33

Zedda, Paulu 77

STUDIA FENNICA ETHNOLOGICA

*Making and Breaking of Borders
Ethnological Interpretations,
Presentations, Representations*
Edited by Teppo Korhonen,
Helena Ruotsala & Eeva Uusitalo
Studia Fennica Ethnologica 7
2003

*Memories of My Town
The Identities of Town Dwellers and
Their Places in Three Finnish Towns*
Edited by Anna-Maria Åström,
Pirjo Korkiakangas & Pia Olsson
Studia Fennica Ethnologica 8
2004

Passages Westward
Edited by Maria Lähteenmäki
& Hanna Snellman
Studia Fennica Ethnologica 9
2006

*Defining Self
Essays on emergent identities in Russia
Seventeenth to Nineteenth Centuries*
Edited by Michael Branch
Studia Fennica Ethnologica 10
2009

*Touching Things
Ethnological Aspects of Modern
Material Culture*
Edited by Pirjo Korkiakangas,
Tiina-Riitta Lappi & Heli Niskanen
Studia Fennica Ethnologica 11
2009

Gendered Rural Spaces
Edited by Pia Olsson & Helena
Ruotsala
Studia Fennica Ethnologica 12
2009

STUDIA FENNICA FOLKLORISTICA

*Creating Diversities
Folklore, Religion and the Politics
of Heritage*
Edited by Anna-Leena Siikala,
Barbro Klein & Stein R. Mathisen
Studia Fennica Folkloristica 14
2004

Pertti J. Anttonen
*Tradition through Modernity
Postmodernism and the Nation-State
in Folklore Scholarship*
Studia Fennica Folkloristica 15
2005

*Narrating, Doing, Experiencing
Nordic Folkloristic Perspectives*
Edited by Annikki Kaivola-Bregenhøj,
Barbro Klein & Ulf Palmenfelt
Studia Fennica Folkloristica 16
2006

Mícheál Briody
*The Irish Folklore Commission
1935–1970
History, ideology, methodology*
Studia Fennica Folkloristica 17
2007

STUDIA FENNICA HISTORICA

*Medieval History Writing and Crusading
Ideology*
Edited by Tuomas M. S. Lehtonen
& Kurt Villads Jensen with Janne
Malkki and Katja Ritari
Studia Fennica Historica 9
2005

*Moving in the USSR
Western anomalies and Northern
wilderness*
Edited by Pekka Hakamies
Studia Fennica Historica 10
2005

Derek Fewster
Visions of Past Glory
Nationalism and the Construction
of Early Finnish History
Studia Fennica Historica 11
2006

Modernisation in Russia since 1900
Edited by Markku Kangaspuro
& Jeremy Smith
Studia Fennica Historica 12
2006

Seija-Riitta Laakso
Across the Oceans
Development of Overseas Business
Information Transmission 1815–1875
Studia Fennica Historica 13
2007

Industry and Modernism
Companies, Architecture and Identity
in the Nordic and Baltic Countries
during the High-Industrial Period
Edited by Anja Kervanto Nevanlinna
Studia Fennica Historica 14
2007

Charlotta Wolff
Noble conceptions of politics
in eighteenth-century Sweden
(ca 1740–1790)
Studia Fennica Historica 15
2008

Sport, Recreation and Green Space
in the European City
Edited by Peter Clark, Marjaana Niemi
& Jari Niemelä
Studia Fennica Historica 16
2009

Rhetorics of Nordic Democracy
Edited by Jussi Kurunmäki
& Johan Strang
Studia Fennica Historica 17
2010

STUDIA FENNICA LINGUISTICA

Minna Saarelma-Maunumaa
Edhina Ekogidho – Names as Links
The Encounter between African and
European Anthroponymic Systems
among the Ambo People in Namibia
Studia Fennica Linguistica 11
2003

Minimal reference
The use of pronouns in Finnish
and Estonian discourse
Edited by Ritva Laury
Studia Fennica Linguistica 12
2005

Antti Leino
On Toponymic Constructions
as an Alternative to Naming Patterns
in Describing Finnish Lake Names
Studia Fennica Linguistica 13
2007

Talk in interaction
Comparative dimensions
Edited by Markku Haakana,
Minna Laakso & Jan Lindström
Studia Fennica Linguistica 14
2009

Planning a new standard language
Finnic minority languages meet
the new millennium
Edited by Helena Sulkala
& Harri Mantila
Studia Fennica Linguistica 15
2010

**STUDIA FENNICA
LITTERARIA**

*Changing Scenes
Encounters between European
and Finnish Fin de Siècle*
Edited by Pirjo Lyytikäinen
Studia Fennica Litteraria 1
2003

Women's Voices
*Female Authors and Feminist Criticism
in the Finnish Literary Tradition*
Edited by Lea Rojola & Päivi
Lappalainen
Studia Fennica Litteraria 2
2007

Metaliterary Layers in Finnish Literature
Edited by Samuli Hägg, Erkki Sevänen
& Risto Turunen
Studia Fennica Litteraria 3
2009

**STUDIA FENNICA
ANTHROPOLOGICA**

*On Foreign Ground
Moving between Countries and
Categories*
Edited by Minna Ruckenstein
& Marie-Louise Karttunen
Studia Fennica Anthropologica 1
2007

*Beyond the Horizon
Essays on Myth, History, Travel and
Society*
Edited by Clifford Sather & Timo
Kaartinen
Studia Fennica Anthropologica 2
2008

www.ingramcontent.com/pod-product-compliance
Lightning Source LLC
Chambersburg PA
CBHW080804300426
44114CB00020B/2826